SATHER CLASSICAL LECTURES
VOLUME FIFTEEN
1938

The POETRY *of* HOMER

The POETRY *of* HOMER

BY

SAMUEL ELIOT BASSETT

UNIVERSITY OF CALIFORNIA PRESS
BERKELEY, CALIFORNIA
1938

UNIVERSITY OF CALIFORNIA PRESS
BERKELEY, CALIFORNIA

———

CAMBRIDGE UNIVERSITY PRESS
LONDON, ENGLAND

COPYRIGHT, 1938, BY THE
REGENTS OF THE UNIVERSITY OF CALIFORNIA

PREFACE

THESE LECTURES were not delivered. Death came gently to Samuel Eliot Bassett in the quiet of his study, on the twenty-first of December, 1936, not long after he had completed his manuscript and only a few days before he was to have begun his journey to Berkeley. Few American Hellenists have made greater contributions to the true understanding of ancient Greek literature, and none has been more beloved and respected.

The Editors believe it is their duty to present the text as nearly as possible in the form in which it was left by Professor Bassett in his final draft. Consequently, their work has been limited to minor revisions of the sort that would ordinarily be made by the author and the insertion of references and Greek quotations from the earlier drafts. Their grateful acknowledgments are made to Mr. Harold A. Small, Editor of the University of California Press, for invaluable services in the preparation of the manuscript, and to Mr. M. P. Cunningham, Hattie Heller Graduate Scholar in Classics, for assistance in proofreading and for the verification of references.

THE EDITORS

BERKELEY, CALIFORNIA
JUNE 28, 1938

CONTENTS

	PAGE
PREFACE	v

CHAPTER
I. An Important Homeric Problem and Its Postulates	1
II. The Epic Illusion	26
III. The Epic Illusion (*Continued*)	57
IV. The Breaking of the Epic Illusion	81
V. The Poet and His Audience	114
VI. The Poet as Singer	141
VII. Homer the Poetic Demiurge	173
VIII. The Poet as Realist and as Idealist	227
Notes	247
Index	261

CHAPTER ONE

AN IMPORTANT HOMERIC PROBLEM AND ITS POSTULATES

THE WORK of John A. Scott will go down in history as a telling blow for the return of Homer the Poet, and for his restoration to kingship in his "wide demesne in the realms of gold." Fewer than twenty years have passed since the publication of Scott's conclusions in the first volume of the Sather Lectures, but this brief period has seen an ever-increasing tendency among Homeric scholars to recognize the essential unity of the *Iliad* and the *Odyssey*, and a noticeable decline in the attempts to reconstruct the origins of the poems. The Homeric Question has ceased to be an attractive problem of classical scholarship. A new Homeric Problem, which began to interest scholars in the early years of the present century, promises soon to take its place. For the solution of this problem Scott cleared the ground and pointed the way.

The basic principle of Scott's book, *The Unity of Homer*, was, "Homer must speak for himself"; its method was a minute and laborious study of philological and other facts in the Homeric poems to test the hypotheses of previous scholars. The next step is obviously to employ a similar method for the purpose of letting Homer speak, not against the Higher Criticism, but for a clearer understanding of the principles of great poetry, and of poetry itself.

The obligation resting upon the Homeric scholar to contribute to this understanding is the greater by reason of Homer's unique position in literature. The *Iliad* and *Odyssey* together are by universal consent one of our greatest works of poetry; they are the oldest surviving literary work of the Western world, and the most pervasive in their influence on its literature as a whole. These three facts make Homer a foundation stone of our entire literary edifice, and for that reason one of the most important literary documents in our possession. This document is large, containing perhaps 200,000 words, and it is complete, not fragmentary. It is hardly an exaggeration to say that Homer is the greatest single literary fact in Western history. The present and the future are children of the past. No sane view of life excludes the unchallenged truths of history; and science in searching for knowledge of man's mental and social life, and of life itself, is carefully studying beginnings. If creative literature is to keep pace with science, if it is to play in this age the important part which it has played in the greatest periods of Western civilization, no argument is needed to prove the need of determining more exactly, with our new knowledge and our new methods, the universal and the particular poetic qualities of the earliest and the historically most dynamic literary document.

This task is the more important because it has been much neglected by Homeric scholars for generations. The giants of nineteenth-century philology used their great knowledge and their fine feeling for language and style, and often for poetry, in the attempt to explain the origin of the poems. To our lasting regret they left the analysis of Homer's poetic qualities partly to lesser scholars, whose voices were unheard in the uproar over the Homeric Question, but chiefly to men outside the confines of Greek scholarship. Poets and critics have a task of their own in the study of Homer. Their duty is to weigh by the principles of their own *métiers* the facts and theories furnished by the Homeric scholar. In the same way the student of Homer must judge the conclusions of poets and critics by the facts in Homer which he knows better than they. During the past century the opposite of this was true. Poets and critics too often accepted the conclusions of Higher Criticism, although these contradicted the implications of their own conception of great poetry.

Homeric scholars, on the other hand, for a century accepted the conclusions of Lessing in the *Laokoön* without examining how far and in what sense they were true in the light of facts available in the Homeric poems. The present century has seen the beginning of a movement, led by Rothe and Drerup, to change the focus of Homeric study from the antecedents of Homeric poetry to the poetry itself. But Greek scholars do not yet universally recognize the need of this change of focus. There still lingers the impression, created by the leaders of nineteenth-century Homeric studies, that the study of Homer as poetry is unscholarly.

There is no sound basis for a charge of this kind. The searcher for the poetic qualities of Homer is impelled by the two aims of the scholar: he seeks the universal by examining particulars, and he expects no reward save the scholar's joy in the pursuit of truth. He is only a journeyman laborer, providing materials and partial truths to be used in some future synthesis. The secret of Homer as a powerful force in literature cannot be discovered by one man. There must be the earnest and concerted labors of many scholars for at least a generation before we can hope to understand the full connotation of the word "Homeric" as describing a certain quality or standard in the work of creative imagination which we call great literature.

The one who labors towards this end is a true scholar if he employs the scholar's method. Such is that which Scott used to prove the flimsiness of the foundation on which Higher Criticism built its theories. It is the deduction of principles from facts which occur often in the poems. This is the method of science. In embryonic form it was used by the grammarians two thousand years ago. There are three steps in this method: collection of facts, brief generalization, and interpretation of the latter's significance. The old grammarians were too often content with the first two steps. The terms in which they generalized have been preserved as priceless heirlooms. Today the commentator is usually satisfied to remark, "Note the chiasmus," and if a beginner can recognize an instance of litotes or hendiadys he is thought to be making progress in his appreciation of Greek or Latin literature. But what really counts is the significance of the generalization. Taking the third step the student of Homer's poetry must diverge in method from the scientist. The available facts in poetry are not to be treated as in a laboratory, because the most important fact, the working of the poet's mind, cannot always be determined objectively from the facts in the poems themselves. Where this is impossible, the conclusions from an analysis of the facts have not the value of a scientific hypothesis. They are only probabilities, whose strength lies in the extent to which they are supported by other groups of facts and are in accord with the generally accepted principles of great poetry.

Every method of research must be based on certain postulates. In most fields these can largely be taken for granted, because of general agreement among scholars. But in the Homeric field the confusion resulting from the countless and conflicting conclusions of Higher Criticism makes a statement of principles indispensable. Therefore, before we discuss the poetry of Homer we must explain the basic assumptions with which we start. They are implicit in the idea of a superlative literary document about whose authorship and poetic antecedents and origins not one single objective fact is known.

We assume, first of all, that the poetic qualities of this document were given to it by one master poet. This cannot be either proved or disproved by any method acceptable to science. But the evidence, as I understand the term, both internal and external, is overwhelmingly in its favor. It is also to be preferred pragmatically. The poetry of the *Iliad* and the *Odyssey* is *sui generis*. Even if the spade should bring to light unquestionable evidence of more than one

Homer, it would still be necessary to determine the qualities of Homeric poetry before studying those of the different Homers.

Our first postulate is not so much in conflict with the still prevailing hypothesis of two poets as might appear at first glance. It is true that perhaps the majority of leading Homerists still maintain, against all antiquity, the "paradox" of two obscure sophists, Xeno and Hellanicus, that the *Odyssey* is not the work of Homer. But, in the first place, they have not seriously considered Scott's argument, which says: It is contrary to Greek tradition that the poet of the *Odyssey*, if he were not Homer, should have vanished without leaving the slightest trace. Again, the rather large number of chorizonts who recognize the single authorship of each poem hold an illogical position. The evidence for two poets is of exactly the same kind as that which was used to prove the multiple authorship of the *Iliad* and of the *Odyssey*—theories which they reject. The Separatist hypothesis is a holdover from the last century; its present strength is due to a time lag. The trend is also away from it. It seems not improbable that soon the hypothesis will be abandoned, or will sink into insignificance. Perhaps we may make clearer the reasons for our first assumption, and at the same time dismiss the Homeric Question so far as possible from our discussion, by putting Plato in Homer's place. Let us imagine a Platonic Question something as follows:

"We have no knowledge of the historical Plato, except that he was the reputed author of the *Republic* and the *Laws*, and that these two dialogues are the earliest works of Greek literature which we possess. Excavations made within the last century have, however, revealed surprising evidence of high culture at Athens and elsewhere in Greece of the fifth century B.C. From this it appears probable that Pythagoras and other pre-Socratics, Socrates himself, the Sophists, and other characters, like Lysias and Alcibiades, had historical prototypes. Of literature after 'Plato' the first extant works are the *Politics* and one or two other works of Aristotle, besides some fragments, all but the *Politics* probably being written by minor Peripatetics. Our great corpus of Greek literature begins with New Comedy and the writers of the Alexandrian period. Of course, we have all of Lucian and Cicero. We also possess a Byzantine summary of Xenophon, Antisthenes, and other Socratic followers, which is an abstract of a lost work of one of the lesser Alexandrian librarians."

On the basis of these imaginings—which the reader may expand and improve at his pleasure—some very interesting conclusions might be drawn. The *Republic* might easily be assigned to at least five authors, plus a *Bearbeiter*. "The Necyia of Book X, for example, would certainly be a later addition, especially as Cicero had made the very natural remark that 592 B (the end of Bk. IX) was the τέλος of the dialogue. But the other extant dialogue, the *Laws*, could not possibly have been written by Plato. Both its style and its conception of government are different. According to most critics, it must have been written at least a century after the *Republic*, when Socrates no longer was supreme in his influence on thought. The whole *Gestaltung* of the philosophical dialogue has changed. There is no Sophist present, and little destructive dialectic. The argument in favor of wine drinking is utterly at variance with the *Republic*. The *Laws* has no great myth and few long similes. The Platonic Separatists are divided into two schools: the Lawgiver school would put the *Urgesetze*, on which the extant dialogue is based, nearer to the time of Solon, Lycurgus, and Charondas, that is, before the birth of Socrates; the other, the Rival school, thinks the author to have been a very great but unknown writer, belonging to the period of decline of the Socratic dialogue, who challenged the author of the *Republic* with a different conception of the philosophy of government. Because of this conception he decided to lay the scene in Crete, and, as Socrates never left Athens, he had to seek a new chief interlocutor. The style of the Platonic dialogue," our imagined Higher Critics would conclude, "can be explained only by assuming that it had been cultivated for centuries before the time of 'Plato,' in whom it either showed a full flowering or a decline from the greatness of earlier and more perfect, but lost, works. We know from the *Republic* itself that a certain kind of dialogue had been used in the mythical Homer and in the more historical Attic drama. At least we can be sure that the Greeks from the earliest times cultivated the art of conversation. A lexicographer tells us that the lesche, a kind of forerunner of the London coffee house, was mentioned by the mythical Homer and by Aeschylus. Pausanias described a famous lesche at Delphi. This is of the greatest importance as showing the intimate connection between the dialogue and Apollo, the god of poetry," etc., etc.

This imagined parallel to the Homeric Question may seem flippant; it is, however, most seriously offered. Its purpose is to illustrate the futility of assuming as objective facts what are only unsubstantiated and oftentimes highly subjective inferences. The *Iliad* and the *Odyssey* are no more unlike each other than are the *Republic* and the *Laws*. The Homeric poems, like the dialogues of Plato, are *sui generis*. The characteristic features of this genus of poetry are within our ken; the authorship of the poems is beyond it. But since all the greatest poetry whose authorship is known—and this includes the dialogues of Plato—bears witness to the singleness of great poetic power, it is reasonable that we should assume one great maker of the Homeric poems until we are confronted with unmistakable objective evidence to the contrary.

Our second assumption concerns the meaning of poetry in Homer's day.

In Homer the only word for poet is "singer." This indicates that in its earliest and purest form poetry was emotional utterance. Song is "the overflow of powerful feelings" in the round of life of primitive peoples when the emotions become too intense for speech. The use of song has no more to do with the purpose of song itself than—as Plato would say—the object of a voyage has to do with the art of navigation. Poetry in its purity, therefore, has no aim other than emotional satisfaction, or, as we say, an appeal to the feelings. What is the nature of this appeal after poetry has ceased to be song? We must divest our minds of the poetry of today, when the encroachment of prose has limited it to a very small corner of the field it once occupied alone. In the time of Homer, so far as we can know, epic poetry was not a kind of literature, but literature itself. Therefore in studying Homer we must understand by "poetry" all that is implied by the Greek word *poiesis*.

A ποιητής is a maker. No one knows the etymology of the verb from which "poet" is derived. It must come from the noun or adjective ποιός, but the origin of this word is unknown. We have, however, a word accidentally of the same form, which may serve to illustrate the meaning of "poet." The Greek pronominal adjective ποιός means "of a certain quality or character." A "poet" is he who gives to material at his disposal a particular, individual quality and existence. The "maker" is the formal cause of what he makes. He brings an entity into being by imparting life to inert matter —if what he "makes" is capable of life. In the world of beautiful thought and its expression in words the "poet" is what the Creator was to the author of the first chapter of Genesis—the illustration is apposite, since both this author and Homer belong to an early era of thought. The Creator gave life and particular qualities to existing matter, and brought our world into existence. The aim of the early poet in thus creating is also illustrated by the Hebrew account of the Creation. This mentions no object in the mind of the Creator except delight in the Creation: "And God saw every thing that he had made, and, behold, it was very good" (Gen. 1:31). The only reason for the creative effort of the early "poet," as poet, was the joy in the making, which, because of his humanity, or for some other reason, he shared with his audience. There is strong evidence that Homer had no other purpose than this—a fact which, if established, gives to our oldest literary document the added value of being poetry in its pure state.

Sainte-Beuve compares the moral teaching of Homer to a fountain in some Florentine garden, whose stream issues from a vase held by the figure of Poseidon. But the god is oblivious of his office. This applies to all the treasures, other than poetic, in the storehouse of the Homeric poems. The poet's mind is on other things. That the genealogy of Aeneas or of Glaucus was introduced to flatter some princely family of Homer's day, or that Nestor and his sons play leading rôles as a compliment to the Neleidae of Miletus, are unsupported conjectures. We know that the story of the Creation in Genesis had a religious purpose, for on it is based the reason for the sanctity of the Hebrew sabbath and of marriage (Gen. 2:3, 24). Both Vergil and Milton at the outset mention a "greater argument." But there is no evidence of this in Homer. It is commonly held that one "purpose" of the epic is to glorify the national past. This is not Homer's aim, if we are to judge by the proems of the two poems. It is the "ruinousness" of the Wrath, the sufferings of Odysseus, which are the themes. A great poet in serious poetry will be true to himself. If he is deeply religious or a man of high moral purpose, he will not present irreligion or depravity attractively: if he is proud of his nation he will not decry, but rather glorify it. But there is no evidence that this was Homer's "purpose." On the other hand, there are many indications that Homer, like the Creator in Genesis, saw only that his poems were "very good." Indirectly, through the words of his characters, and more modestly and therefore more effectively, he shows his confidence in the future fame of his poetry. This is more definitely expressed in the *Odyssey*, when, we may be sure, the *Iliad* had already been received with acclaim. The shade of Agamemnon says of Penelope,"The fame of her virtues shall never die: the immortals will fashion for earth-dwellers a lovely song for true-hearted Penelope" (ω 196-198). Many scholars see here, as elsewhere, only a reference to the songs of bards in general. But this assumes as true what is only a conjecture, that Penelope belonged to familiar tradition. It also neglects the cumulative force of the evidence found in the poems themselves. We select a passage of particular interest in this connection.

The nearest approach to a *raisonneur* in Homer is the hero of each poem. An ancient commentator notes, as evidence of the poet's love for Achilles, that the latter, alone of the Heroes, sings, and that his theme, κλέα ἀνδρῶν, is that of Homer himself.[1] In the *Odyssey* Homer shows still more clearly his attachment to his hero. When Odysseus pauses in the middle of his Apologue, Alcinous says,"With the skill of a bard thou hast told thy tale, the grievous woes of all the Argives and thine own" (λ 368 f.). By "all the Argives" Alcinous must mean the comrades of Odysseus, but his choice of this word, instead of "comrades,"[2] would remind the poet's listeners of the sorrows of the returning army, described by Nestor and Menelaus. The Apologue was the poet's masterpiece; why should he not unconsciously fuse himself with the hero who is his mouthpiece? The whole speech of Alcinous (λ 363-376), in which he bestows the highest praise on his guest's skill as a narrator, serves also to deepen the interest of the poet's audience in the rest of the Apologue. It is a delicate but effective "blurb" of the

---

[1] Superior figures refer to notes which will be found on p. 247.

Wanderings, and the inclusion of "all the Argives" makes the praise apply to all the *Odyssey* up to this point.³

Homer was not content merely to share with his audience his "delight in the making," if we may judge by the effect of the Apologue upon Odysseus' listeners. When Odysseus paused, and after he had finished, "a hush fell upon them all; they were caught by the spell" (κηληθμῷ δ' ἔσχοντο, λ 333 f., ν 1 f.) The lays of the bard are called "charms of mortals" (βροτῶν θελκτήρια, α 337, cf. ρ 514-521). The ancients, of course, like ourselves, used language figuratively; the word "charm," although it comes from the verb which describes Circe's transformation of the Comrades into swine, must not be taken as evidence that in Homer's day the bard was still a medicine man. The words "a spell fell on them all" and "the story he [the beggar Odysseus] tells would 'charm' your dear heart," mean that in the days of Homer a good tale, well told, made the listeners for the moment forget the real world about them and for the nonce enter a new and equally real world. Our second assumption is, therefore, that Homer's only poetic purpose was to make an imagined experience real, and that, as master poet, he succeeded so well that the listeners under his spell were charmed into being partakers of the life which his imagination created.

Our next assumption deals with Homer's materials. Here the analogy to the Creator in Genesis ceases, for the human maker finds his stuff already partly formed. It seems certain, especially since Nilsson's studies appeared, that the legends of the Heroes grew from historical facts, through the imagination of succeeding generations of bards. Scholars differ with regard to Homer's place in the succession. For a century Homer has quite generally been placed long after the zenith of the Greek epic: the *Ur-Ilias* and the *Ur-Odyssee* were the works of its prime. This seems altogether unlikely. It can hardly be owing to accident that we have the works of the three great tragic poets, not of Thespis and Phrynichus; of Aristophanes, not of Chionides and Magnes; and of Herodotus and Thucydides, not of the Logographoi and the Atthidographoi. We therefore assume that Homer came at the peak of the early Greek epic, and that his poems superseded all previous epics because they were both more complete and, in all respects, greater poetry.

It follows that we must adopt a view of Homer's use of his sources which differs from that which has prevailed in modern scholarship. The quest for Homer's *Vorlagen* has magnified their importance, and has given them an objective existence in more or less definite form, far beyond the bounds of probability. Professor Lowes could rebuild the Road to Xanadu because *Purchas his Pilgrimes* and other works read by Coleridge are available to scholars. But of the Road to Troy and Ithaca there remains not one literary trace. In positing the *Vorlagen*, scholars adopted the method of physical science without first proving that it can be applied to poetry. Geologists can construct a picture of the Palaeozoic Age because they can prove that certain remains which can be studied today belonged to it. This process of reasoning cannot apply to Homer's sources, since it is equally possible that post-Homeric features of myth and legend originated in the Homeric poems themselves. We therefore postulate as a basic principle of our study that facts found in the literature after Homer are not to be used as evidence of Homer's sources unless they are vouched for in other ways. For example, until very recently most Homeric scholars saw in the Tricking of Zeus Homer's use of the ritual of the Holy Marriage of Zeus and Hera,[4] and some have even asserted that Homer's description of the couch of the divine pair was taken bodily from the hymn used in this ritual. But—aside from all other objections—we have no evidence that this ritual antedated Homer. Herodotus vouches for the great influence of Homer on the later conception of the gods. It is quite within the limits of probability that the rite of the Holy Marriage owed its origin to Homer's mention of the first union of the king and queen of Olympus (Ξ 295 f.). The great corpus of Greek myth and legend is sufficient evidence of the creative imagination of Greek bards and poets, and the conflicting versions imply some freedom to vary tradition. The greatest poet of all may reasonably be assigned a freedom and scope of invention commensurate with his greatness, except where archaeology points to the probable historicity of tradition. How far one can go within these limits will depend partly on the extent to which he discovers in the poems themselves the indications of creative imagination. The evidence is cumulative, and, unfortunately, too likely to be subjective. But of one thing we can be certain. There is no reliable evidence, either in Homer or elsewhere, that any Greek poet before Homer had told the story of the wanderings of Odysseus. The opposite view, so prevalent today, is based on the poet's address to the Muse (α 10), εἰπὲ καὶ ἡμῖν, which is interpreted, "Tell us, as thou hast told others." The scholiast's explanation,"that we, too [as well as the Muse], may know," is supported by one passage in Homer and at least two in Plato. Odysseus says to Alcinous (ι 16 f.), "First I will tell you my name, that you, too, may know it." This cannot mean, "you, as well as others," for Odysseus adds, "and that one day you may be my guest." This idiomatic use of καί is found in Plato. (1) *Republic* 344 E,"Nay, kind Sir, consent to enlighten us, too." Here there is no reference to "others"; Jowett renders,"Prithee, friend, do not keep your knowledge to yourself."(2) *Republic* 573 D, Socrates asks how the tyrannical man lives. Adimantus replies,"That, to speak facetiously, you will tell me, too" (καὶ ἐμοὶ ἐρεῖς). Shorey translates, "As the wits say, you shall tell *me*." The same interpretation of Homer's words to the Muse is not only true to the Greek idiom; it is also the only one which is in keeping with the poet's manner. Homer is most careful to catch the attention and arouse the interest of his listener. It is therefore unreasonable to think that at the very beginning he needlessly announced that he was telling only an old story.[5] On the contrary, it is more in keeping with Homer's way that the words of Telemachus to his mother, "Men acclaim more highly the *newest* song" (α 351 f.), should have been intended as an indirect "blurb" of the *Odyssey*.

But even the greatest of poets is limited in his freedom to invent. The poet must present "both the old and the new."[6] Great and universal poetry must unite harmoniously these two elements. The old is the familiar, the accepted, the admired and loved. The old is, in fact (in an age when books and libraries are unknown), largely the contribution of the poet's listeners to the success of his recitation. Their interest and their knowledge are valuable assets on which the poet can count. Hence we cannot categorically either assert or deny the existence of *Vorlagen*. But, since it is the poet's task to present also the new, in subject-matter as well as in other things, to limit Homer too strictly to the imaginative material supplied by earlier bards is to deny his supremacy as an epic poet. Furthermore, the same suppositions must apply *a fortiori* to Homer's predecessors, and Greek myths and legends would thus have come into being fully developed, like Athena from the head of Zeus. Not only does our reason deny this; Pindar and Attic tragedy prove that it is poetically impossible.

For a similar reason we must also grant to Homer some degree of originality in the use of poetic language. In recent years the opposite view was supported with great ability by the late Milman Parry, whose untimely death brought irreparable loss to Homeric scholarship. Parry denied to Homer any individuality of style whatsoever.[7] This conclusion he reached by a masterly study of certain formulas in Homer, and from corroborating evidence in the folk poetry of Jugoslavia. His inferences from these facts have greatly increased our understanding of an essential and distinctive feature of Homer's style, namely, its oral character. But he carried these inferences so far beyond what the evidence seems to justify that his chief thesis awakens the gravest doubt.

Parry seems to me to have established more firmly and more clearly than anyone had ever done before[8] the fundamental difference between the style of Homer and that of most later poetry. Technically, Homer's style was the result of concentrated attention by countless bards, for generations untold, to oral, and often extemporaneous, narrative in verse with heroic themes. Like Demodocus, a bard might be called upon to recite upon a theme upon which he had never meditated. Hence the bard must have in memory a stock of formulae of various kinds adapted both to the various metrical and rhythmical phrases of the hexameter and to oft-recurring details of every tale of Heroes. It follows that neither the bard nor his listeners could have felt the slightest aversion to the repeated use of the same formula for unimportant parts of the narrative, or to repetitions in general. The broadcaster of an athletic contest uses the same technique, and for the same reason.

Thus far Parry seems to me to have made one of the most important contributions of recent years to our understanding of Homer's poetry. Hereafter, the fact that Homer composed solely for oral recitation must be given an importance which, without Parry's work, it might never have received. In the future, likewise, no verse or passage in Homer can be regarded with suspicion merely, or largely, because it is also repeated elsewhere.

But Parry went much farther, and held that not only the style but also the language and the ideas of Homer were purely traditional. Poetry in Homer's time, he says, was composed "only by putting together old verses and old parts of verses in an old way."[9] "At no time is he [Homer] seeking words for an idea that has never before found expression."[10] Parry's interest in the traditional phrase made his conclusions about Homer largely negative. If he had lived longer he might have considered the positive aspect of his observations by examining with equal acumen evidences of originality in Homer. As it is, his theory, if I understand it correctly, is based on two assumptions, neither of them sufficiently supported by argument or evidence, which prevent me from accepting it.

(1) Parry assumed that the memory is used only to retain what the mind receives from without; he denied an equal use in holding fast the product of the mind itself. The poet, "not having the device of pen and paper which, as he composed, would hold his partly-formed thought in safe-keeping while his unhampered mind ranged where it would after other ideas and other words, ... makes his verses by choosing from a vast number of fixed phrases, which he has heard in the poems of other poets."[11] This assertion, that a poet without the help of writing cannot originate phrases and ideas, is denied by indisputable evidence of the function and power of the memory in Greek historical times. In Plato's *Phaedrus*, King Thamus tells the god Theuth that the latter's invention of writing will ruin the memory. "Letters," he said, "are an aid not to memory, but to reminiscence, and you give your disciples not truth, but only the semblance of truth; they will be hearers of many things, and will have learned nothing."[12] These words imply that one of the functions of memory is to aid in the mind's search for truth, without reliance on what comes from other sources. To this function the unusual capacity of memory in the ancient Greeks contributed. The modern reliance on "black and white" makes us forget the ability of men in Plato's day to grave upon the tablets of the mind. Shorey calls Antiphon's recitation of the conversation between Parmenides and Socrates, which Antiphon had heard from Apollodorus, "an im-

possible *tour de force* of memory."[13] It could not seem so in the fourth century B. C. Plato was too great an artist to give to Antiphon—and to Socrates when he repeats the *soi-disant* speeches of Aspasia and Diotima—a power of remembering which would seem unusual then. The boast of Niceratus, in Xenophon's *Symposium*, that he can repeat the *Iliad* and *Odyssey* from beginning to end, provokes no surprise at this feat of memory. This remarkable power of memory, so abnormal as it seems to us, was used not only, as in the examples just given, to retain in the mind the utterances of others, but also in the process of independent and original thinking. Neither Themistocles before Salamis, nor Pericles before delivering the Samian oration, wrote out their speeches. The brilliant utterances for which Socrates was famous were made without "the device of pen and ink." It cannot have been more difficult for Homer to tell his tale in hexameters than for a brilliant conversationalist to express an original thought in beautiful language, if the hexameter was the only poetic medium and if bards had composed in this meter from early youth. Even today, when prose has entirely supplanted verse in speech, there are many individuals who can improvise verse without using either the pen or a remembered poetical cliché. Therefore, while Parry seems to have proved that the prevalence of a traditional style tended to favor the traditional phrase, his assumption that it barred all—or virtually all—invention of new phrases and diction is not logical or convincing.

(2) His second hypothesis is still less reasonable. Parry assumed that Homer's poetry was only the result—except for its choice of phrase among those of tradition—of an infinitely long, exceedingly slow, and apparently entirely uniform, development.

"It may occur to some to ask how the diction was ever made if one thus grants the Singer no power to change it. It is to be answered that the years of its first making belong to a very dim past, and were also those of its least perfection; then, that we may well suppose for the single poet a very few cases where the play of words has suggested some new epithet, or phrase, or verse, which the other Singers found worth using and keeping, but that there could never be more than a few such creations for any one Singer, and they could win a place in the diction only as they were in accord with what was traditional, and fitted the habits of verse-making of the other poets. . . .

"At no time is he [Homer] seeking words for an idea which has never before found expression, so that the question of originality in style means nothing to him."[14] (We may remark that the last statement denies to Homer even a spark of originality; it follows that if the long line of bards who preceded him had not been more original than he, *none* of the ideas in Homer were ever expressed! And if superior bards had expressed new ideas, they must have coined new phrases, without reference to those of tradition. *De nihilo nihil fit.*)

Parry was reviving the nineteenth-century hypothesis that Homer was not, at least in ideas and diction, a great creative poet, but rather the last of a long series of ever-inferior bards. In fact, Parry's hypothesis is a restatement of Herder's theory of Homer the *Volksdichter*. Parry found external evidence for his theory in the methods of composition used by the South-Slavic guslars. This is not direct evidence, but analogy, which is convincing in proportion to the importance of the elements present in the two objects of comparison. South Slavic folk poetry lacks the most important element: it produced no Homer. History has provided us with another analogy. It has shown us that every work of poetic art comparable in greatness to the *Iliad* and *Odyssey* bears the stamp of a single great creative mind. The analogy of Homer to the great historic poets is greater. Since we cannot know, we choose the greater parallel. All the great creators of literature are alike in one respect: they take the old and make of it the new, in ideas and language, in incidents, characters, and action; and they add and invent out of their imagination. We must believe that Homer was no exception.

The same analogy gives us the right to assume further that Homer was not a single poetic mood, a single view of life, a single literary point. The extension which was given in the last century and by Parry to Homer's antecedents must not be denied to the poet himself. We are justified in thinking that Homer did not differ essentially, as poet, from great historical poets and other men of literary genius about whose lives and works we have more knowledge. Even the greatest poet is a mortal, and subject to the ups and downs and the changes of human life. He works in different ways at different times. His poetic potential is now high, now low; his views and his style may change to some degree; he is more interested in some minor themes than in others, and for different purposes and with different themes he may use different poetic means. Finally, a great and large work of poetic art—like the *Iliad* of Homer or the *Republic* of Plato—is often the work of years, with all the possible changes and the minor imperfections which this implies. In our lack of all external knowledge of Homer we should as far as possible look within the poems for the explanation of differences in his poetic art. We should try to relate these to the theme and to the tone of their context, or to the importance of the episode in the scheme of the whole poem. And when an imperfect juncture is found, as at the end of the Catalogues and the Doloneia in the *Iliad*, or at the beginning of Book V of the *Odyssey*, we should assume the possibility that a late insertion or substitution never received the poet's finishing touch.

We have next to ask, To what extent do we possess in our Homeric poems the work of the great poet? The "spurious" verse or the "late" passage was one of the pawns in the game of making the text of Homer prove something about Homer. Nitzsch used this pawn to prove his unity; the Dissectors and Separatists, to prove his multiplicity. Both adjectives imply that a verse or passage is not the work of the creator who gave form to the poems, and both have been used, with differing meanings, of more than half the verses of the two poems. But we cannot study Homer's poetry without first deciding how much of it we are to regard as "Homeric."

Today, when so much is known about the transmission of literature, we are aware that we cannot read either the exact language of the poems as their author left them, or only what he composed. There must have been weathering of various kinds and slight repairs, and there is always the possibility of well-meant improvements by the insertion of verses. But there is danger in the free and categorical rejection of verses. Certainly the studies of Rothe and Parry conduce to extreme caution in rejecting a verse as a "weak imitation" or a "repetition" of some other verse.[15] Nor can a metrical or linguistic fault or a *hapax legomenon* justify rejection: the fault may be due to weathering, the new word to the poet himself. The poetic tone of a verse or passage, upon which Aristarchus and Wilamowitz at times relied, is no sure test. Until we know more about the poetic soul of Homer—which will require years of intense and concerted study of his poetry—we shall have no final criterion for the rejection of verses in the Homeric poems. Furthermore, the *pruritus expurgandi* tends to become acute and uncontrollable; at best it is a dangerous affection.[16] No two text critics agree. The result is that today, after more than a century of text criticism by the ablest Greek scholars of modern times, we have many *texts*, but no *text*, of Homer. Yet if you want to study Homer a text is indispensable. It seems to me that the choice of the student should be pragmatical, within the limits of scholarship. He must use the traditional text as far as his studies prove it to be consistent with the rest, accepting the conclusions of the critics where the consistency is thereby improved, rejecting them otherwise. Let me illustrate by an extreme instance.

In Book XIII of the *Iliad* Idomeneus plays the star rôle. The ethos of this hero is made clearest to us in his conversation with his friend Meriones, the longest dialogue of the episode. When the two meet, Idomeneus speaks first: "Meriones, fleet son of Molus, why have you left the battle?" (vss. 249 f.). Meriones replies (in the vulgate text), "Idomeneus, counselor of the bronze-clad Achaeans, I go to my quarters for a spear" (vss. 255 f.). Most editors reject verse 255, Ἰδομενεῦ, Κρητῶν βουληφόρε χαλκοχιτώνων, as not found in some of the best texts, both of Alexandrian and later times. Let us test this rejection by the rest of Homer. His characters are by nature courteous folk. They normally use a vocative in their first address to one another. This vocative is omitted only about seventy-five times, and then only because the person addressed is unknown or a menial, because the occasion requires haste or brevity, or because of the character or the mood of the speaker. None of these reasons for the omission is found here. Therefore the omission of verse 255 makes Meriones inconsistent with other heroes of his rank in a similar situation. Again, in the *Iliad* the honorific vocative which fills a whole verse—a sort of titular address—is used of every major Greek hero, including Patroclus.[17] If verse 255 be rejected, Idomeneus is the only major Greek hero without such title, and that, too, in the episode containing his *aristeia*. Therefore it seems that the verse was accidentally lost from the archetype of some of the MSS or else inserted by some excellent text critic who saw that it was needed. It is Homeric either in fact or in spirit. For reasons like this we should be slow to accept the rejection of verses which make good Homeric sense.

On the other hand, the fact that a verse has been suspected by great critics should make us more careful in testing its consistency. More than this, it should guard us against maintaining with certainty the truth of conclusions so far as they rest on moot points in Homeric scholarship. And since these cover so much of the Homeric field, the result will be that we shall state our conclusions only as observed tendencies, which, taken together, may help to clarify the connotation of the word "Homeric" in its application to poetry.

Our final postulate is based on the title which the ancient Greeks gave to Homer, "The Poet." The *Iliad* and the *Odyssey* are poems par excellence. Now a poem, a thing created by a human "maker," especially when severed from all connection with music and dancing, is in its essence a mythos (not a logos). It is not an account of what men have said and done; it is not human speech so ordered as to convince men of truth or error, of right or wrong, of the expedient or the unprofitable, nor is it the utterance of cold reason about fact and experience. It is the presentation in language of the elements of experience, selected and ordered, colored and harmonized, and warmed with the breath of life, not as truth, but as an image of truth. Mythos presents life figuratively. It is a simile on a grand scale, but an inverted simile. The simile uses a familiar experience to illustrate a new and unfamiliar act or situation. The mythos, on the other hand, offers a new experience of life, which throws a fairer light on the life we know and, by increasing our sensibility to this life, gives to it a deeper meaning.

The poet par excellence is he who creates the truest and most dynamic image of life. This poet sees life steadily and sees it whole. He is also gifted with a preternatural vision. Our own senses and thoughts are blunted from use in the dull round of life. We see life mistily and in monochrome because we have injured the eyes of the imagination by using them to read the cold print of the world about us—a world that seems to be growing old. But it is our eyes that are aging, not the world. When we go hand in hand with the poet, we are like one leading a little child into the country: we see with his young eyes.[18] The great poet is like one of Plato's souls that darts back to earth after a thousand years amid the indescribable sights and experiences of heaven. His eyes behold the splendid sights and colors and magic landscapes that we have lost the power to see. His ears can catch the overtones and the undertones of the human world that never grows old. So he creates for us a new world of beautiful thought, and quickens our senses to detect new beauties in our own world.[19] In doing this the poet par excellence enlarges the dimensions of the human spirit and shows us the grandeur and the sublimity of life. This quality has always been recognized in Homer's poetry. Today we understand what made this possible.

The eternal war between poetry and science,[20] between the mythos and the logos, between truth and the image of truth, is in a certain way a conflict between the past and the present. Science draws from the present all the material which it uses at first hand, for the present alone consists of many particulars which the physical senses can perceive and weigh and measure. But the present has no abiding value, for it is full of change and uncertainty."The past, at least, is secure," and it has always been the great storehouse of poetic material. It is the most extensive realm of human experience, which, as John Dewey tells us, is the peculiar sphere of art. The Muse of Epic Poetry was the eldest daughter of Mnemosyne, because man has always regarded as "memorable" chiefly those bygone experiences which seemed to have permanent value.

The same difference between poetry and science is seen in the use of language. Science must ever coin new words, translate old terms into new, or at least remove from old words the connotation which the past has given them. But poetry loves the old words because, like old wine, they have a bouquet. They are packed with the experiences of other lives and with meanings in other poetry. Old words give to the poet's simile of life an enchanting strangeness and at the same time a universal significance so far as the cumulative meaning, gained from their varied use in the past, helps to summarize human experience.

History shows a certain correlation between interest in the past and poetry. The greatness of the poetic material has often inspired the greatest of poetry. In this respect Homer is like Vergil, Dante, and Milton. His material is taken from one of the great chapters of human history. But Homer differs from these poets and from all the other great poets who were directly or indirectly influenced by his poetry. In the *Aeneid* and the *Divine Comedy* and *Paradise Lost* the greatness of the poet's own day leads him to relate the past to his own present. But Homer lived, as it were, in a lowland of Greek culture, between two peaks, Mycenae and Athens. He does not relate the great past to his own times. He sees in the past only a permanent value superior in all ways to that of the present. The *Iliad* and *Odyssey* are a tale of human greatness which glorifies an important era of civilization in the Western world. This tale sums up the human achievement of that era. It pictures the Trojan War as the greatest exploit of its greatest heroes. It is a story of war and peace, whose two keynotes are like the only two "harmonies" which Plato admits into his ideal State: "one, warlike, to sound the note or accent which a brave man utters in the hour of danger and stern resolve, or when . . . he is going to wounds or death . . . , and another to be used by him in times of peace . . . when by prudent conduct he has attained his end, not carried away by his success, but acting moderately and wisely. . . . These two . . . the strain of courage and the strain of temperance."[21]

To Plato the State was the individual writ large. This is what the past meant to Homer. In the *Iliad* and *Odyssey*

Homer presents as an image of truth Human Life Writ Large. He is "The Poet" because he possessed the "divine" vision to see the grandeur of human existence, and because, like the Creator in Genesis, he breathed the breath of life into the image which he had made. Homer pictures the Life Writ Large so dynamic with vitality that his poetry from the beginning to the present day has "charmed" innumerable audiences and has cast upon them the "spell" of reality.

In the next chapter we shall consider some of the ways in which Homer weaves the spell of reality.

CHAPTER TWO

THE EPIC ILLUSION

ALL GREAT POETRY at its best transports us to the realms of gold. If for the moment we can put reason in abeyance, we are "enthralled." The spell of poetry can make the hearer forget both himself and the poet and the real world about him. It can banish all awareness that an image of life is being presented, because of its magic power to make the image seem the only reality. This spell is the poetic illusion. The term is usually confined to the drama, but it describes also the effect of lyric poetry and still more of the Homeric epic. In all three genres the illusion can never be quite complete if print draws a curtain between us and the poetry. If we remove this curtain and think of the lyric as sung, the epic as recited, and the drama as acted, we can readily see wherein the illusions created by the lyric, the epic, and the drama at their best differ from each other.

In lyric the contact between poet and listener is direct, with no personal intermediary; yet if we submit to the spell of the poetry we forget the poet himself.

> Teach us, sprite or bird,
> What sweet thoughts are thine.
> I have never heard
> Praise of love or wine
> That panted forth a flood of rapture
>   so divine.

If we should hear these verses sung, and if we ignore the influence of the music, the "I" that has "never heard" is not Shelley, but, as it were, the emotion of rapture itself, which we make our own. The ego of the lyric is so impersonal that the hearer by its spell is fused into one with it. Lyric speaks in an ideal first person. Its illusion is produced by the immediate stirring of an emotion by an ideal self.

In the drama the eye aids the ear, but the poetic source of the illusion is the thought of the poet. This comes to us through the words of characters in our presence. In their relation to us the characters are impersonal, yet as carriers of the poet's message they speak directly to us. The dramatic poet speaks in the ideal second person.

In the epic the source of the poetry's magic power is still farther removed from us. In its Homeric form the epic comes to its audience from an unsubstantial third person. The story seems almost to tell itself. The words which transport us to the world of heroes come from a source so submerged from view that the heroic life seems to move of its own vitality. The epic illusion in Homer thus depends more completely on poetry itself than does the effect of any other great poetry. Lyric poetry requires the mood of song, and originally used musical accompaniment; drama loses its greatest power without the assistance of visible persons and scenes, and in all other great epics of the Western world the subtle effacement of the poet is not so nearly complete. Homer is unique, like Socrates (Pl. *Symp.*, 215 E); by the words of his poetry alone, he awakens in the hearer, as Socrates did in Alcibiades, a stirring of the soul. This is the epic illusion of which Homer himself speaks when he says of Odysseus' Phaeacian listeners, "The magic spell was upon them" (λ 334).

Such perfection of the epic illusion is rare in the real world. It is not only one of the supreme triumphs of the poet's art, but indeed its crown. A poet may create by his imagination a beautiful and glorified new world, but he is not a true creator unless by his art he beguiles us into the momentary acceptance of that world as our own. Homer is said to have done this even for the sophisticated Athenians, if we can believe Plato (*Ion* 535 B-E). The rhapsode Ion admits that he is ecstasized by the verses of Homer which he recites, and that the tears of his audience, and their strange looks of awe and wonder, prove that they are similarly affected.

The perfection of the epic illusion in Homer is one of his chief claims to an exalted place in literature, and is an excellence in which he has no superior. Hence we must examine some of the basic principles of narration on which largely depends the spell of Homer.

The epic illusion in its entirety results from the creation of three minor illusions. We shall consider these in the order of increasing importance.

(1) The first is the Illusion of Historicity, which removes from the mind of the hearer every doubt that the characters of the tale once actually lived and that the events are historically true. The grandeur of a glorious past always thrills the listener, who can never hope to see its equal; but no picture of that past equals in power the picture which the listener accepts as true. Socrates describes the "bewitchment" which the narrative of great historical events may cast upon the hearer. In speaking of the funeral orator's account of Athens' great past (of which the greatest exploits are vouched for by history), he says, "As I listen, the spell falls upon me, I feel that I have become at the moment a greater, nobler, finer man, and this feeling persists for three or four days" (*Menex.* 235 A-C). Socrates' accustomed playfulness of tone here, as often elsewhere, only disguises the utterance of a profound truth. Only when the hearer has the unshaken conviction that the life which he is to enter emotionally was once actually lived can he for the moment live vicariously in all its fullness the great life that is denied to him. Only then can he rise above himself in a brief moment of exaltation, and experience a catharsis of the aspirations which he cannot otherwise satisfy. In Homer the unquestioned authority for the truth of the story is the Muse, whose function, according to all the evidence in the Homeric poems, seems to be for the most part confined to the creation of the illusion of historicity.

The Muse of Homer's impersonal narrative is not the

Muse of all poetic tradition since Homer. She does not inspire with a divine frenzy. Of the latter we find a hint, it is true, in the Catalogues (B 594-600), where Thamyris vied with the Muses and paid heavily for his presumption. But these, as we shall see, are not the Muses invoked by Homer. The earliest description of the power, sphere, and function of our traditional Muses of Poetry is found in the proem of Hesiod's *Theogony* (vss. 21-30). The Muses met Hesiod as he watched his lambs at the foot of holy Helicon, and said to him, "We can utter many a fiction, and make it seem true; and when we will, we can voice the truth." Then they gave him a wand of laurel and they inspired in him a divine utterance, that he might glorify the past and the future. The Muses of Hesiod inspire; their sphere is both truth and fiction; their function is to confer "divine utterance." But they are the Muses of Helicon (*Theog.* 1 f.), although fused by the poet with the Muses of Olympus. At Helicon there was from early times a cult of Dionysus, as there was in Thrace, where Thamyris sang. Dionysus represents the mystic, ecstatic aspect of poetry, which justifies Plato in ascribing ecstasy, frenzy, and possession to the influence of the Muses, and in calling poets inspired (*Ion* 534 E, *Phaedr.* 245 A). The place names, Helicon and Leibethrum, haunts of the Muses of Boeotia, are found also in Pieria, the home of Orpheus and, therefore, of ecstasy. The traditional Muse of Poetry is therefore almost certainly Orphic and Dionysiac in origin. The Heliconian Muses largely displaced their Olympian sisters. Pindar always calls the Muses Heliconian or Pierian,[1] never Olympian. Callimachus and Ennius received their inspiration from Mount Helicon,[2] and Quintus Smyrnaeus makes the Muses who sing the dirge for Achilles come from Helicon and return thither.[3]

The Muses, and the Muse, of Homer are revealed by the Homeric poems in a completely different character and

---

[1] Superior figures refer to notes which will be found on p. 248.

function. In the first place, there is no evidence in either poem for the rather common statement that in Homer the poet is the "spokesman of the Muse," that is, possessed and inspired by her, as the Pythian prophetess was by Apollo. This conception of the Muse is Heliconian; the first to employ it is Pindar: "Give thine oracle, Muse, and I will be thy spokesman" (Frg. 150). All the evidence in Homer makes against this view of the Muse. Alcinous says that Odysseus is not like the roving impostor, "telling stories that no one can believe." "You, on the contrary [he continues] have charm of speech and an honest heart; you have told your tale as well as if you were a bard." Compliments aside, Alcinous means that he believes the story of Odysseus to be true. The bard in Homer "is taught by the Muse or by Apollo" (θ 488); the Muse (θ 64) or Apollo (θ 498) bestows on him "the gift of song"; the god has implanted in his heart "lays of all kinds" (χ 347 f.). The implication of these passages is that to Homer the source of human superiority in achievements of all kinds is divine, not that the individual thus favored represents the divinity and interprets his will. The gift of Heaven or of the Muses naturally includes the poetic manner and charm, for those taught by a divinity always "fashion pleasing works" (η 108-111). But when Odysseus tells Demodocus that the Muse or Apollo must have taught him, because he has sung of the sufferings and the mighty deeds of the Achaeans "*comme il faut*" (κατὰ κόσμον), he adds, "as if you were present yourself, or have heard the tale from an eyewitness." So when the poet invokes the Muses before the Catalogue, he adds: "Ye are present and know the truth; we have no knowledge, only hearsay." Homer calls on the Muses and the Muse, not for inspiration, but only for the facts.

Homer's Muses do not dwell in the Pierian valley, but on Olympus. They are in no wise chthonian; their power is not mysterious and their gift is not transcendental. The Muse is the daughter of Zeus, whose voice is authority (α 282-283, β 216-217). The Muse of Homer thus becomes the authentic Voice of the Past. When historical truth is the chief object of a narrative the narrator himself vouches for it, as did Hecataeus (Frg. 1a Jacoby = Frg. 332 Mueller) and Herodotus (I, 1); we accept it according to our estimate of the author's information and veracity. But the Voice of the Past in Homer's day could not be thus challenged. It was perfectly adapted to produce the illusion of historicity.

The Muse, once she has played her part in the proems of the two poems, fades unobtrusively from the picture, like the crowd at the feast of Poseidon at Pylus, or Athena's immortal spear which Telemachus placed with the other spears in the hall at Ithaca (γ 386-387, α 99-101, 121-129, 320). It seems very questionable whether commentators are justified in basing arguments on the consciousness of the hearer that the Muse is telling the story. Once convinced that the tale was of a real past, the audience could forget its source and feel only that the story told itself. This is implied by the fact that later in the *Iliad*—after we have been reminded (A 604) that the Muses are many, not one—the poet casually invokes the Muses to emphasize the reality of a particular action or episode. This he could not do if his audience were still conscious of the Muse as the narrator of the tale.

Furthermore, the Muse in Homer is never called upon to explain causes, as in Vergil and Milton; she is never invoked to aid in describing a work of art, not even the shield of Achilles, nor before any account of Olympian action. It is worth noting that in the *Odyssey* Demodocus is prompted by the Muse, or by "the god," when he sings of the Trojan War (θ 73, 499). But he begins the *chronique scandaleuse* of the Loves of Ares and Aphrodite without such prompting (θ 266). The sole contribution of the Muse in Homer, aside from the grace and charm which accompanies all divine instruction, is the facts about the Heroes. The novelist has invented many devices for making fiction pass for truth.[4] The two most essential are described and used by Homer. Demodocus has told of the exploits and sufferings of the Achaeans "as if he were present himself, or had heard the tale from another." The tale of the Wanderings, so full of monsters and magic, the poet and audience "hear from another," Odysseus, a mortal, and gifted with the art of making fiction seem true, as he proves often in the sequel. The poet does not vouch for the truth of the Wanderings. But the poet's own tale of the long-vanished past has the supreme sanction for its veracity. The brief appeal to the Muse in the proems makes the audience hear, as it were, the voice of one who was present, the daughter of Zeus, "who above all others bringeth true tidings to men." How better could the hearer be made to feel—all unconsciously—that he was to view with the eye of the imagination the reincarnation of great human lives?

(2) The poet who has the divine gift of anabiosis must, like Homer, be master of the art of creating a second illusion, the Illusion of Vitality. This does not concern particular events or circumstances of the story; it has nothing to do with the vividness of narration or depiction of characters. It is the realism, in the most literal sense, with which the tale from beginning to end conforms with the essential and most universally felt characteristics of life itself. Three of these manifestations of all life that we know, Homer embodies in his narrative with surpassing skill and consistency. They are progressiveness, continuity, and movement. The first two are intimately related to the category of time, the third to that of place.

Time and place are, as it were, the frame of every picture of life that a poet presents to our imagination.[5] Together they define the boundaries within which our attention is to be held and beyond which it must not be allowed to stray. Like the frame of the Sistine Madonna, this frame of the narrative must be worthy of the picture, but it is always subordinate and must never intrude upon our attention.

One of the unchanging and universally observed facts about life is its progressiveness. Our own experience and the experience of mankind assures us that life never goes backward.

Early in the development of the human mind, the forward movement of life was marked by its stages and its smaller divisions. Still later, the concept of time was evolved, an abstraction which seemed, and which was treated more and more by the ordinary man, as a concrete fact. Professor Einstein has shaken the conviction of scientists that time exists as a separate and distinct attribute of being. Homer unconsciously agrees with Einstein. In Homer, as with Einstein, time is relative. If a modern Lucian should meet the disembodied Homer, and should ask him how many days are included in the action of the *Iliad* or the *Odyssey*, or how there could be two mornings on the third day of battle in the *Iliad*, it is probable that the modern necromancer would receive no answer at all, for the poet could not understand what the question meant. Professor Hermann Fraenkel has made it clear that Homer means by time measured by a certain number of days or years merely short or long duration, with a certain emotional connotation.[6] Intervals of time, whether hours, days, or years, are therefore qualitative, not measurable by the clock or calendar. The use of our commensurable concept of time in the analysis of the Homeric poems has been one of the most naïve errors of the *historische Methode*. Historically considered, the Homeric narrative is timeless. The Attic tragedy in its disregard of objective time[7] is only following Homer, who treats the linear dimension of existence as undefined in a wider sense than Aristotle meant (*Poetics* 1449b 14).

The indefiniteness of time in Homer is due to a certain relativity not to place, as in physics today, but to action.

The action of the Homeric narrative is like a river, ever flowing onward. A generation ago Zielinski seemed to have proved that the Homeric narrative never retraces its steps to describe a second main thread of the narrative, because the account of two actions which take place at the same time is not possible for a primitive period, before the awakened reason permits a more abstract and reflective conception of events.[8] Axel Olrik shows that in the folktales of Western Europe two actions are never narrated as parallel; when parallel actions are recognized as such, "es ist litteratur."[9] We need not be surprised to find much that is primitive in Homer. We care only to ask whether the primitive in the Homeric poems is good art, and whether it contributes to the "spell of Homer." We also expect that reason, as Plato implies, is sometimes inimical to art, and that the result of too much reflection often mars the effect of a work of the imagination. Because reflection tells us that many different actions occur simultaneously, it does not follow that a master narrator will select and arrange the accounts of action so that his audience must finish one and then go back and begin another. This is clearly bad art; it substitutes a literary convention for a subtly realistic conformance to a law of nature; it diverts our attention from the story to the fact that a story is being told, and it requires of us a mental effort which does not increase, but lessens, our pleasure. Some years ago a play was given in New York City in which the opening scene was laid in 1934, and the closing scene sixteen years earlier in 1918. The result was a "befuddling of the audience."[10] This is a *reductio ad absurdum* of any unnecessary breaking of the illusion by reversing the current of life.

We have abundant evidence that Homer chose the more "primitive" method because it was the best, and not because he knew no other. Zielinski found in the *Iliad* (p. 441) no examples of the "advanced" method, that is, of narrating parallel actions as occupying the same time, and only two "embryonic" traces of it in the later books of the *Odyssey* (p. 443: ρ 48 ff., ω 222, 386). But there are many clear examples of it in both poems,[11] and the better ones are in the *Iliad*. These, like the "embryonic" instances found by Zielinski, concern the entrances and exits of characters. For example, after the account of the death of Hector and of the laments of Priam and Hecuba, the scene changes to the palace of Hector (X 437-446). Andromache had not yet heard aught of Hector. She was at home, weaving a patterned cloak, and had told her maids to heat water for Hector's bath. She heard the wailing on the Walls and started toward the Tower. This concerns the entrance of a character on the main scene. A still better illustration, this time involving both an entrance and an exit, occurs after the parting of Hector and Andromache (Z 495-516). Andromache goes home and bids her maidens mourn for the foreboded fate of Hector. "Nor did Paris linger at home," but put on his armor, hastened towards the Gate, and overtook Hector *just as he was on the point of leaving the spot where he had held sweet discourse with his wife*. Here the movements of Paris and the conversation between Hector and Andromache are clearly concurrent actions,[12] and so conceived by the poet. But with the intuition of the good narrator he sacrifices the reality of the reason to gain the illusion of reality in the imagination, and preserves the impression of the onward movement of time. He is bound by no law or technique of narration. He is guided only by the universal principle of art whether primitive or advanced, the use of the best means for the most perfect result. How subtly he contrives to preserve this realistic onward movement, and how unerringly gives the impression of life to the most pathetic situation, is best seen in the account of the lamentation on the Tower for the slain Hector.

Hector falls, it will be remembered, near the two springs

where, before the Achaeans came, the Trojan women gathered to lave their shining garments. The spot was not near the Scaean Gate, for Hector had run some distance before he reached it (X 145-147). After he breathes his last, Achilles strips him of his armor, and waits for the Achaeans to gather about the body and glut their rage upon it. Then he binds it to his car and drives toward the ships. Only then—and not at the moment after Hector dies—do Priam and Hecuba catch sight of their son's body and know the fatal outcome of the combat. The encounter did not take place within sight of the Scaean Gate, and Homer has spared a mother from seeing her son's death agonies.[13] Andromache enters after Priam and Hecuba have finished their lamentations. This has taken some time, and she must now strain her eyes (X 463, παπτήνασα) to see the chariot whose swift horses were dragging Hector to the hollow ships. After her long lament, with which Book XXII closes, the Achaeans have reached the camp (Ψ 1 f.). The choice of the chariot with its gruesome pendent to link the action and preserve the onward movement of time is of more value in estimating the method and the genius of Homer than all the places in the two poems where the action is less intense and where scholars have challenged both the method and the genius.

Long generations of specialization in telling a story of the great past doubtless revealed the best methods, and a genius would select the best of these. But Homer, after all, was playing on an instrument of infinite capacity, the human imagination. This functions in a realm where reality has no place, but where the illusion of reality is the only goal. This illusion is broken by a single false movement; only the genius can maintain it, or reach it perfectly. When epic narrative was the only form of literature, and when many poets were practicing this form, there must have been developed a very delicate susceptibility to the receptivity of the hearer, and this determined the means which the poet employed.

THE EPIC ILLUSION 37

He has arts of all kinds, but, more than that, he knows the instrument on which he plays.

The slight inconsistencies caused by describing the movements of an entering character are not noticed by the hearer, because his attention is thus engrossed by this character itself. The gain outweighs the loss, as we can see in the drama. Because the theater cannot show off-scene action, entrances are abrupt. They often for a moment confuse the spectator, and at best they require a certain pause in the action while the entry is explained. How much would be gained if the theater permitted us to see the character approach and to share the feelings of this character, was shown by the performance of the *Bacchae* at Smith College in 1934. There was no stage building. The spectators saw behind the orchestra a great lawn stretching out towards the distant Mount Tom—an excellent Cithaeron. Over this green lawn Agave and her Theban Maenads approached from the direction of the mountain. Their coming could be observed for many minutes before they entered the orchestra. The spectator had time to prepare his mind for one of the most horror-inspiring entrances in the history of the drama. Realism proved its superiority over the artificial convention of the theater.

It is not only in a character's exits and entrances that Homer permits the narrative to retrace its steps. Bougot (*Etude sur l'Iliade d'Homère* [Paris, 1888], 531) notes an instance in a simile (P 657-663). The omen at the first Ithacan assembly (β 146-156) provides an instructive example. Telemachus has just threatened to call on Zeus for vengeance upon the Suitors. In response to his words far-voiced Zeus sent a pair of eagles flying from the mountaintop. These for a time sped on the wings of the wind, side by side, on eager pinions. But when they came over the assembly of many voices, they wheeled about; their plumage ruffled; they looked down on the heads of the men, and their look boded destruction. Then they tore at each other's cheeks and throats with their talons, and flew away over the houses of the city. The Ithacans gazed in wonder at the birds, AS SOON AS THEY SAW THEM (vs. 155), and in their hearts they pondered the meaning of the omen. This Halitherses the seer then interpreted for them. Here are two parallel actions, and the poet is conscious that they are parallel: the assembly gazed in wonder after they caught sight of the birds. The eagles must have begun their flight while Telemachus was still speaking. This, however, our quantitative conception of time tells us is impossible, for Zeus did not send the eagles until Telemachus had ceased speaking. But if time is felt merely as relative to action there is no inconsistency. Zeus cannot act until after Telemachus has ceased speaking, and the eagles cannot appear to the assembly without having started from somewhere. It is the action of the eagles that is important and Homer follows it from beginning to end. He does not synchronize it with the main action, because the slight "anachronism" is utterly insignificant for the interest in the action, and to rationalize the time element would break the illusion. It is undoubtedly choice and not naïveté that leads Homer to adopt this method. For when a minor parallel action is not interesting in itself, but is important only for its results, Homer uses the modern method of synchronization and introduces the minor action by "Meanwhile." After the sacrifice to Athena at Pylus, the roasting of the meat is described (γ 459-463). "Meanwhile" Telemachus bathed, dressed, left the bathroom, and took his seat near Nestor. The meat is now ready to eat and the dinner begins. (Cf. also γ 303, θ 438, ψ 289, ω 365, N 83, O 343. In the narrative in the first person the use of the "Meanwhile" is different; the parallel action is only inferred by the narrator from its results, e.g., δ 435). So at Phaeacia, Odysseus, and on the farm, Laertes, bathe while the dinner is preparing (θ 449-456, cf. 470; ω 365-370, cf. 364, 384). While Laertes and the rest are eating, the scene in Ithaca takes place; when the Ithacans approach the farm (489), dinner is over. At Sparta, Menelaus goes with Helen and Megapenthes to the storeroom for the gifts while Eteoneus is making ready the meal (*o* 99-183; cf. 97 f., 134 ff.). The account of the dinner at Ithaca on the day before the Slaughter (*ρ* 170-257) is particularly illuminating in this connection. The Suitors are throwing the discus and casting the spear in a level spot before the palace. When it was dinnertime and the livestock for the feast had been brought from the fields, Medon said to them: "Young Sirs, you have had sport enough. Come to the palace, and let us begin the preparations for the feast. It is not a bad thing to be prompt about meals." So they left their contests, went in and laid their cloaks on the seats, and then began to butcher the animals, preparing them for the feast (vs. 182). But out in the country Odysseus and the Swineherd were bestirring themselves to go to town. Odysseus slings his shabby wallet over his shoulders, borrows a staff from Eumaeus, and they set out. At the public fountain Melanthius, on his way to the city, meets them, reviles Eumaeus, and viciously kicks Odysseus as he passes on. When he reaches the palace the meal has already begun (vs. 259). Soon after this, as Odysseus and Eumaeus draw near, the Suitors have finished eating, for Phemius has already begun his song (vss. 261 f.). The speech of Medon has no justification except to draw particular attention to the preparations for the dinner, which leaves a sufficient interval for the arrival of Odysseus and still sets the scene for his dramatic entrance into his own home after an absence of twenty years. To use a sporting phrase, the poet's "timing" is faultless. But it is equally so in the *Iliad*, in the use of the two springs as the scene of Hector's death.

These minor parallel actions are treated almost exactly as the most familiar kind of parallel action in Homer, the avoidance of a "flat stretch" in the main narrative by the introduction of a parallel episode, like the well-known Meeting of Glaucus and Diomede. Hector leaves the battlefield to go to the city. While he is on his way Glaucus and Diomede meet on the field and exchange arms. At the end of the episode Hector has arrived at the Scaean Gate.[14] This is true of Telemachus' bath while the meat is roasting for dinner, a rather "flat stretch." In the other minor parallel actions that we have discussed, the only difference is that the poet has *created* an empty stretch in the main action, into which he puts the minor action. The main narrative has reached a point where a slight pause is unnoticed. This is the end of a speech or of a conversation or of a lament. This being true, the question arises whether scholars are right in holding that Homer inserts the episode *because he wishes to avoid a "flat stretch."* Is it not truer to say that Homer *takes advantage of any proper place* to insert the account of parallel action which is of importance for the story? There are many flat stretches in Homer (as Lucian recognized, *Diss. cum Hes.* 5) which are not thus avoided, and Homer has other ways of avoiding the "flatness."

In a similar way scholars affirm that Homer narrates two significant parallel actions of the main story because he is so "primitive" that he has never reflected that the two actions must take place at the same time. This conclusion is then hypostatized and we are asked to believe that "in reality" Iris and Apollo performed their errands at the same time (O 169, 237), and that "in reality" Hermes went to Calypso on the same day that Athena went to Ithaca. But since, as we have seen, Homer knows how to describe two actions as parallel, it is more probable that he chose to send Hermes to Calypso in the *Odyssey* after the events described in Book IV because it made the story better.

This is easy to test. Let us assume that at the close of the Olympian scene with which the action of the poem begins both Athena and Hermes had started on their respective errands, and that at the beginning of Book V, with Telemachus busy with the banquet at Sparta and the Suitors in ambush on Asteris, the narrative had returned to Hermes, whom we last saw starting for Ogygia. Homer could have resumed this narrative in three ways. First, he might have given a brief summary of the situation: "While Telemachus was lingering at Sparta and the Suitors were waiting to slay him." This is the modern method. Homer uses it once. In his only account of an event after the close of his story, the obliteration of the Greek wall, he summarizes the chief events up to the close of the *Odyssey*. This is the only way in which future action can be described as actually occurring. The entire passage (M 1-33) satisfies neither the critics nor those who read Homer for pleasure. It manifestly mars the effect of the tale itself, and Homer never uses this method elsewhere. Instead, he employs one of the two methods already mentioned. If the intervening events are insignificant, he uses the shorthand adverb, "Meanwhile"; otherwise, he inserts the new action in a "flat stretch," real or assumed, of the main action. Either of these devices would have required an elaborate mechanism to synchronize the two extended and important actions. The opening scene on Calypso's isle must be omitted, or must be described as "pluperfect" action, which is always less real: "Hermes had arrived; he had gazed with delight on the lovely prospect." Worse than this, the listener, who could not refresh his memory by turning the pages back to Book I, must recall the Olympian scene and the instructions which Hermes must have received there, or else the poet must repeat them —either effort a wasted one. But worst of all, the effort which the hearer must make to conceive of the two actions as occurring simultaneously would give him time and cause to feel that he was listening to a story, not that he was sharing in it. The epic illusion would be broken and must be established anew. Homer avoids this necessity. The new day on Olympus, with which Book V opens, comes in the course of nature after the evening scenes of the previous episode. Hermes starts for Calypso's isle, and we accompany him till his errand is done. Our attention is neither diverted nor burdened, and the tale is true to nature because its current of life flows onward.

(3) Life not only goes forward; its progress is continuous. Even in sleep, "the brother of Death," there is no pause in its current. This continuity Homer observes with the utmost care. From beginning to end of either poem there is no diaeresis in the action. There are, however, different degrees of fullness in its presentation. The simplest account of life is like that of the obituary, which does little more than record its progress. This is linear narrative, for it reduces life to a thread linking its most important points and has no breadth to make a picture. In its strictest sense it is a summary of action which occupies more than one day. Such linear narrative Homer uses with the greatest freedom at need, yet creates the need sparingly, seven or eight times in the two poems.[15] These "flat spaces" have received from critics a rather undue amount of attention. They enter into numerous day plans of the poems. Dörpfeld rejects the flat spaces as late and inferior work, and brings the action of both the "original" poems within exactly ten days each. Some scholars have counted exactly forty days of action in each poem and see in this round number a favorite folk motif.[16] The intervals of 9 + 12 days in the first book of the *Iliad*, and of 12 + 9 days in the last, are very commonly treated as evidence of the formal symmetry of the poem. Finally the brief compass of the action, seven weeks in the *Iliad* and six in the *Odyssey*, are universally treated as marks of Homer's unequaled approach to epic unity of time. All these views, however true some of them are, put too much emphasis on abstract principles. A genius, as we recognize

in Homer, creates the methods which a more critical age reduces to theory. The use which Homer makes of "flat spaces" is their sufficient justification.

Let us consider first the symmetrical arrangement of the time intervals, 9+12 and 12+9 days in the first and last books of the *Iliad*. The plague must last nine days—"a week or ten days," as we say—for two reasons: it must continue long enough to show that it is a heaven-sent scourge, and it must also make clear to the army that Agamemnon, the commander-in-chief, will do nothing to remove it. If Agamemnon, instead of Achilles, had called the assembly and had asked some seer to explain what should be done, the quarrel would have lacked sufficient cause. A week or ten days is necessary for the plot. But it is hard to see how the nine days before Hector's funeral could have been chosen because of any desire to make a symmetrical balance between the beginning and the end of the story. Hector was the pillar and hope of Troy, and he had endeared himself to the listener. In heroic days the funeral of a great hero was a formal function, not to be hurried. The funeral of Achilles occupied twice the time of Hector's. Only one day was spent in the burial of Patroclus, but the poet took pains to make this haste natural. The shade of Patroclus entreats Achilles, "Bury me with all possible speed; let me pass the gates of Hades" (Ψ 71). There was no reason to shorten the funeral of Hector. Its duration is a natural detail, a usual mark of honor, and little more.

The twelve days' absence of the gods in Book I, and the the twelve days' interval in which Achilles drags the body of Hector daily, are undoubtedly contrasting intervals, but the relation between them is functional rather than formal. In Book I the anger of Achilles, "the lion-in-the-man," requires time to lash itself into a fury so great that no offers or entreaties can prevail against it. So in Book XXIV, when this rage has been turned with far greater vehemence against

Hector, time must again elapse before it can wear itself out on the unresisting body sufficiently to make Achilles amenable even to the command of Zeus. Twelve days, perhaps our "fortnight," is none too long for this; but the number twelve is a mere detail.

Finally, unity of time, as applied to Homer's poems, is hardly more than a makeshift, for the idea is based on Aristotle's observation of contemporary Attic tragedies, and it is confronted with an obstacle in the voyage of Odysseus on leaving Ogygia. He sails for seventeen days, the longest continuous sail in Greek literature until Lucian (*True Hist.* I, 6: seventy-nine days' voyage). The poet who created the miraculous Phaeacian ship, "swift as wing or thought," could have shortened the first stretch of Odysseus' homeward voyage if "unity of time" had been one of his chief considerations. Instead of "unity," a more accurate term is "continuity" of time, which intervals of all lengths tend to efface and are, therefore, avoided or condensed.

The sureness with which Homer creates the illusion of continuous time is seen when, as is usually the fact, the thread of life broadens into a ribbon or frieze, which permits scenery and figures. The continuum of human life is made possible by routine matters which even in the most intense and hazardous periods cannot be neglected: sleep, dressing and undressing, bathing, and meals. These are so familiar that when we see them invariably occurring in their proper places in the story, we are unconsciously impressed with the reality of its life. But the fact that they are so familiar makes it unnecessary to describe them in detail. Our interest is not in the menu or in bedroom and bathroom scenes of the stage and the cinema. Details of the diurnal circumstances of life give too much intrinsic importance to matters that belong only to the frame of the picture, which must never be at the focus of our chief attention.

The formulaic language in the account of meals contributes

greatly to this subordination of importance. The formula imparts its meaning instantly, demanding no mental effort to understand its significance; and Homer knows how to vary the formula so as to prevent the monotony which is the worst enemy of interest and attention. The care with which he avoids unnecessary repetitions is seen in the second dinner of the Suitors, in Book II of the *Odyssey*. After the dinner in Book I no meal of the Suitors can interest us until the Beggar appears in Book XVII. Hence the poet skillfully keeps us otherwise occupied while the second dinner goes on. Telemachus finds the Suitors preparing the meat (vss. 299 ff.); he goes at once to the storeroom and arranges for the provisions for his journey. When he joins the Suitors (vs. 381) the narrative shifts to Athena and the getting ready of the ship. When this is done the dinner is over. Homer has avoided another bare stretch.

As the meal varies from the normal, either in circumstances or in importance, the ribbonlike narrative broadens and fills with content. This, however, very rarely includes details of the food itself or of the accessories of the table. This lack is commonly called "primitive," because the early mind does not carefully observe nature, but rather relies on the generalized memory picture which does not preserve particulars. But it is based on one of the soundest principles of narration. Details produce a strain on the mind of the listener, who must translate words into an imagined picture. The strain is greater if the objects described are unfamiliar. Lessing explained the difficulty as arising from the inability of words to present the details together, as painting does: they must succeed each other, and we forget the earlier when we try to combine them with the later. This is not the whole truth. The animated cartoon has at last added to painting the time element which Lessing found only in the verbal description. The multiplication of details in some of these cartoons defeats its own purpose. Instead of increasing our pleasure, the details divert our minds from the chief figures and weary our attention by the burden laid upon it.[17] This is illustrated in Greek vase paintings—for example, two parting scenes, the leavetaking of Persephone on a volute krater in Munich, and the parting of a warrior from his wife, on a fifth-century Attic vase (Furtwängler and Reichhold, *Die griechische Vasenmalerei*, pls. 10, 35). After a hasty view of each of the two—which is all the time allowed by oral description—we find that our impression of the first is blurred and ineffective, because the scene is too full of content and detail. The second, suppressing all detail and using only a few lines, impresses its significance at once, and gives us time to enter into its meaning. So Homer's refusal to crowd even an important dinner scene with details of food and other objects not only gives the setting its proper subordination, but also makes a clearer picture and gives our imagination time to appropriate it.

There are some threescore meals in the action of the two poems. The taking of food, like retiring for the night and arising in the morning, is at least mentioned, if not described, in the account of every day whose action is presented two-dimensionally.[18] The reason usually given[19] is Homer's naïve delight in everything in life, a characteristic of the primitive mind. If so, why do we fail to find these commonplace matters always described or mentioned in poems like the *Kalevala* and the epics of India? Certainly Homer shows no interest in eating for its own sake; a single verse suffices to describe this: "They stretched out their hands for the ready viands." The heroes never eat with gusto. Even Odysseus, always so attentive to food, when he breaks his fast of more than two days is given only one additional verse: "[He ate] ravenously, for long had he been without taste of food" (ζ 250). Arend remarks (*op. cit.* 70) that it was the delight in hospitality, not the joy in eating, that inspired Homer's description of meals. This is doubtless partly true. But the primary function of meals in Homer, as of the other universally observed actions that mark each round of the sun in human life, is to create the illusion of continuous, and, therefore, of real life.

(4) Vitality expresses itself most characteristically by movement. Utter lack of movement, when the heart ceases to beat, implies death, the negation of life. When Matthew Arnold wrote, "Homer is rapid in his movement," he was thinking of style rather than of content; yet every reader of Homer thinks of the action in the poems as rapid. This is especially true when a "flat space" is to be covered. Heroes walk quickly; horses "fly"; a ship runs before the wind with a bone in her teeth; and divinities pass from place to place with seven-league boots, or like a shooting star, or with the speed of thought. But it is movement, not swiftness, which universally marks both the Homeric narrative and life, for "movement includes every real occurrence in the universe" (Hobbes).

Movement is in space and is most easily noticed by reference to its spatial background. Sudden movements of the body without change of place are more difficult to present to the imagination with words, possibly because language conveys the picture too slowly to keep time with the movement. We picture in our minds most clearly, and retain best in memory, the sculpturesque figures and groups in Homer in which the movement is not that of the Discobolus, but in which, rather, a longer moment of rest can hold our attention. Such are Thetis clinging to the knees of Zeus, Priam before Achilles, kissing those dread hands stained with the blood of his sons, Achilles recognizing the goddess, who had seized his golden locks, and many others. The slower and more familiar movements of the body, like sitting, standing, stretching out the hands in prayer, are more characteristic of Homer. The quicker movements when there is no change of place, the poet often suggests instead of describing in detail. When a hero falls in battle the poet often employs a simile, an indirect way of stimulating the imagination: the dancing of the Phaeacian youths is interpreted for us not by description, but through its effect on the chief spectator, Odysseus (θ 264 f.). At the climax of the *Odyssey*, the leap of Odysseus upon the threshold is undoubtedly the most thrilling moment, but one may query whether we picture it as vividly as the more deliberate stringing of the bow and the spreading out of the arrows before him. However this may be, a movement from one place to another demands the least effort of the attention, and thus establishes most simply and imperceptibly the illusion of physical vitality.

Herein lies one of the most fundamental differences between epic and drama. Realistic change of scene is barred from the stage. Where strict unity of place is not observed, resort must be made to a convention. In the *Frogs* of Aristophanes, Dionysus and Xanthias before our eyes proceed to the temple of Heracles, then along the road to Ceramicus, then to the Acherusian Lake, and finally to Hades. Only the Muse of Old Comedy could dare thus to challenge the evidence of our senses. The modern curtain utterly disregards the reality of continuous time. The Attic tragedy by means of its chorus kept the illusion of this reality, but thereby sacrificed change of scene. Diametrically opposed to this unity of place is Homer's multiplicity. The two poems take us to Heaven and to Hell; to sea as well as land, and to widely separated parts of the world, both the known and the unknown. The cinema has at last made possible an epic drama, but must go to Homer before it can fully realize it.

For unity of place Homer substitutes continuity of place by means of the movement of the characters. This continuum of place, like that of time, freed Homer from all artificial "laws" of unity, and made his narrative true to that oneness of the external world which our own experience recognizes. Let us take as a single example the second book of the *Iliad*, in which we are told how the Greek army came to be marshaled. In this account, consisting of nearly five hundred verses, there are ten changes of scene, with only one break in the continuity. The narrative begins with the same scene as at the end of the previous episode, the bedchamber of Zeus. We follow the Dream to the bed of Agamemnon, then Agamemnon to the council (53); with the Elders, Agamemnon goes to the assembly, and the crowd follows (84-86); they accept his proposal to return home, and rush to the ships (150). At this moment, while they are taking away the props of the ships, to launch them, the scene changes for the only time, to Olympus, by a device which we shall consider in a later chapter. From Olympus we follow Athena to the ship of Odysseus (167-169), then Odysseus as he passes along the ships through the crowd. With the crowd we go back to the assembly, where one of the crowd, Thersites, for a moment holds the center of the stage. At the close of the assembly "the Argives rose, and, hurrying to the ships, prepared dinner." The meal in Agamemnon's quarters is singled out for special attention, and at its close the princes move to the parade ground, the crowd following, and in their midst Athena, inspiring in the heart of every soldier an eagerness to fight.

For static unity of place Homer substitutes a totality of many parts linked together by the moving characters. The one scene of many an Attic tragedy is before a palace. In the *Odyssey* we come to know, with little or no description by the poet, at least ten places in the palace at Ithaca, by visiting them in turn with one or another of the characters. The result is not unity, but reality: the palace is filled with life because men and women are moving about in it. Unity of place would have robbed the Homeric poems of much of their charm. This is easily seen if we compare the *Iliad* with the *Odyssey*. Before doing this, however, we must consider another important aspect of place in Homer, its distinctness.

In realism of scene Homer has one feature in common with Attic tragedy in the days before Sophocles introduced scene painting, and with modernistic scenery, which, however, does not vary with the circumstances, as Homer's does. Where action often occurs in the same or in similar surroundings, and also where a crowd is on stage, Homer gives little attention to the setting. In the former case the place becomes sufficiently clear to us by a sort of *Einfühlung* as the action goes on; in the latter, perhaps, the crowd occupies most of our attention. So in Attic tragedy, where the backgrounds are few in number, and where no change is made throughout the play, too great detail might easily become wearisome to the spectator, just as intricately patterned wall paper once disturbed us when as children we had to see it continually from a bed of illness. And when the chorus is always present, it keeps our attention from straying to the scenery. But whatever may have been the reason, the Homeric narrative follows this general principle. The battlefield, the place of assembly, the great hall of Ithaca, are never made distinct by detailed description. But when the setting is new, and especially when a single character, or at most a small group of not more than three or four, engage our attention, there will be description. The palace of Priam is described when Hector alone stands before it, not when the Trojan assembly meets near it (B 788); that of Alcinous as Odysseus approaches, as are the quarters of Achilles when Priam is about to enter. Our only knowledge of the splendid interior of the palace of Menelaus is gained from the whispered words of Telemachus to Pisistratus. Distinctness of background seems to be sought by Homer when a small group of characters is to appear before it, or when it is isolated from a large crowd in any way. Both of these considerations help to lend to the *Odyssey*, as compared with the *Iliad*, that charm which made Lowell say that "the *Odyssey* is the only long poem that reads of itself."

The social instinct of man gives to the crowd a universal appeal in all fiction. Tragedy in Athens, being denied the direct use of the "mob," had recourse to the epic, and introduced the large crowd in the tale of off-scene action; for example, in the *Septem* and the *Persians* of Aeschylus, and in almost every Messenger's tale of Euripides. Homer uses the crowd at will, but with this general difference in the two poems, that in the *Odyssey* the crowd tends to act as the background of the action; in the *Iliad*, as one of the *dramatis personae*. The crowd at Pylus is merely mentioned and then fades from the picture. The assemblies at Ithaca and Phaeacia do not indicate their will as do most of those in the *Iliad*. Even the band of Suitors does not assume large proportions until Odysseus begins to plan his vengeance. Then (π 245-255) we learn from the words of Telemachus that there are more than a hundred of them. The very fact that they are so numerous makes the account of the Slaughter, in the opinion of many critics, less vivid. On the other hand, the climax of the *Iliad*, the death of Hector, gains much of its power from the concentration of our attention on the chief actors, because the crowd, the two armies, and all the Trojans and all the gods, are no more than a background. But in most of the *Iliad*, since it is a tale of war, the armies cannot be ignored. This fact tends to diminish the clarity and distinctness of the scenes of battle. (See below, Chap. IV.)

Besides its greater use of the crowd, the *Iliad* is also handicapped by its closer approach to a greater unity of place. The scenes of the chief action are laid in one of five regions: the city, the Greek camp, the Trojan or the Greek side of the battle, and Heaven. All these regions are close to each other. Even Olympus is so near that from it the gods see what happens on the Trojan plain: it is *ex hypothesi* near. The nearness to one another of these five regions permits frequent change of scene. This frequency of change offers less time to give reality to the background, but it tends to keep us conscious of the other regions. Our attention is unduly burdened. Hence the greater unity of place in the *Iliad*, added to the frequent presence of the two armies, handicaps the poet. He finds it necessary to resort to many poetic devices which have given Separatists many of their arguments. (See below, Chap. IV.) In the *Odyssey*, until the climax approaches, the scenes are widely separated and are less thronged with crowds. Our attention is more clearly focused on each scene, with little intrusion of the others. Instead of unity of place there is unification of places by means of the journeys of the characters. During the first fourteen books—more than half the poem—this continuity of place is broken but twice in the main narrative: the scene changes once from Sparta to Ithaca, and once from Ithaca to Olympus. Otherwise, places as far from Ithaca as Pylus and Sparta, Calypso's isle and the land of the Phaeacians, are linked together as realistically as London and Canterbury, and Bombay and Tokyo, would be in our experience if we visited them personally on a voyage round the world.[20] From the opening scene on Olympus we go with Athena to visit Telemachus, and with the latter to Pylus and then to Sparta. From Olympus again at the beginning of Book V, Hermes takes us swiftly to Calypso's isle, where we meet Odysseus and then make the return voyage to Ithaca more slowly, and with a delightful break in the journey, the three days' stop at Phaeacia.

The remoteness from Ithaca of the scenes in which fully half the action takes place is, as I have said, one of the secrets of the eternal charm of the *Odyssey*. It is human nature to observe more carefully new and strange surroundings, and to find refreshment from the absence of the more familiar sights. All the first-class storytellers recognize this. But few of the best of them have equaled Homer in the amazing skill with which he invents and uses scenes which vary the monotony of the action at Ithaca. Recall the famous tales: *Treasure Island, Robinson Crusoe, Don Quixote*, the *Faerie Queene*, the *Inferno*, and the *Aeneid*, and think of the introduction of the hero. Is there in any long story that you know a more dramatic entrance of the major character than that of Odysseus, on an island at the world's end, alone on the shore looking out over the sea and longing for home? Think of an *Odyssey* without Phaeacia, or the remote steading of the Swineherd, which in turn loses its significance without the journey of Telemachus.

Journeys in Homer not only make the action continuous; they interest us of themselves. In the Tricking of Zeus in the *Iliad*, Hera might have gone straight to Mount Ida; for Sleep, like all minor gods, is at hand when needed (cf. II 682). But instead, the Queen of Heaven, after making the most elaborate toilet described in either poem, leaves Olympus with the swiftness of a modern airplane, drops to Pieria and Emathia, sets her course for the snow-capped mountains of Thrace, which she just clears, and, passing Mount Athos, drops again, this time to the sea, and soon reaches Lemnos, where she finds the God of Sleep. After some haggling over the price of his assistance and the security for its payment, the two fare onward, past Imbros to Lectus, a peak of Ida. Here Sleep perches on the top of a towering pine tree, and Hera goes on alone to Gargarus. By this time we have forgotten the long battle described in the last three books, and are intent only on Hera's trick. But notice the return of Hera to Olympus (O 79), "like the flash of thought in the mind of a widely traveled man" which carries him in memory instantly as far as he will. Homer loves these contrasts in journeys. The voyage of Odysseus from Calypso's isle to Phaeacia takes three weeks and includes storm and suffering; but from Phaeacia, still on the edge of faeryland, to Ithaca, Odysseus voyages in a few hours, peacefully slumbering, forgetful of all that he had suffered (ν 92). On the voyage from Ithaca to Pylus, Telemachus and his crew rely on the experience of the older Mentor (=Athena). They broach the wine and spend the night in good cheer. But on the return journey, Telemachus, with no one to counsel him, sails on through the night wondering whether death awaits him at the rising of the sun.

Shorter journeys are often made full of interest and emotion. Hector on his way to the city is surrounded at the Scaean Gate by the Trojan women, asking for news of their men, "and sorrow had befallen many of them" (Z 237-241). The journey of Eumaeus and the beggar Odysseus in Book XVII, from the piggery in the country to the palace, is broken by three scenes: the gross insult by the Goatherd at the city fountain under the shrine of the Nymphs; the first sight which the hero has had of his home in twenty years; and the death of the old dog Argus, the only mortal being in the whole poem who at once recognized Odysseus.

If journeys can thus be made full of interest, why does the account of a long voyage from beginning to end, like *Two Years Before the Mast*, or the Argonautic Expedition of Apollonius, fail to have the keen interest of a good yarn? Even without the wearisome footnotes of the mythological periegete, the *Argonautica* could not hold our interest. We feel that we must follow the journey from beginning to end, and that with the last casting of the anchor stones and the final making fast of the stern hawsers the tale is done. The voyage for its own sake lacks the unity that Aristotle found wanting in a tale of the labors of Heracles. The feeling that we must follow the voyage to its end robs us of one of the essential prerequisites of pleasure, which is a certain freedom. Most of us after much travel feel a certain nostalgia. Homer guards against this by interrupting the ten-years-long homeward journey of Odysseus by periods of rest. We may hazard the conjecture that a clear recognition of the principles on which rests the keenest interest in adventures on a long voyage had quite as much to do with the way in which Homer describes the Wanderings of Odysseus, as any conception of the advantage to be gained by "unity of time." The account is twice broken, once by the three days at Phaeacia, and again, this time in a different way, in the Necyia. Furthermore, the hearer knows that the tale will not be too long, for the most exciting part is to come after the Wanderings are over. This seems clear evidence that Homer knew that even the most interesting voyage must not be too long or be told solely for its own sake. The Wanderings of Odysseus, if told as a separate poem, could never have had their present fascination.

We have at some length contrasted the use of place in the two poems to show that the *Iliad*, not only because of its larger cast of characters, which includes the two armies, but still more by reason of its greater unity of place, presents a more difficult problem in narration. A few statistics will illustrate and confirm our conclusion. These show that both the number of "scenes" and the abrupt change of scene are proportionately greater in the *Iliad*. For this purpose we define a "scene" as action, with place constant, which is narrated graphically or with speeches by the characters. We also disregard battle scenes in which place is irrelevant. Of scenes thus defined the *Iliad* contains at least 225, the *Odyssey*, without the Apologue, 98; proportionately the *Odyssey* should contain 149. This is not surprising when we remember the numerous scenes on Olympus and Ida, and the four different regions of earth: city, camp, and the two sides of the battle. But what is noteworthy is that in the *Iliad* the scenes which change without one of the characters going from one place to another, are more than three and one-half times as frequent as in the *Odyssey* (76:21; the proportionate ratio would be more than double, i.e., 76:47.5). This testifies not so much to the greater mastery of the art of narrative in the *Odyssey* as to the circumstances of the latter tale, and especially to the great importance of the widely separated places of action. Pylus and Sparta, Ogygia and Scheria, the Swineherd's steading and the farm of Laertes, are inventions of a master narrator.

Place and time; life presented as it were by the impersonal Voice of the Past; life flowing ever onward; continuous life; and life revealed to us chiefly by movement: these are matters which deal with the reality of all human existence. They are elements in every story, but they do not concern the story itself. In the creation of the Epic Illusion, the spell of the Human Life Writ Large, the most important constituent is a third illusion, which we shall consider in the next chapter, the Illusion of Personality.

CHAPTER THREE

THE EPIC ILLUSION—(*Continued*)
PERSONALITY—THE DRAMATIC IN HOMER

No POETIC PICTURE of past human life can produce the illusion of reality if it does no more than convince us with its general likeness to life. The real world that we know is peopled with other human beings no two of whom are identical. The more intimately we enter into the lives of others, the more we feel the uniqueness of their individualities. The universal human interest is never in typical "man"; it is in persons—because individuals, not types, belong to life. The most universally human presentation of life must therefore create above all the illusion of personality. This is the life principle of every great mythos. The biology of literature may abstract the elements of personality and describe them, but the secret of its synthesis has never been discovered. It differs from moral character as the story from its plot. It is not physical appearance or peculiarities of action. Shylock is a real personality, but who knows how he looked or moved? Much less is it revealed by an analysis of the contents of the mind. Personality is a complex intangible. It has been called a "fourth dimension,"[1] a term which in the theory of relativity describes ultimate physical reality. Literary art produces the illusion of the ultimate human reality chiefly by means of the form of self-expression which is most characteristic of our race. Man has been articulate ever since he became human. He makes known the uniqueness of his individuality best by his *ipsissima verba*.

The power of direct speech to create this illusion is seen in the Apologue, where the theme carries us far from reality. When Polyphemus says to Odysseus that he does not recognize the rights of suppliant and stranger (ι 273-277), he tells

---
[1] Superior figures refer to notes which will be found on p. 249.

us little more than we have learned from the poet's description of him: "Respect for the right had no place in his heart" (ι 189). But the Cyclops does not become to us a living personality until we not only see him, but also hear him speak. The speech both in Homer and in Attic drama is again and again used as the final and the supreme way of producing upon us the emotion caused by the illusion of personality. In the *Ajax* and in the *Oedipus Rex* of Sophocles the sufferings of the hero are first described, then we see him, and finally we hear from his lips the expression of his agony of mind. In the *Alcestis* of Euripides the handmaid describes the queen's farewell to her home and her failing strength; then we see her with her husband and children, taking her last look at the light of day, and, finally, she speaks, and becomes for the first time a real person. (The Attic drama uses the recital by the Messenger from within and from off-scene to prepare the minds of the audience and so to heighten the impressiveness of a scene of pathos.) Here, as often elsewhere, Homer showed tragedy the way. Homer first describes Cyclops; then after an interval we see him enter the cave and perform his evening tasks; and at last, when these are done and his fire is lighted, we hear his terrible voice and his brutal words. It is the words of Polyphemus to Odysseus, to the other Cyclopes, and to his pet ram, that made him a personality, destined to live throughout classical literature. The king of the Laestrygonians, on the contrary, and his wife and daughter, all silent actors, lack this reality, and do not appear as characters in later literature. The hospitable Axylus and handsome Nireus are like interesting characters who are merely pointed out to us as they pass on the street. But Thersites and Phoenix are real persons, because we hear them speak. Out of the abundance of the heart the mouth speaketh; and the heart not only is the center of the physical life but also has become for us the center of personality.

THE EPIC ILLUSION

The urge to create the illusion of personality through direct speech is primitive. It falls entirely within the sphere of the sensuous; it accords with the naïve personalization of the external world, and it results directly from the childlike tendency to imitate. Aesop's animals speak. The tales of the Old Testament abound in direct discourse. (In the Book of Ruth the story is told in seventy-five verses, I 6-IV 17; only fourteen verses contain no direct utterance, and of indirect discourse there is not a trace.) But the persistence of direct speech as the most universal characteristic of the imaginative picture of life expressed by means of words we cannot explain without recognizing in direct utterance the chief component in the illusion of personality. The term "dramatic illusion" disregards its origin and its debt to Homer. Plato identified Homer with drama in his use of the speeches (*Resp.* 394 B). His discovery of this most potent ingredient in the "charm" of Homer—under which Plato himself fell (*Resp.* 607 D)—has been too much overlooked in recent years, especially by scholars in other fields than Greek. Both the *Aeneid* and the *Nibelungenlied* have been called more "dramatic" than the Homeric poems.[2] It is true that the adjective is thus used in a derived sense. It describes the effect rather than the manner of drama. But its frequent and ambiguous use has obscured the significance of Aristotle's observation that in the use of the dramatic manner Homer was supreme among epic poets (*Poetics* 1460a 5).[3] For this reason, in examining the illusion of personality in Homer we shall discuss at some length the use of speeches, calling in the aid of statistics.

Homer employs direct speech more than any later Western epic poet. Of the three poetic manners in Homer, the objectively narrative, the subjectively explanatory, and the dramatically "imitative," the last is used more than the the first two taken together. If the verses which introduce the speeches and are little more than the stage direction "loquitur" of drama are included, three-fifths of Homer consists of speeches. This is almost exactly the same proportion as that of speech to choral lyrics in the *Suppliants* of Aeschylus.

Homer not only uses direct speech more than any other epic poet of Western literature; he uses it in a more dramatic way.

The characteristic feature of drama is the dialogue. This is literary mimesis in its truest sense, since conversation is the most common accompaniment of all human intercourse. Because Aeschylus added a second actor and thus made true dialogue possible, he was regarded as the father of tragedy. His debt to Homer has not been sufficiently recognized. His remark that his tragedies were "portions from Homer's great feasts" (*Athenaeus* 347 E), if taken at its face value, should mean that what he added to the embryonic drama of Thespis and his immediate successors was due to the inspiration and pattern of Homer. The evidence is worth considering here, since it also testifies to the dramatic character of Homer.

(1) The first great renascence of Homer fell during the formative years of Aeschylus. The recitation of the Homeric poems was made an important feature of the Panathenaic festival sometime in the sixth century, most probably by the Pisistratids, and was followed by a deep and widespread enthusiasm for Homer. During the fifth century the Homeric poems were familiar to every Athenian; they are likely to have been still more popular before they had to share with the drama the public interest. During the life of Socrates the rhapsode wore a festal costume and employed all the histrionic artifices: Plato makes no distinction between rhapsode and tragic actor (*Ion* 532 D, *Resp.* 395 A).[4] These features were most probably introduced in the sixth century. Homer was the only poet to whom Aeschylus in his early years could have turned for suggestions of the way to

handle a tragic plot and present it dramatically. (2) Plato identifies Homer's epic with tragedy in its effect: ". . . the authors of tragic poetry in iambic and in heroic verse" (*Resp.* 602 B); "When we listen to Homer or any other tragic poet" (*Resp.* 605 C); "Next, consider tragedy, and its leader and guide, Homer" (*Resp.* 598 D); "Homer, the first of the tragic poets" (*Resp.* 607 A). Plato, himself a poet, must have had good reason for this identification. (3) Aristotle says that tragedy "has all the elements of the epic" (*Poetics* 1462a 15). Chancellor Throop has shown that most of the characteristic features of the tragic plot are found in Homer.[5] Finally, Aristotle frequently illustrates from Homer a principle of the structure of a tragic plot. The recognized similarity between Homer and tragedy in plot, in mimesis, and in effect, the lack of other similar poetry (for the cyclic poems were rich in material, but poor in its use), and the great popularity of Homer at Athens just before Aeschylus began to write, seem sufficient to prove that his remark about the influence of Homer upon tragedy was literally true. We notice also that Athenaeus contrasts Aeschylus with a certain Ulpian: the latter took, not "slices" of meat, as Aeschylus did, but a bone or a thick piece of gristle. The *pièces de résistance* of Homer are the dialogues, which Aeschylus, by adding a second actor, introduced into the nascent tragedy.

In the use of the dialogue Homer is unequaled in Western epic. After Homer, Greek epic shows a steady decline in this respect, until in Nonnus there is an average of less than one dialogue to a book, and in the whole of the *Dionysiaca* only three which consist of as many as four speeches. The third book of the *Argonautica*, which is the most dramatic, falls far short of Homer.[6] Vergil, too, restricts the dialogue within far narrower limits than Homer does.[7]

A comparison of Homer's dialogues with those of Attic tragedy is illuminating. Of course, since stichomythy is barred from the epic, we cannot compare the number of speeches per dialogue. Yet Homer has one dialogue of 26 speeches (in τ), a greater number than is found in either of the first two epeisodia of the *Prometheus Bound*. We can, however, make the comparison with respect to length of dialogue. In the *Ajax* of Sophocles the six dialogues average about 185 verses each. Homer has seven dialogues, each of which is longer than this. In the *Medea* of Euripides there are eight dialogues containing from 79 to 196 verses each, averaging 131 verses. Homer has 30 dialogues of more than 79 verses each, and 15 of more than 131 verses. The dialogue which contains the Apologue (θ 536-ν 15) contains 2298 verses, and is undoubtedly the longest dialogue in verse in Greek literature.

In the number of interlocutors Homer's dramatic manner is more free than that of either the primitive folk tale or Attic tragedy. The former limits the number to two,[8] the latter practically to three—for where three actors participate, the words of the Coryphaeus are for the most part a pure formality. In Homer's dialogues three or four speakers often take part, and nine times there are from five to eight, most frequently without a single new entrance.[9] It is noticeable, however, that where Homer is dramatic in effect as well as in manner, the number of speakers is limited to two or three or, at most, four. Plato observes the same freedom and the same limitations.

The *Odyssey* makes a more extensive use of the dialogue than does the *Iliad*. Hirzel[10] virtually denies this. He accepts the view of the Author On the Sublime (IX, 13, cf. 11), that the *Odyssey* was the work of the poet's old age: the *Iliad* is "full of action and conflict; the *Odyssey* is largely narrative"—which is characteristic of old age. Hirzel believes that dialogue belongs to youth, whether of the individual or of nations, because passionate youth delights in the external and make-up, while age withdraws within itself, and relates the external to its own ego. Aside from the preponderance of speaker's narratives in the *Odyssey*—which we shall discuss presently—Hirzel's chief argument is that the *Odyssey* has no dialogues which compare in dramatic power with those between Hector and Andromache (Z), between Achilles and the Envoys (I), and between Achilles and Priam (Ω). This view confuses theme and situation with the poet's manner of presenting them. The theme of the *Iliad* is more tragic. Hence the situations of the three dialogues just mentioned give rise to deeper emotions. In their effect some of the dialogues of the *Iliad* are more dramatic. But if "dramatic form" is proper to youth and not to old age, as Hirzel thinks, the inference that the *Odyssey* was composed in Homer's later years is not supported by the facts, as a few statistics will show.[11]

The comparative compass of the *Iliad* and the *Odyssey* without the Apologue is expressed by the ratio 8+: 5. By this ratio let us test the formal dramatic mimesis of the two poems.

(1) The most undramatic speeches are those outside of the dialogue,—single speeches without a reply. Of these the *Iliad* has 357, the *Odyssey* 72, a ratio of 25:5.

(2) The *Odyssey* has a relatively larger number of dialogues (*Iliad*, 125; *Odyssey*, 102; ratio, 6−: 5).

(3) In the length and freedom of the dialogue the difference between the two poems is still more marked. Less than one-sixth (i.e., 20 dialogues) of the *Iliad's* dialogues contain more than 4 speeches each, only one consists of as many as 13 speeches, and there are never more than 4 interlocutors, unless we include the "Voice from the crowd" (B 272). In the *Odyssey*, more than one-third of the dialogues consist of 5 or more speeches, there is one of 16 and another of 26 speeches, and 7 named speakers are heard at the Ithacan assembly (β 25 ff.). Table 1 shows in summary form how far the *Odyssey* excels in dramatic manner.

The advance in the technique of the dramatic epic exhibited by the *Odyssey* is clear. That it is largely due to the theme and the resulting situations is almost equally so. We considered in Chapter II the importance which Homer gives to movement. He gives equal attention to rest, and it is here that the dialogue plays its part. On the battlefield

TABLE 1

QUANTITATIVE AND RELATIVE USE OF SINGLE SPEECHES AND DIALOGUES IN THE ILIAD AND THE ODYSSEY (WITHOUT THE APOLOGUE)

	RATIO
Number of verses (16,696:9960)	8+:5
Number of single speeches not in dialogue (357:72)	25:5
Verses in single speeches (about 2200:600)	18+:5
Number of dialogues (125:102)	6—:5
Number of verses in dialogues (about 4800:5400)	4.4:5
Proportion of verses in dialogues to total number of verses (30 per cent : 54 per cent)	2.8:5
Short dialogues: of two speeches (54:35)	8—:5
Short dialogues: of three speeches (40:22)	9—:5
Short dialogues: of four speeches (11:10)	5.5:5
Long dialogues: of five or more speeches (20:35)	3—:5
Proportion of short dialogues to total number (84 per cent:66 per cent)	4—:5
Proportion of long dialogues to total number (16 per cent:34+ per cent)	2.3:5

combatants may speak as they approach, but if a dialogue ensues we must assume, and the poet often tells us, that they then stood still. On a journey or voyage there is rarely conversation in Homer, except when a halt is made.[12] Priam and Idaeus pause at the river to let their steeds drink, and the long conversation with Hermes ensues. But as they drive on, no word is spoken until they reach the quarters of Achilles. The exchange of speeches at the assembly and the council, in the quarters of Agamemnon, Achilles, and Nestor, and in the palaces of Priam and Paris points to the conclusion that speech and action, the logos and the ergon, tend to exclude each other. Hence the *Odyssey* offers greater opportunity for the dialogue. The scenes at Ogygia, Ithaca, Pylus, Sparta, and Phaeacia are better adapted to the dialogue than is the battlefield at Troy.

The alternation between movement in the narrative and rest in the dialogue has its counterpart in the stasima and epeisodia of tragedy. The evolutions of the chorus offered a pleasing diversion after the comparative lack of action and movement of the actors, except in the entrances and exits. Homer, however, introduces action, even off-scene action, into many of his longer dialogues. The dialogue between Achilles and Priam is thrice interrupted thus: Achilles leaves the hall and prepares the body of Hector for its return; the meal is prepared and eaten; and a couch is prepared for Priam. Attic tragedy had no place for eating and sleeping: the *Alcestis* is "rather like comedy."

This blending of action with dialogue is particularly noticeable in the *Odyssey*. It is less appropriate in the *Iliad* because the violent action of the battlefield demands for the listener's relaxation more completely motionless scenes between the accounts of fighting. Yet the manner is the same in both. In Book XV, in Hera's return from Mount Ida, her chief errand is postponed by the angry exit of Ares to avenge the death of his son Ascalaphus, and his recall to his senses by Athena. This adds much to the picture of the unhappy Olympian family, but has nothing to do with the chief purpose of the episode. It would be impossible in Attic tragedy. Nor could Hera give her message to Iris and Apollo off-scene. Yet these off-scene words, and Athena's "big sister" interference with the plan of Ares, undoubtedly deepen the perspective in which we view the Olympians, and also contribute to the realism of the story.

Let us test the closeness with which Homer in his long dialogues approaches drama in both manner and effect. At the same time let us try to see how nearly alike the two poems are in both these respects by taking an episode from each, the Presbeia and the Niptra.

In the Presbeia (I 186-668), the scene is laid in the quarters of Achilles. Achilles, seated, is singing of exploits of heroes, accompanying himself on the lyre. Opposite to him sits Patroclus, listening to his song. Automedon and perhaps other squires are clearing away the dinner. A knock is heard, one of the squires opens the door, and Odysseus and Ajax enter, followed by Phoenix and the two heralds. Achilles and his friend spring to their feet and warmly greet the two envoys. The latter sit while food is prepared and eaten. Then there is an awkward pause—Odysseus, as always, is "the deliberate." Ajax nods to Phoenix to speak, but Odysseus is now ready and begins. The dialogue continues for more than four hundred verses, with six long speeches, a speech by Odysseus, by Phoenix, and by Ajax, and the reply of Achilles to each. This long dialogue is interrupted only by the "loquiturs" and by six verses of stage directions, describing the silence that followed Achilles' rejection of the plea of Odysseus, the emotion of Phoenix (430 f., 433), and the gesture of Achilles to Patroclus to prepare a bed for Phoenix, thus telling the envoys that the interview is over. With the usual libations the envoys and heralds exeunt.

This episode contains nothing that makes it unsuitable for presentation on the stage. It shows not only Homer's ability to dramatize action, but still more his manner of selecting the essential details of setting, of action, and of speeches. If the effect of a narrative is to be deep it must be distinct. Therefore the attention of the hearer must not be diverted by unessential details nor overburdened by too many. We know that Phoenix and the heralds accompanied the envoys; hence no mention is made of their entrance, just as Automedon's presence is not indicated until he is brought into the action (vs. 209). The exchange of greetings and the conversation during the preparation of the food are reduced to a minimum. As listeners we can follow at one time only the action of a single person, or of a small group acting together. Hence our attention is focused on Achilles. His two short speeches—one expressing his glad surprise and his joy at the coming of his friends, the other bidding Patroclus assist in giving them a hearty welcome—are sufficient to create the emotional atmosphere of the action which follows, and to impart to it reality. Of course, we are not to suppose that the envoys maintained an absolute silence until Odysseus spoke, or that there was no conversation while the meal was being prepared and eaten. But realism here would defeat the poet's aim. His interest, and ours, is in the play of spirit on spirit in the debate.

This episode could be presented in a Greek theater by laying the scene before Achilles' door. The envoys would enter and summon him forth from within—at least, this would be the simplest arrangement. Instead of the meal, there must be a brief dialogue to introduce the Debate. It seems unlikely that even Sophocles could have created a greater emotional tension by this dialogue than Homer does by the meal and the two short speeches which precede it.

In the Niptra (τ 51-601), Odysseus, a ragged beggar, is for the first time in twenty years alone in his own hall (51 f.). He is standing at one side, at some distance from the fire. Penelope enters (from the other side) with her attendants, who place for her, near the fire, a chair with a fleece for a cushion. She sits (53-59). The house servants (including Eurycleia) enter, remove the food, the goblets and the tables, and replenish the braziers. Melantho taunts Odysseus because he lingers. He chides her for failing to remember that ill fortune may come to any mortal, and warns her of her own fate if she persists in her disloyal conduct. Penelope overhears the conversation and sternly rebukes Melantho for her unnecessary insolence to the Beggar. He remains, she says, by her own command. She bids Eurynome bring a cushioned stool for the stranger. The stewardess does so. Odysseus takes his seat by the fire, and the conversation with Penelope begins, and continues through eleven speeches, ending with the Queen's command to the old nurse to bathe the Beggar's feet. Aside from the "loquiturs," the poet interrupts only three times to indicate the emotions of the three chief characters. He describes (1) Penelope's burst of tears, called forth by the fictitious account of Odysseus' visit to the Beggar twenty years before, and the pity of Odysseus for his wife—which he stoutly conceals (203-213), (2) her second burst of tears when the Beggar describes the garment and brooch which she herself had given Odysseus at his departure (249-251), and (3) the gesture and tears of Eurycleia when told by Penelope to wash the feet of the Beggar (361 f.). At verse 385, after a speech by Eurycleia, the poet narrates: "The old slave woman took a shining basin and poured in cold water, then hot, until it was the right temperature. Odysseus, sitting at the hearth, quickly turned away from the bright fire, for suddenly the thought came to him that when she took his foot in her hands she would know him by the scar. She came near her master, and began to bathe his feet, and quickly recognized him by the scar, which——" The narrative pauses at this tense moment while the poet tells how Odysseus came by the scar (393-466). The listener is tense with interest, not so much in the outcome, for he knows this will be "happy," as in how the critical situation will be treated. The poet postpones the solution for seventy-four verses, while he narrates this incident of the past, deliberately, with details, and even with direct speech (404-412). Yet even this part of the Niptra, like all the rest, could be produced on the stage. The water for bathing the feet, we know from verse 503, must be brought in from without. For the stage version, when Penelope bids Eurycleia bathe the stranger's feet, the nurse must leave the hall to get the basin and water (the poet omitted this action as unessential). Odysseus suddenly moves away from the hearth and turns toward the darkened part of the hall, expressing his fears about the scar in a long soliloquy in which he tells the story of the Boar Hunt. Penelope has no interest whatsoever in the act of hospitality to a stranger, and therefore falls into a deep revery—possibly she even nods. Hence she would not hear the soliloquy of Odysseus, nor would she notice the agitation of the old slave when she recognizes her master, nor the look with which Eurycleia tries to draw her attention to her discovery (vss. 476 f.). The poet has a briefer, and altogether sufficient way of indicating the inattention of the Queen: Athena turned her thoughts elsewhere (vss. 478 f.). When Eurycleia has brought fresh water and has bathed and dried the feet of her master, the latter resumes his position by the fire, and the conversation with Penelope is taken up once more and continues until the exeunt of Penelope, the women servants, and, finally, Odysseus (vss. 600 f., υ 1).

In external form the two episodes are remarkably alike. They are of the same length.[13] Time (evening) and place (a hall) are the same. There are four speaking actors and mutes or supernumeraries in both. In both the Crowd (the army and the Suitors) are absent. Both begin with the entrance of chief characters and end with "Exeunt omnes." Both lack off-stage action. On the scene the chief movements are due to the proximity of a meal, and minor actions by the chief characters—the lyre song of κλέα ἀνδρῶν and the spinning of Penelope—contribute to ethos.

But the themes are contrastingly different, and this difference is sufficient to account for many of the dissimilarities. The *Iliad* is a tale of war, unmarked by trickery: the *Odyssey*, of domestic intrigue. Odysseus is the only man in the Niptra, and Eurycleia's rôle is in many ways like that of Phoenix. Achilles is the straightforward, peerless champion. Odysseus excels in δόλος. This complicates the situation. The path of the lie is always devious. The Debate in the Presbeia takes the straight course of truth. Its theme is single: Shall Achilles return to the fighting? Hence the speeches of the episode can be limited to seven, and the Debate is not interrupted by action. The Niptra contains twenty-six speeches, all concerned with the intrigue which arises from the return of Odysseus. The main dialogue falls into three parts. Two questions are to be answered: Is it likely that Odysseus will return? and Shall Penelope select a new husband by the ordeal of the Bow? Between these two "debates" both action and dialogue are inserted which deepen the impression that Penelope's first question has already been answered happily, and that the ordeal will not result as she forebodes.

The themes determine the kind and the degree of emotion aroused by the two episodes. The Presbeia consolidates its effect because the emotion which it arouses is strictly tragic. But the tragedy with a happy ending may also be highly dramatic in its effect. The Niptra does not suffer by comparison with the famous recognition scene in the *Iphigenia in Tauris*. In both, the situation permits two recognitions. Euripides presents them both, because both situation and plot demand the second, inferior though it is. The Niptra, like the *Oedipus Rex*, successfully postpones the second and major recognition, and the resulting suspense enhances the effect. Now, as the recognition in the *Iphigenia* is as "dramatic" but not as "tragic" as that of the *Oedipus*, so the Niptra is quite as "dramatic" as the Presbeia though not equally "tragic." In the same way the parting between Hector and Andromache, and the scene between Achilles and Priam, are no more "dramatic" than the Argus episode and the recognitions of Odysseus by Penelope and Laertes. The theme of the *Iliad* is the greater one: the dramatic art of the poet is essentially the same in both *Iliad* and *Odyssey*.

The theme of the *Odyssey* also explains sufficiently its greater use of the narratives contained in the dialogues. We need not resort to the explanation offered by the Author On the Sublime, that the love of tales is a token of the old age of genius. These tales, with very rare exceptions, are told only in the dialogue. Like the dialogue itself, they bulk larger in the *Odyssey*, but the technique of their use is found in the *Iliad*.

Corinna's advice to the youthful Pindar to use more myth in his odes contains a universal truth. Poetry, prose, and every speaker, use the tale because it illustrates one's thoughts, from experience real or imagined. Thus Agamemnon tells the tale of the birth of Heracles as an instance of the infatuation to which great kings, whether of Olympus or of Argos, are liable. The modern public speaker's tale or anecdote has a similar use, and often the story is remembered long after its moral has been forgotten. Hephaestus told the story of his fall from Heaven to illustrate the danger of crossing the purpose of Zeus. The tale is firmly embedded in literature; its moral is usually forgotten.

Men must converse about something, and small talk is not "memorable speech." The tale gives body to many of the longer dialogues of Homer. Remove from the only speech that Phoenix makes, the allegory, the story of his own youth, and the tale of Meleager, and the residue is too meager to justify the speech. What else could the Swineherd and the Beggar do during a long day and a long night, except to tell of their own past lives? Without these long conversations the two episodes would lack both extent and content.

In addition to the three uses just described—to give body to the dialogue, to enrich it with matters in themselves interesting, and to illustrate an argument or strengthen a plea—the tale within the tale is employed to give the needful exposition of the past. It is this function which explains its more extensive use in the *Odyssey*.

The *Iliad* and the *Odyssey* contain each about a score of these narratives, but in the *Odyssey* their average length is much greater (including the Apologue, about six times as great; without the Apologue, at least twice). In the *Iliad* the account of the past is of comparatively little importance. With a few exceptions, the previous years of the war are for the most part ignored. We are told of incidents in the previous fighting of Achilles, and of the negotiations for the return of Helen. Aulis is mentioned in one episode. But for the reconstruction of a history of the earlier years of the war we must rely on casual references. It is the same with the past lives of the major heroes, except Achilles, Diomede, and a few others. Hence (in the *Iliad*) the tales which enrich the dialogues are largely taken from, or include, well-known myths and legends, like those of the Centaurs and Amazons, Heracles, and the Seven Against Thebes.

The *Iliad* tells of a tragic incident near the close of the war. The *Odyssey* includes the events of the next ten years. It is a Nostoi as well as a Nostos, for it tells of the death or the safe homecoming of every major Greek hero of the *Iliad*. Of this part of the theme we are given a hint at the beginning of the poem (a 11 f., 35-43). Now it is significant that of about twenty tales within a dialogue in the *Odyssey* fourteen are of events, real or fictitious, in the lives of Odysseus or of some major hero of the *Iliad* between the end of the *Iliad* and the beginning of the *Odyssey*, and five more concern Odysseus or some member of his family. Only the tale of Eumaeus is of matters outside the theme.[14]

The richness of the dialogue in tales ἔξω τοῦ μυθεύματος is undoubtedly due to the Ionian *Lust zur Fabulierung*, but the art with which the tales are inserted is one of the many indications that with Homer the intuitive power to impart to a narrative the reality of life reached an all-time peak. The German term *Rahmenerzählung* fails to do full justice to this innate power. In Homer the frame and the tale blend into one, so that the tale becomes an organic element in the conversation of living persons.

Herein Vergil shows the decline of the storyteller's art. Perhaps it is fairer to say that Vergil shows the essential difference between the oral and the written narrative. Vergil inserts his Apologue in a love story, to which it contributes nothing. If both the questions of Dido which introduce the narrative of Aeneas (I 753-756), and the narrative itself (Bks. II, III), were omitted, the love story would be improved. The three questions of Dido are the frame and nothing more. The three themes suggested by her do not follow from her previous questions about Memnon, the horses of Diomede, and the stature of Achilles. They originate too clearly in the mind of the poet, not of Dido, and the first two questions do not concern Aeneas, in whom is centered all the Queen's thought: "a prima dic, hospes, origine nobis [1] *insidias Danaum*, [2] *casusque tuorum*, [3] erroresque tuos." The feast itself has made no preparation for Aeneas' speech. The cosmological song of Iopas, "errantem lunam solisque labores, unde hominum genus," contributes nothing either to the Apologue or to the love story. It is an external enrichment. Finally, at the end of Aeneas' narrative there is an abrupt pause in the chief story of the poem. At the beginning of Book IV the poet starts afresh with his own account of Dido's lovelorn heart.

In Homer the Apologue grows out of the previous action and blends imperceptibly with what follows. Its setting and its beginning and end are truer to life. Odysseus, always "the deliberate," has avoided telling his name. But he knows he must do so, as Alcinous says, if the Phaeacian ship is to carry him home. The time for this has come. So he asks Demodocus to sing of his greatest δόλος, the Wooden Horse. This is, as it were, the overture to the recognition. The questions of Alcinous spring naturally from the situation: "Who are you? Where is your home? Where have you wandered? [He knew from the conversation of the previous evening that his guest had suffered much (η 211-214).] Why do you weep when the bard sings of the Trojan War?" The reply of Odysseus contains more than the tale of his wanderings. It is treated as an after-dinner speech. There is first the delicate compliment to host and bard; then the modest hint that the speaker can add nothing to the enjoyment of the feast, and the equally modest and tactful remark that one's own simple home is far dearer than luxury in a foreign land. At the middle of the speech—also at the one point where the narrative threatens to become wearisome—the speaker suggests that he has spoken long enough, and is complimented and urged to go on. At the end the dialogue is continued, with the appreciation of the speech, and the life which the poet is presenting goes on without a break. Homer's *Rahmenerzählung* is not an artifice; it is the unconscious result of the consummate art of the master of oral narrative, which relies for the illusion of reality chiefly on the *ipsissima verba* of individuals.

The oral narrative uses the direct utterance of its characters also for other subordinate purposes. A reader with print before his eyes can reread the words if their full import is not clear at first, or if he wishes to enjoy again the emotion which they arouse. But the "winged word" cannot be thus recalled. This is perhaps one reason why Homer uses the single speech, either in or outside of the dialogue, which might easily be omitted in written narrative. Sometimes the single speech does little more than "hold the picture" and give the listener time to enter it emotionally. The speeches of Odysseus to the leaders and the common soldiers in the Diapeira are quite unnecessary for the printed narrative: "Whenever he met a prince or a man of prominence, he would stop and with gentle and courteous words check his flight to the ships [the words of the speech follow]. But if he saw a common soldier and found him joining in the cry [to launch the ships], he would smite him with his scepter and with harsh words rebuke him [the harsh words follow]. Thus with authority he went through the camp, and the army rushed back to the assembly." The *ipsissima verba* of Odysseus (vss. 190-197, 200-206) bring him more closely before our attention, and present him less as a fact than as a personal character in the story. But they also give us time to picture the turning back of the army from its purpose to sail home.

The words of exultation over a fallen enemy often serve the same purpose. When Othryoneus, suitor for Cassandra's hand, is slain by Idomeneus (N 370), or Cebriones by Patroclus (Π 737), or Iphition by Achilles (Υ 386), the victor's boast tells us almost exactly what we have learned just before from the poet about the importance of the slain warrior or the manner of his fall. But the repetition of the same idea helps the listener to grasp them better. Similes are used for a similar purpose. But rarely do we find both the victor's boast and the simile used together. The fall of Asius, slain by Idomeneus just after Othryoneus (N 387 f.), is pictured with the aid of a simile; that of Alcathous, which follows soon after, not by a simile, but by a speech of exultation. The fall of Sarpedon is described by a simile, and Patroclus does not exult over his body; but no simile is used when Hector falls; instead, Achilles exults over him. Both simile and speech of exultation "hold the picture" and, in different ways, present the death of a warrior as the carrier of some emotion, and not merely as a historical fact.

Perhaps the commonest secondary use of single speech is to make clearer the action which is to follow. On these single speeches the poet, or the bards who preceded him, seem to have bestowed special attention. With all their variety they show a far greater tendency to be typical than do the dialogues, especially the longer ones. It is the same technique of specialization which Euripides shows in his speeches of prologist and messenger, and in his δικανικοὶ λόγοι. Fully 90 per cent of the 350-odd single speeches of the *Iliad*, and 80 per cent of the 70-odd in the *Odyssey*, fall into one or other of the following categories: (1) the prayer; (2) the soliloquy; (3) the "Voice from the crowd"; (4) the Messenger's repetition of a command; (5) the exhortation of a general to his army, or of a warrior to his comrade; (6) the flyting of a foe, or the exultation over his fall; (7) the dirge; (8) the command.

Of the more than 400 single speeches in the two poems, about 40 per cent are commands. Furthermore, the last speech of a dialogue often expresses a command or a purpose. By this means the listener is informed of the action which is to be described. The speeches of Zeus in the *Iliad* and of Athena in the *Odyssey* serve this purpose. Helenus thus twice announces the program of the following episode (Z 77 ff., H 47 ff.). Nestor often plays the rôle of announcer (B 362 ff., H 327 ff., K 204 ff.). In the *Odyssey*, Nestor's command to his sons is carried out almost to the letter in the account of the sacrifice to Athena, which follows (γ 418 ff.).

The repetition of the same command by other single speeches often helps to emphasize action which is of unusual importance in the plot. The thrice repeated description of the proposed journey of Telemachus (α 280-286, β 214-217, 359 f.) gives the listener fair warning that this episode is to bulk large in the sequel. We, who find in a novel a table of contents and often chapter headings, are apt to forget that to the simple and unsophisticated listener this kind of information must have been very welcome. The tendency of some readers to turn to the last pages of a novel to see how it ends, shows how this kind of curiosity may interfere with the enjoyment of the immediate action. The latter is always Homer's chief concern. If the narrator had given the information *in propria persona* and at length, he would have diverted the attention of his hearer to the fact that he was listening to a story. The illusion would have been partly effaced.

Speeches which forecast the action of an episode often add its ethos, which likewise gains by repetition. The "baneful Dream" repeats to Agamemnon, and Agamemnon to the council, the command of Zeus to arm the long-haired Achaeans with all speed, for now Hera has prevailed over the Olympians, and Troy may be captured. Homer has prepared for the "baneful Dream" by the ironical words of Achilles to Agamemnon (A 63): "[Consult some seer or priest,] aye, or a reader of dreams, *for the dream comes from Zeus.*" The first Olympian episode has made it clear that Zeus is deceiving Agamemnon when he says that Hera's entreaties have won over all the Olympians to the side of the Greeks. The first speech in Book II therefore not only gives the program of the marshaling of the troops, but also helps to create the atmosphere with which the poet surrounds Agamemnon throughout the poem.[15]

The terms of the truce are recited four times: by Hector, by Iris, by the Trojan herald, and by Agamemnon. They are of extreme importance, because after the Trojans have broken the truce—and not till then,—Greeks, Trojans, and the listeners are sure that Troy is doomed. The truce and its violation add an undertone to the rest of the story.

Whatever their secondary functions may be, the speeches have as their major purpose the presentation of the characters as living personalities. The reality of the characters is shown by the way they live today. Homer gave them, indeed, a kind of immortality. In this respect his only rival in Greek literature is Plato. The Platonic Socrates and his friends and acquaintances still live for us, because we hear them converse as men of that day must have spoken. The illusion of personality is not created best by the analysis of a few characters, possibly because one's nature is best revealed by the varied contact with many other individuals. Dickens, with fifty or more characters in some of his novels, portrays personality quite as well as Thackeray with far fewer. The half-dozen characters of an Attic tragedy cannot compare in this respect with Shakespeare's far more numerous *dramatis personae*. There are about seventy-five speaking characters in the *Iliad*, and nearly as many in the *Odyssey*, if we include the Apologue and the tale of Proteus. No two of these are alike. As Aristotle says, by their words they all reveal different individual traits. We should not mistake Eidothea for Leucothea if we could talk with these two sea nymphs. The more we hear the characters speak, the better we know their personal peculiarities. As an illustration let us take Hector, who speaks more than any other character in the *Iliad* except Achilles.

Hector is a man of sentiment and imagination. He cannot think out a plan of action for his army, but he can picture a desired or dreaded future. "There will come a day" is more than once on his lips. On the morrow he will drive the Greeks into the sea (Θ 535 ff.). His horses will easily leap the trench (Θ 179). He will give Dolon the horses of Achilles. He will face Achilles, though he has never dared to do so in the past. He has a clear vision of Andromache as a menial slave of some Greek princess, and of his own fall from an object of adoration to that of scorn among the people of Ilios. A man of feeling, he acts before he thinks. He is quick to rebuke and rash in promises and in boasting too soon.

The predominance of feeling in his nature gives him the soul of a poet. He uses language more picturesquely than any other of Homer's characters except perhaps Achilles in his passionate replies to the Envoys. Hector says that Paris deserves to "put on a tunic of stone" (Γ 57); Troy is in danger of becoming "a furnace of destroying fire" (Z 331); "If ever we set up a bowl of freedom" (Z 528); "My spear shall devour your lily-white flesh" (N 830 f.); "I will face Achilles, though his hands are hands of fire, aye, hands of fire, and his strength as the strength of steel" (Υ 371); "There can be now between Achilles and me no talk of sweet nothings, like a lover and his lass, a lover and his lass exchanging love talk" (X 126-128). Hector is not a type, nor can one find his like in literature. He is a living individual. Homer, his creator, as Scott thinks, breathed into him the breath of life.

The two old men of the *Iliad*, Nestor and Priam, offer additional evidence that Homer's characters are not types. Nestor is one of the solidest characters in Homer,—in this respect not unlike Sophocles. After a brilliant youth, and a prime of life that saw him everywhere influential, he lives to a green old age. When his knees cease to ply nimbly beneath him, the substantial qualities of his personality give him a high place in the war. He supplies the brains of the army. Like Sophocles, he is even-tempered, and therefore popular everywhere. He never loses his temper, and rarely his *sang-froid*. Not loved by many readers of Homer today, —Gildersleeve used to say that the mention of Nestor always made him think of a "mare's-nester,"— he yet served as the human stabilizer in the storm of passions let loose by the Wrath.

Priam offers the most striking contrast to this youthful old man. He is hardly more than the shell of the mighty warrior who fought the Amazons on the banks of the Sangarius in vine-clad Phrygia. He lets Hector marshal the army without his consent. He shivers with apprehension at the thought of going down to the plain to conclude the truce. The only word that he utters on the field is that he cannot bring himself to watch the combat between Paris and Menelaus. A mere husk of a man! Hence at the Trojan assembly he cannot even remonstrate with Paris for his refusal to abide by the terms of the truce. He weakly acquiesces in the proposal of Paris, without even giving a reason, and leaves to the herald Idaeus the diplomatic presentation to the Greeks of this unsatisfactory message. Idaeus by contrast reflects the weakness of the king by the skill with which he translates the curt words of Priam into the proper language of the envoy. The senility of Priam is best seen at the river where he and Idaeus have stopped to let their steeds drink. Darkness with its terrors is coming on. Idaeus catches sight of Hermes approaching, and says: "Son of Dardanus, bethink thee! There is need of all thy wits. I see a man, and I fancy we shall soon be torn in pieces. Shall we turn our steeds in flight, or throw ourselves at his feet and beg for mercy?" So he spoke. But the old man's wits left him. [One of Homer's fine touches!] "A panic of terror seized him. The hairs on his gnarled limbs stood on end. He stood there in a daze as the Helper drew near."

Priam lives only in Hector. So when Hector is slain he can call back something of his old power, and brave all if he may recover the body of his "one" son. He is the true father of this son. He can resolve upon a desperate undertaking, but cannot picture its risks. He is quick and needlessly harsh in rebuke. Like Hector, too, he can picture vividly the future. He can see the approaching sack of Troy and his own body worried by his own dogs at the outer door of his palace. It is Priam, more than any other character, who personifies, with ever-increasing pathos, the certain issue of the War—the end of a great kingdom. Nestor, on the other hand, stands for the Greeks, "eternally young."

The primitive man personalizes his thoughts of the world. The oral narrative must present a tale dramatically both because it is primitive and because its method of presentation lends itself to pure mimesis. Long generations during which the attention of bards was concentrated on this one genre would, with fortune, produce ever greater attention to the persons of the tale. It is not surprising that in Homer there are more numerous, more varied, and perhaps more living characters than we find in the work of any other poet before Shakespeare.

CHAPTER FOUR

THE BREAKING OF THE EPIC ILLUSION THE SUBJECTIVE ELEMENT— DESCRIPTION

THE TERM "epic illusion," which we have used to describe the effect of Homer's narrative, is included in the word "objectivity," which since the end of the eighteenth century has been commonly held to be the most distinctive characteristic of Homer.[1] But objectivity, like all abstract terms, permits widely diverging definitions.[2] The failure of theorists to agree on a single meaning has led to erroneous views of Homer's poetic art.

Any imaginative picture of life, such as poetry presents, may be objective in two ways: in its effect on its audience, and in the means used to produce this effect. A play of Shakespeare's has both kinds of objectivity. The audience, as spectators and not as critics, have no thought of the poet, and the latter cannot speak directly to them. Poe's Annabel Lee is subjective in both ways, because we see the girl through the poet's eyes and hear only the poet speak. Objectivity may thus mean (1) the presentation of imagined action and characters with such perfect mimesis that we forget the medium of presentation, and for the moment feel the imagined life as real. In this Homer excels all epic poets. But the term may also mean (2) that the poet in creating the illusion never intrudes, as poet, by words of his own. On Homer's objectivity in this sense erroneous views have been, and are still, widely held.

Schiller's famous remark that the "naïve" poets, Homer and Shakespeare, are as invisible behind their material as the Creator behind his universe,[3] is true in one sense: neither poet presents himself as "Homer" or "Shakespeare." But

---
[1] Superior figures refer to notes which will be found on p. 250.

this is due to the medium. Shakespeare used actors; Homer, his own, or a rhapsode's, oral delivery. Herodotus signs his name at the beginning of his Histories because they were written and published. When he recited from them at Athens there was no need of this. His audience saw him and knew who he was. The four verses prefixed to the *Aeneid*, and removed by Varius, are un-Homeric only because Vergil's medium differed from Homer's. Ariosto may address his patron because he does so in writing. Homer "vanishes behind his poetry" because, as "Homer" theoretically, he is always present before his listeners. But Schiller is wrong in implying that Homer, as poet, commonly refrains from addressing his audience.

Schiller's view is widely held today. "Epic is, in style, objective. It narrates habitually *without interposition* [italics mine], by images visual, auditory, motor. . . . The object of epic being persons, its commonest descriptive details are of personal activity: attitude, movement, speech, gesture. The method is to suggest that heroic life *by its physical sensations* [italics mine], to make the characters, as Aristotle says (Ch. XXIV), reveal themselves."[4]

This description, as a moment's reflection shows, is not of the epic, but of the dramatic, manner. Only drama is "without interposition." Only the drama confines its presentation to "visual, auditory, motor" images; to "persons," and their "attitude, movement, speech, gesture." And only the drama employs solely "the method . . . to make the characters reveal themselves." An epic, however much it may employ the dramatic manner, cannot produce its proper effect without something more. A remark of Aldous Huxley on his first reading of the dramatized version of a novel suggests why this is so. He says: "When I first read the script the difference from the book seemed disturbing; at first sight the play seemed only a bald sketch of the original, but at rehearsals I have been intensely interested to see how the producer and the actors 'fill in' the characters and supply so much that is in the book and is missing in the script.". . .The chief difference between writing plays and writing novels seems to be that the novelist is solely responsible for the effects he achieves, whereas the dramatist has to depend on other people to help him out.[5] The epic poet, too, is "solely responsible for the effects he achieves." He aims to produce some kind of effect for which a description, in words, of attitude, facial expression, gesture, and movement, is inadequate. Moreover, his wider compass of time and place, and his larger cast of characters, make it impossible to put all the exposition, description, motivation, and explanation of various kinds into the words of the characters, as drama must do. Therefore the epic poet must often personally interpose.

We must remember the difference between the epic poem and the simple account of facts. The child or the primitive savage is purely objective in his report of a highly emotional incident. It is only by repeated questioning that he yields the details from which the scene may be reconstructed in the imagination. The oral epic poet must anticipate such questions in the mind of his audience; he must furnish the details along with the facts, and he must do this in such a way as both to facilitate the imaginative construction of the scene and to heighten its emotional effect. Hence any tale worthy of the name cannot be by any means purely objective. We may test this statement by the Book of Ruth.

The interpositions of the narrator are as follows: the introduction, 1:1-5, gives time, place, circumstances, and describes Naomi and Ruth; purpose is mentioned in 1:6,"that she might return from the country of Moab"; also the reason for the action,"for she had heard," etc.; Boaz is briefly described, 2:1; the ancient custom of sealing an agreement is explained, 4:7, in order to make clear the action of the kinsmen of Boaz; a cross reference to an earlier passage is found once, "the kinsmen of whom Boaz spake came by," 4:1; emotion is once described, "the man was afraid," 3:8. Lack of objectivity is also found in plurality of speakers—the reapers, 2:4, the elders, 4:11, and the women, 4:14, 17; in explaining the contents of the mind of a character, "when she saw that she was stedfastly minded to go with her," 1:18; and in giving the substance of the speech of Ruth, which is followed by her actual words, "And she told her all that the man had done to her. And she said, 'These six measures of barley gave he me,' " 3:16 f.

The tale of Ruth is a brief episode. Aside from Ruth herself, the characters have little ethos; the action is unimportant; and the emotions are not deeply stirred. Furthermore, the tale is told with a purpose, to describe the immediate ancestry of David, as the concluding verses show. The need of author's contributions is both limited and simple. But Homer's poems have no aim save the satisfaction of the hearer's desire to hear them. They are long and complicated tales, each with a distinct plot; there are many changes of scene, characters innumerable, violent action, and emotions of high potential. Hence we expect—and we actually find—that the subjective element, the poet's manifest and undisguised contributions, are far from being as negligible as the words of Professor Baldwin, quoted above, imply: they are numerous and greatly varied in kind; without them the poems could never have attained their exalted place in the world's literature.

This is to be expected when one considers the implication of Andrew Lang's remark that Homer in a certain sense includes all Greek literature. In literature, as we have seen, the author may address his audience in one of three ways: in the first, or the second, or the third person. These three manners may be used together, as Goethe said, in the shortest poem, but the kind of literature is determined by the predominance of one or another of these three. The epic, the tale, history, require the third-personal manner, because the past is by its nature removed from our presence. The second-personal manner belongs to the drama and the dialogue; the author addresses us through characters in our immediate presence. But in lyric and the oration the author speaks directly to us.

Homer's dramatic epic employs also the first-personal manner, albeit in the epic or impersonal way, to a surprising degree. Speaking very roughly, the impersonal narrative, chiefly the account of action, objectively presented, occupies one-fifth of the poems, the speeches three-fifths, and the direct personal utterance of the poet, or his interpretation or explanation which the objective narrative cannot give, one-fifth. Thus the Muse, the *dramatis personae*, and the poet himself form a trinity each member of which contributes a share in re-creating the past for the hearer.

Homer addresses the Muse or the Muses, and also, by name, five of his characters: Menelaus, Melanippus, Patroclus, and Apollo in the *Iliad*, and Eumaeus in the *Odyssey*. Why, we do not know. It seems probable that he thus heightened the interest of the hearer. Today an excitable spectator in the bleachers often thus cries out to a contestant. The poet's engrossment in a character would be communicated to his audience. But the fact is more important than the reason, for it shows his willingness to interpose directly for the sake of the increased effect of his tale.

This effect is upon the *listener*. To him, therefore, most of the poet's interpositions are addressed. Even the rare rhetorical question in Homer[6] cannot be addressed to the circumambient ether, much less to the poet himself. These, and other remarks by the narrator, are made to the audience which is immediately before him. If the reciter were an expert in his art, he would have made his interpretation recognized as such by altered tone of voice. But, keenly alive to the delicate intangible, the hearer's attention, on which his success depended, he would have contrived to interpose as unobtrusively as possible.

His manner, therefore, must be indirect. Homer never addresses his audience as "gentle hearer." No more does a character in Homer directly address his listener in the tale within the dialogue. The vocative is confined to the introduction and the conclusion, to the reason for telling the tale or to its application, or to the continuation of the conversation. This is true of all the tales of Nestor, Menelaus, and Odysseus; of the story of Glaucus told to Diomede (Z 152-211; the vocative is in vs. 145); and of the two tales of Phoenix (I 447-491, vocatives in vss. 444, 485, 494; the tale of Meleager, I 529-599; ἐν ὑμῖν ἐρέω, 528, ἀλλὰ σύ, 600).[7] This is evidence that in Homer's time the illusion of any tale was not to be needlessly broken.

It must be broken, however, as we have seen from the simple story of Ruth. Neither the speeches nor the account of physical action suffices. For example, if all the characters of Homer revealed by speeches as much of their feelings, thoughts, and purposes, and of their past histories, as the tale requires, the poems would be interminably long and utterly wearisome. Nor can this information, and much else, be included in an account of rapidly moving action. Besides, every listener, especially the naïve listener, enjoys a tale more if he can compare with or relate to his own experience the life which is presented to his imagination. The oral narrative gives him little time to pause for this. Hence the narrator must assist him.

A large number of Homer's interpositions are so brief as not to be noticeable. Where they form a considerable digression, the poet frequently resumes the narrative with a pointing word, "Then," "There," "This man," which takes the place of Sir Walter Scott's more cumbersome phrase, "The place [or man] we have been describing," or "To return to our story." Sometimes, too, Homer adds a repetition in different words, of the action described or implied at the point where the narrative stopped; for example, ο 223, σχεδόθεν δέ οἱ ἤλυθεν ἀνήρ,—the digression on the ancestry of Theoclymenus follows (vss. 224-255),—256, τοῦ μὲν ἄρ' υἱὸς ἐπῆλθε, 257, ὃς τότε Τηλεμάχου πέλας ἵστατο, Β 811-814 (the hill Batieia is described in the present tense), verse 815, ἔνθα τότε Τρῶές τε διέκριθεν, κτλ.

The word τότε is most used for this purpose. It marks the return to the narrative after a digression (1) on what had happened before, or was (only once, Μ 35) to happen later, or (2) describing what is true in the experience of the listener's own day. The first use is commonest after the description of minor characters[8] like Theoclymenus, or of the history of objects which enter the action.[9]

The slight digressions just considered affect the epic illusion but little, for they deal with matters which belong to the story. The interruption is greater when the poet refers to his own day. The illusion is plainly broken when Homer says that Diomede easily hurled at Aeneas a great boulder which could not be carried by two men "of our own day" (Ε 304), or that Leucothea was once a mortal, but "today" (νῦν, not τότε, "at the time of our story") she is a sea goddess. After such references to the present the word τότε often recalls the listener to the narrative. Achilles at the trench shouted "like the clear voice of the trumpet, when it blares as the bloodthirsty foemen rush to the assault of a city. So clear at this moment in our story (τότε) rang out the voice of Achilles." (Σ 219-221). The trumpet was not used in the Trojan War; it belonged to the time of Homer and his audience. This reference to the present is in a simile. In his similes Homer never refers to the past; he always uses the present or the gnomic aorist tense,[10] and after the simile he frequently uses the pointing word of recall. This is sufficient evidence that whenever the poet uses the present tense outside of the speeches, he is speaking directly to his audience of what is either a part of their own experience or is as true for them as for the story. This principle not only removes the so-called anachronisms of the similes; it explains other supposed difficulties, two of which are so much discussed that we must consider them at some length.

The first is "The Garden of Alcinous" (η 86-132), a description of place. Homer has two ways of describing places. He may use past tenses, picturing the scene at the moment of the action. This method is objective in that it continues the epic illusion. It is used in describing Calypso's cave (ε 63-74). Hermes found the nymph at home; she was singing at her weaving before a lighted fire. The poet continues: "Round the cave *grew* a luxuriant grove, alders and poplars and the fragrant cypress. Here the long-winged birds *were wont to roost* at night. . . . Four springs *poured forth* streams of clear water, in different directions. . . . All about [the grove and the springs] soft meadows *bloomed* with violets and parsley." We see the lovely spot where the hero had been an unwilling prisoner for seven years, but we see it through the eyes of Hermes, who has just arrived.

The other method is subjective. The copula largely supplants the main verbs of action, and the present tense is used. This is perhaps the nearest approach in Homer to the historical present, so common in Vergil. It differs chiefly in presenting a place rather than an action which is, as it were, before the poet's eyes. This method is used in the description of another cave, the one at the head of Phorcys Harbor (ν 96-112). Just before dawn the Phaeacian ship bearing the hero, fast asleep, *drew near* the island. Here the narrative stops, and the poet speaks: "Now there *is* in the land of Ithaca a harbor, the harbor of Phorcys. . . . at its head *is* a slender-leaved olive tree, and hard by *is* a cave, lovely, but dimly lighted, sacred to the nymphs. . . . Inside *are* mixing-bowls and jars of stone; bees store their honey in them. There *are* also looms of stone, very tall, at which the

THE BREAKING OF THE ILLUSION 89

nymphs weave their purple robes. . . . *At this place* the Phaeacian sailors drove their ship ashore." We see this scene through the poet's eyes; and the pointing adverb, ἔνθα, means "the place which I have been describing."

In the description of the palace of Alcinous the two methods are combined. Odysseus approached, and, before he reached the threshold, paused to think—like Socrates in Plato's *Symposium*. The poet now describes what gave pause to the hero: it was the splendor and the gathering within. The interior gleamed, with walls of bronze, doors of gold with doorjambs of silver, and gold and silver watchdogs, the work of Hephaestus, on both sides. Within, along the walls were placed armchairs, spread with bright cloths of fine texture, on which sat all the princes of Scheria, at dinner, "and on finely wrought pedestals stood youths of gold, with flaming torches in their hands, turning night into day for the feasters in the hall." The poet perhaps marks the conclusion of this part of his description by his return to "the gleam" that made Odysseus pause.

It is at this point (vs. 103) that the supposed difficulty arises. The poet changes to the present tense, which he keeps to the end in telling of other marvels in this faery region. He begins, as usual, with the credible: fifty housemaids, to grind the yellow wheat and to weave the fine linen. Then he passes to the marvelous: orchards, where "pears and pomegranates and shining apples, sweet figs and big olives," ripen throughout the year, summer and winter; a vineyard, with grapes at all stages of growth, some drying for raisins or being trodden in the wine presses, others just forming where the blossoms have fallen; neat garden beds, also ever-bearing. And there are two springs, one irrigating the gardens, the other supplying the public fountain. "Such were the gods' gifts at the home of Alcinous."

From the time of Bergk and Lehrs, scholars have been troubled by the change to the present tense. As late as

1924, Eduard Schwartz[11] found it "inexplicable." But the whole description is quite in the Homeric manner. At verse 103 the poet has finished describing what interested Odysseus.[12] The rest of the passage is the poet's direct contribution to the entertainment of his audience.

The other supposed difficulty (ζ 41-47) is of far greater importance, for on it the chorizonts base one of their strongest arguments, holding the passage to be unmistakable evidence of a much later view in the *Odyssey* of the home of the gods. Athena has spoken to Nausicaa in a dream. The narrative continues: "*With these words Bright-eyed Athena departed to Olympus*, where, *men say*, the gods' abode standeth fast forever. It is neither shaken by winds nor wet with rain; no snow falls upon it; only the clear sky is above it, without a cloud, and dazzling light spreads over it. *Thither went Bright-Eyes, after she had given her message to the maiden.*" This is a more idealized conception of Olympus than we find in the *Iliad*. There Olympus belongs to the story, as the scene of many interesting episodes. Here the poet presents the popular conception of his own day, "as men say,"[13] and because his interposition has interrupted the narrative, he picks up his tale with the pointing word and a repetition of the last action before his digression.

The subjective present tense is commonly used to characterize and describe the gods and everything that belongs to them. They are "ever-living," and nothing in Heaven perishes. Hera and Athena in their chariot start for the Trojan plain. "Unbidden roared open the gates of Heaven, which the Seasons tended [thus far the narrative], in whose care are the vast heaven and Olympus, to roll back the thick cloud and to put it in place again." This picture is as subjective as that of any lyric poet, and as directly addressed by the poet to his audience.

The armor of mortal heroes is described by imperfect tenses: it belongs to the story, and has passed away. But divine armor and attributes require the present tense: the aegis of Zeus, Athena's spear, Aphrodite's cestus, Poseidon's sword, and the wand of Hermes.[14] The stars, too, are eternal, and the poet loves to contemplate them, and to express his lyric fancies about them. "What time the Dawnbringer goes forth to proclaim light over the earth, whom saffron-mantled Dawn followeth, spreading over the sea, *at that time*," etc. (Ψ 226 ff.).

The interpositions we have been considering have been chiefly descriptions of persons, places, and objects. Homer is chary of these interruptions of the narrative. The principle which seems in general to govern his use of description is sound. Homer does not describe the chief characters, the scenes of frequently recurring action, or the objects which often enter the narrative. He tells us more of the raft of Odysseus than of any ship; of the setting of the Cyclops episode than of the Greek camp or of the Trojan plain. How much do we know of the external appearance of the major characters? That Hector has beautiful jet-black hair; that Odysseus was long-waisted, and that Ajax was a giant. We know as much of the appearance of Euphorbus and Amphimachus, and more of Thersites. Homer takes it for granted that we shall become sufficiently familiar with his chief characters. We know them by meeting them repeatedly. This is the way we become acquainted with Patroclus. After the Quarrel, Achilles goes to his camp "with Menoetiades and his comrades." This tells us no more than that a hero whose father is named Menoetius is an intimate of Achilles and is important in the story of the Wrath (A 307). The next time we see Achilles, thirty verses later, he is with a companion whom he addresses as "High-born Patroclus," and whom he bids fetch Briseis and give her to the heralds (A 337-345). Patroclus obeys his "dear comrade." Achilles appears next in the Embassy, and the narrative makes still clearer his intimate association and friendship with Patroclus (I 190-220, 620, 658-668). Achilles has appeared in three episodes. In each one Patroclus has been with him and has played an increasingly important rôle with each succeeding appearance. We now know him well enough to be prepared for his mission to Nestor and for the rest of the Patrocleia. His personal looks would contribute little to the tragedy of the *Iliad*.

When Homer does describe a major hero or anything connected with him, the description is purposeful and pertinent to the immediate action or effect. We are not told of Hector's beautiful locks until they are trailing in the dust behind the chariot of Achilles. This chariness and casualness of description of persons is perhaps primitive. Elijah the Tishbite is not described until it is necessary to identify him to King Ahaziah. Then we learn that he is "an hairy man, and girt with a girdle of leather about his loins" (II Kings 1:8). So in Homer: the only horse of which we have a visual image is one of the pair which Diomede captured from Aeneas and drove in the chariot race, "solid bay, with a white spot on the forehead." This description is given only to explain why Idomeneus knew that Diomede was leading.

The picture of this horse and of Thersites seems to show that the scantiness of Homer's description of physical appearance was not due to lack of observation. The explanation may be that the *swiftly moving action* in the oral narrative gives the listener too little time to synthesize the visual details, or that the plastic arts had not yet schooled the poet's public in attention to the individual differences of persons and objects as presented to the eye. So far as we have evidence in Homer, however, the reason seems to be that the interest in an object is due rather to its source or history. It is personal rather than visual. Palaces, robes, furniture on Olympus are not pictured; it is enough that Hephaestus or Athena made them. Ornaments and metal works are held up for admiration, not by describing their details, but as *objets d'art phénicien*. The cup of Nestor, the baldric of Heracles, the breastplate of Agamemnon, and a few other objects which offer exceptions to this principle, merely show that Homer could have described physical appearances in detail if he had so desired. But he does otherwise as a rule. It is the history of an object which chiefly interests him. Homer does not help us to visualize the scepter of Agamemnon, the Pelian ash of Achilles, the mare Aetha, or the bow of Odysseus; instead, he gives us their history, especially the persons of note with whom the objects had been associated.

This interest in persons rather than in things is strikingly illustrated by the vignettes of the minor warriors in the battles of the *Iliad*. Since large masses of men in conflict can never present a clear and distinct mental picture to the ordinary listener, the poet resorts to the personal encounter or the personal casualties. A few of these are episodes, but the majority are casual features of the fighting. The little vignettes of minor warriors are like the similes in their use. Both interrupt the narrative and are often followed by the resumptive τότε. Both may be very simple, a single word, or may be expanded into a little story, and both are a very characteristic element in the account of battles. There are about 240 similes, long and short, in the *Iliad*, and 243 named persons are slain, of whom perhaps ten are heroes in extended episodes. Sometimes only the name is given, or with patronymic or tribal name; or with a brief two-verse description without details or characterization—for example, Bathycles, slain by Glaucus, was "the dear son of Chalcon; his home was in Hellas, and in wealth and prosperity he was preëminent among the Myrmidons" (Π 595 f.). But often this is expanded into a brief biography, of about the same length as the longer similes, as of Othryoneus, suitor for the hand of Cassandra (N 363-369), or of Menesthius, a Myrmidon leader (Π 174-192). In function these miniature portraits are a complement to the similes. The latter point the hearer to the present, and lead him to relate his own experience of normal life, outside of war, to the tale of the past. The miniatures give a glimpse into the life of the past, not in its crises, but in its peace and happiness, so that the Trojan War gains perspective by a background in a real world where war is only an incident, not the main business of life. Finally, in the miniature portraits as well as in the similes an emotion is suggested which heightens the interest in the tales of battle. Iphidamas, son of Antenor, was reared by his grandfather in Thrace. When he grew "to the measure of glorious youth," he married a wife, and prepared to spend his life in Thrace. But the wedding was scarce over when tidings of the war came. He sailed to Percote, entered the fighting, and was slain by Agamemnon. "So he fell asleep on the battlefield in the bronze-fettered sleep of death, poor fellow, defending the people of his city—far from his bride, of whom he had no joy" (Λ 221-245).

In these miniatures the poet only twice mentions details which help us to form a visual image of the minor hero, and then only casually (B 872, P 51 f.). This fact, added to the paucity of Homer's detailed description of objects, seems to show that the oral epic narrative was less interested in giving a distinct visual picture than an emotional impression; in other words, that Homer cared less for the surroundings of human life than for that life itself. Let us test the truth of this conclusion by the *pièce de résistance* of description in the Homeric poems, the Shield of Achilles (Σ 478-608.)

The scenes on the shield have often been considered as evidence that Homer was acquainted with similar scenes in plastic art, whether Minoan, Phoenician, or Geometric, and for more than two centuries scholars have attempted to show how the scenes could be arranged plastically on a shield of various shapes.[16] On the other hand, scholars who examine the poems rather as poetry, for example, Bougot,

H. F. Grimm, Cesarotti, Rothe, Finsler, and Drerup, tend to reject these attempts, wholly or in part. We think the evidence is in their favor, and should like to direct attention to a few points not sufficiently recognized.

(1) The scenes are filled with life, action, and movement. In other works of art described by Homer there may be motion of a living creature in one place, but there is no movement from one position to another, much less a succession of scenes in time.[16]

(2) The poet has carefully prepared his hearers for accepting the divine artificer's power to give life and movement to objects of metal. His tripods are automatic (vs. 376); the bellows act personally (vss. 469-473); his handmaids, although wrought of gold, are like living maidens; they not only move from place to place, but also have intelligence and speech (vss. 417-421). The expression ζωῇσι νεήνισιν ἐοικυῖαι (418) is exactly like that used of the plowed ground on the shield, ἀρηρομένῃ δὲ ἐῴκει, χρυσείη περ ἐοῦσα, to which the poet adds, τὸ δὴ περὶ θαῦμα τέτυκτο (548 f.). The divine smith could miraculously make gold appear like black earth.

(3) The interest in technical details is almost *nil*. The only tools of Hephaestus are bellows, crucibles, hammer, anvil, and tongs. The only metals, bronze, gold, silver, tin,[17] are those used elsewhere in the poems in making armor.

(4) There is no hint of the arrangement of the scenes on the shield, except that Oceanus flows around the edge. On the shield of Heracles there is a serpent in the center (*Aspis* 144), the City at War is "above" the Gorgons (237), and the City at Peace is "beside" the City at War (270). The scenes on Jason's mantle (Ap. Rh. *Argon.* I, 728-729) are on the border.

(5) The likeness of the scenes on the shield of Achilles to those of the similes has often been noticed, but the inference from this fact has been ignored. The scenes are those which are familiar to the poet's audience from their own expe-

rience. The only reference to the past is the mention of Daedalus, and this is no more than an epic superlative: τῷ ἴκελον, οἷόν ποτ' ἐνὶ Κνωσῷ, κτλ., means nothing more than that the dancing place on the shield was as wonderful as the most famous in legend. The greatest contrast with the heroic past as described in the story of the two poems is the concentration of attention on the common people. The youths and maidens in the dance belong to the wealthy class, it is true, but the scene closes with the enjoyment of the crowd looking on. And this reference to the upper class is exceptional. There is no mention of commanders of the two armies in the City at War, nor of the owners of the flocks, herds, vineyard, or of the fallow land under the plow. The Harvest begins with the laborers, and ends with the preparations for their supper. The βασιλεύς and his banquet under the oak add festal splendor to the scene, but the βασιλεύς is motionless and silent, hardly more than a lay figure. Modern scholars understand βασιλεύς to mean a "heroic prince," but in the only two passages in Homer where the word occurs outside of its heroic setting, here and in a simile (Δ 144), the ancients rendered it "lord of the estate."[18] The prevailing tone of the scenes suggests a poet of the people, reciting to a popular audience.

Eustathius saw a didactic principle governing the arrangement of the scenes, and Professor Myres has with great skill worked out their plastic symmetry. There is at least an equal poetic symmetry, not of form, but of emotion.

The scenes give a picture of human life. Of the two obvious orders of presenting life—from the primitive to the artificial, or the reverse—Homer chooses the second. He begins with the polis, where harmony or disharmony may prevail. The first scene is of harmony: weddings, festivity, music, and dancing. The second is of discord, within the city, and not serious: a lawsuit. Then disunion between cities, leading to war, siege, and discord within the besieging armies, and the battle at the river. The convoy of cattle, with the herdsmen all unaware of their danger, and playing the pipes, provides the transition to the next group of scenes, in which the city is forgotten as we pass to view three large estates in the country. In the first many plowmen are turning the rich black soil; it is morning and they plow eagerly. There is no mention of sweat or weariness, and a cup of wine is waiting at the end of every furrow. Next we see a deep field of ripe grain with harvesters working briskly: their master is looking on and their supper is being made ready. Then comes the vintage. We see only young men and maidens at work, and work to them has become play: their feet dance for happiness to the music of the Linus Song. The next group of scenes brings us still nearer to nature. With the cows we leave the homestead with its barns, and rush to the pasture by the river. There is disunion in nature, too, brute against brute, as well as man against his fellow. But in the next scene all is harmony. In a lovely valley is a great pasture dotted with white sheep, and steadings with shepherds' thatched huts and sheepfolds. The picture of life seems about to end with a note of quiet loveliness and peace, but the poet adds the Dance. This has been suspected on various grounds, among them (by Rothe) that it ruins the symmetry. This argument demands of Homer a symmetry which is cold and formal. Attempts to see this kind of symmetry in Homer tend to rob him of his chief claim to greatness. The poet of genius uses the element of form to make a thing of beauty which is like any human body or any of nature's creations. No individual specimen is exactly like a geometric or numerically expressed form which may be abstracted from many specimens taken together. Nature's forms are organic, not machinelike. The Dance, the final scene on the shield, completes an organic unity which without it would be lacking. The scenes have painted the lights and shadows of life, but the former receive all the emphasis. Our attention is not drawn to the emotions aroused by discord and war—there are no groans or cries in the fighting, and death is personified, not described. Even labor is not toil. The music, whether of flutes or harps or shepherds' pipes, whether song of the boy at the vintage or of the wedding chorus, brings only joy. Without the Dance the shield would lack that periodicity which marks Homer's literary architecture, a periodicity consisting in the return, at or near the end, to some fact or person or motif prominent at the beginning. The motif at the beginning of the Shield is joy and gladness, and to this the Dance at the end returns. Youth and its joys are in the foreground. The Shield, in its prevailing atmosphere, reminds us of the scenes of the Meidias Painter. In spite of its occasional contrasting tones, it is, as it were, a symphony of the rapture of living. This is suggested in the overture, the first scene of the City at Peace. The Dance is the finale, repeating this theme *molto vivace*.

There are certainly Cretan elements in the Dance. The poet must have known the tradition of Minoan culture. It is maintained with good reason that in the Phaeacian episode we have a poetic version of memories of the court of Minos. Both Phaeacians and Minoans made much of dancing. If Homer wished to convey the impression that life at high tide is, as Havelock Ellis believes, a dance, he would naturally add to the two dances on the shield, the dancing at weddings and at the vintage labor, a third picture, of dancing for its own sake, and in rich costumes and with trained and formal movements. This dance, too, would remind his hearers of the dancers par excellence, the Cretans, in whose cultured life the joy in nature for its own sake reached an apex.

The Shield is an epic *hyporcheme* intervening between two of the most poignant moments of emotion in either poem. At Hector's death Andromache swoons and Priam wishes to risk his life that so perchance he may hold the body of his "one" son in his arms. But when Achilles learns of the death of Patroclus, Antilochus fears that he may take his own life—the only suggestion of suicide from grief in the action of the two poems. The second deeply emotional moment is described immediately after the Shield. Thetis brings the armor to her son at daybreak. She finds him lying with his arms around the body of Patroclus. She lays the arms on the ground beside him. "And as he saw them, so much the more did rage enter into him, his eyes shot forth as it were a flash of terrible fire from beneath his eyelashes." This is a fine psychological touch, like that after the death of Hector. There the momentary exultation over his victory makes Achilles forget his dead friend, but only for an instant (X 378-387). Here the thought of vengeance momentarily banishes his grief for Patroclus: νῦν δ' ἤτοι μὲν ἐγὼ θωρήξομαι (T 23), "Now I will arm myself"—to slay Hector, and then to die (Σ 91 f., 98). It is between these two outbursts of passion that the Shield is inserted. It differs from the *hyporcheme* of tragedy in being limited to the effect upon the audience. The emotions stirred by the scenes do not concern the action. This shield of Achilles has no device. The description is an interposition of the poet in which he lyrically contrasts the rapturous joy of living with the grief which makes Achilles say, "Let me die," and the hate which makes him add, "But not until I have slain Hector."

The Shield is the best example in Homer of the introduction of extraneous matters to enrich the objective narrative, particularly in its effect upon the emotions. We have still to examine the poet's brief and still more personal interpositions which either enhance the listener's emotional participation in the action or clarify and explain the action itself.

The first group leads us aside for a moment into Greek syntax. As the Trojans advance after the treacherous arrow of Pandarus has broken the truce, the poet continues: "At this moment you [my hearer] cannot picture Agamemnon asleep or terror-struck or unready to fight."[19] The ancients[20] and most modern grammarians and commentators treat the optative with ἄν (οὐκ ἄν ἴδοις) as if it were a "past potential," but they do not explain how the optative can have this meaning. Plato, however, gives a clear hint of the way Homer used this optative. In the *Menexenus* Socrates says one must *see* the bravery of the Athenians of old *by placing himself in thought* in those days. If he will put himself back into that time, Socrates says, he can understand how brave they were who faced the Persians at Marathon.[21] This is just what Homer calls upon his hearer to do a score of times, always at a crisis or a moment in the action of intense interest. "Aeneas may be slain!" (E 311). "The horses *can't* descend into the trench!" (M 58 f.). "Menelaus may easily carry off the splendid armor of Euphorbus" (P 70). "You can't imagine that vast army moving forward so silently" (Δ 429). "A hawk can't keep pace" with the Phaeacian ships (ν 86). "No supper can be more joyless than that which the goddess and the mighty man were to make for the Suitors, merrily dining" (υ 392). This optative is not a "historical present," as van Leeuwen calls it. The historical present presents a past action objectively; the "potential optative" is the most subjective form of the Greek verb.[22] It leaves the degree of possibility to the one who makes the estimate. Hector sprang through the gate of the Greek wall, "his face like swift-coming night, his terrible armor agleam, and with two spears in his hand—no one save a god *can* face him and drive him back—when he leaped through the gate" (M 463-466).

The potential of the past is used in a similar way, and much oftener—more than one hundred times in the narrative portion of the two poems. What might have been, or what could not have happened, is purely subjective. The objective narrator would not say that Agamemnon's testing of his army would have sent the Argives home before the fated time if Hera had not interfered, or that Menelaus would have gained great glory by dragging Paris from the lists, if Aphrodite had not saved him. He would have described what actually happened: Menelaus was dragging Paris away; Aphrodite broke the helmet strap of Paris and carried him off to the city. The objective method, however, would not mark the critical situation. The listener would grasp this in retrospect, but by that time the narrative would have passed to other matters. Homer's way concentrates the emotional tension and relieves it, all within the compass of two verses. So this method becomes a shorthand way of treating less serious situations, a critical point in an athletic contest, or in an altercation; to terminate any series of similar actions. Odysseus has killed seven Lycians; he would have killed more, if Hector had not come to their rescue (E 679). Finally, it is used to bring to an end an emotional impasse: "They would have gone on weeping [for joy or grief], if something had not stopped them."

This marking of a critical situation before relief comes is often done by the imperfect of δύναμαι, always with the negative. The Trojans could not wound Antilochus (N 552), or break the Achaean ranks (O 408), or fire the ships (O 416), or make Ajax retire (Π 107). The verb does not describe action or advance the account of it, but only suggests the issue. This is done more distinctly by the verb μέλλω, which is often used to prepare the listener for the death of one of the heroes, Dolon, Asius, Lycaon, Antinous and other Suitors, and even of Sarpedon, Patroclus, Hector, and Achilles; and less frequently, to foreshadow a happy outcome: Zeus was to drive the Trojans back from the ships (O 601); the Achaeans were not long to be held back from the body of Patroclus, that is, they would soon protect it (P 278). Where the approaching crisis is unsuspected by a character, it is often marked by the close approach to apostrophe. The Suitors thought the Beggar had slain Antinous by accident;

"poor fools, they knew not that the meshes of death had closed upon them all" (χ 32).

All these interpositions seem to be adapted to the oral narrative. They give the listener time to grasp the significance of an important moment in the story by suggesting the crisis, or by hinting at the sequel. Moments of lesser import are introduced by the emotional particles ἦ, ἦτοι, μήν, μάν. These are hardly more than articulate equivalents of physical gestures, appropriate rather to oral than to written expression, as the dialogues of both Homer and Plato show.

There remains to be considered the subjective feature of Homeric narrative which in principle is that of history and the modern novel. This is the substitution of indirect for direct presentation of action, feeling, and thought. Homer, however, uses the indirect method much more sparingly, confining it to situations which are of minor importance or are unsuitable for direct presentation.

The young child or the primitive adult uses little more than pure diegesis and pure mimesis. He describes action as he has observed it, and without explanation except in the words which he has heard the speakers use. His version of the appearance of Athena to Achilles in the assembly (A 194 ff.), if he used Homer's facts, would be something like this: Achilles started to draw his sword. Hera, on Olympus, saw him, and said to Athena, "Agamemnon and Achilles are both dear to me. Go and restrain Achilles." This is objective narrative. Homer is purely subjective: Athena came to Achilles, for Hera sent her, because she cared for both heroes. This presents a minor action in the reverse of the real order, by introducing causality. This is seen in the use of γάρ. The reason for an act belongs to history, and above all to oral utterance. In the *Funeral Oration* of Pericles γάρ is used three times as often as in the *Pentecontaetia*; in the speeches in Homer more than twice as often as in the narrative.[23] The primitive narrator gives few reasons. In Genesis 1:1-31, he gives none; in Ruth (outside of the speeches), but one (1:6). But Homer uses some expression of cause for many purposes; for example, (1) to give information which a modern historian would place in a footnote. The Aetolians had Thoas for a leader: (for) Oeneus and his sons, including Meleager, were dead, and Thoas was sole king (B 641-643). (2) He also uses it to tell with the utmost brevity—usually in a single verse, and more often in a half-verse—the thought which moved the character to act, or the reason for his emotion. Menelaus came to Agamemnon's dinner uninvited: (for) he knew how busy his brother was (B 409). The Suitors were dumfounded: (for) they had said to themselves that Telemachus had not gone to Pylus, but was with Eumaeus or Laertes (δ 638). (3) Sometimes the reason is given as a brief comment to mark the impressiveness of the situation. Behind the bier of Patroclus walked Achilles, in the anguish of grief: (for) goodly was the comrade he was escorting to the tomb (Ψ 137). Odysseus sallied forth from his covert to meet Nausicaa and her maidens with only a leafy bough to hide his nakedness: (for) need was come upon him (ζ 136).

Purpose, like cause, may be presented both directly and indirectly. Homer uses the objective method when the action is important. Achilles' purpose in calling the assembly (A 62-67), Agamemnon's in sending the heralds to fetch Briseis (A 322-325), Thetis' in going to Olympus (A 419 f.), and Athena's in going to Ithaca (α 88-95), are expressed in speeches. But for incidental action Homer uses the subjective method. Telemachus seats Mentes at a distance from the Suitors to prevent their noisy behavior from disturbing the guest, and that he may ask Mentes about Odysseus (α 133 ff.). He bends his head towards Mentes that the Suitors may not hear his words (α 157). Homer seems inclined to explain the purpose of a divinity more often than that of a mortal. Sometimes he thus announces the theme of the following episode. Athena gives Diomede courage and strength

(E 2) that he may distinguish himself and win fair glory—the theme of Book V. The same goddess goes to Sparta to cause Telemachus to return at once (ο 3); his return is the theme of the greater part of Book XV. It is noticeable that the indirect expression of purpose very rarely gives the hearer new and important information which is not implied in the context: Athena darts to earth to find Pandarus—the first mention of the way in which the truce is to be broken (Δ 88), and Hector was dragging the body of Patroclus to cut off the head and throw the body to the dogs (P 126 f.). Usually the purpose is unimportant or can be inferred from the context. The purpose of Polites (B 794), to watch for the approach of the Greeks, is implied in the statement that he was a scout. The cap of Hades is of course intended to make its wearer invisible (E 845). The purpose of Dawn in leaving the couch of Tithonus is, naturally, "to bring light to the immortals and to mortal men" (Λ 2 = ε 2).

The statement of a purpose gives us a glimpse into the mind of a character—which is one of the chief marks of the subjective narrative. Homer reveals the thoughts of his characters indirectly, that is, in other ways than by the *ipsissima verba*, more than is generally recognized.

There are three ways of chronicling the utterances of a person. The simplest and most indirect method is to sum up the gist of the utterance. "He commanded the clear-voiced heralds to call to assembly the long-haired Achaeans." The wives and daughters of the Trojans asked Hector for news of their men, and he bade each in turn to pray to the gods. This is indirect and undramatic dialogue. Homer has few of these; but many dialogues are partly indirect. "Nestor bade Patroclus be seated, but he refused, saying," etc. (Λ 644 ff.). The indirect method is common to Homer and to all narrators, whether they incline more or less to objectivity. The opposite method is direct and dramatic. It presents the words of the speaker in the first person. Between these is the method of so-called indirect discourse. Cauer thought that Homer avoided indirect discourse because of a certain lack of flexibility of thought, which made him loath to translate a character's words into the third person.[24] This view seems to confuse indirect speech with the form of indirect discourse, and to ignore the unsuitability of this kind of utterance to narrative in general and oral narrative in particular. Homer often presents a character's thoughts indirectly, and often his speech. The account which Odysseus gives to Penelope of his wanderings is the longest passage in *oratio obliqua*, and has been rejected by Aristarchus and by modern scholars. But in form it does not differ from the two songs of Demodocus about the Trojan War (θ 76-82, 500-520), except that, since Odysseus has not one but many themes, the particle of indirect discourse (ὡs) must be used oftener. Shorter indirect speeches, introduced by the verb φημί, are not uncommon in both poems, in the narrative and in the speeches. "He [Agamemnon] said that he would that very day capture Priam's city" (B 37). " 'Patroclus, I ween thou didst say thou wouldst sack my city, rob the Trojan women of their day of freedom, and carry them in ships to thine own dear native land' " (Π 830-832)."They [the Suitors] said he [the Beggar] had slain the man without intent" (χ 31 f.). " 'I said that he would suffer many hardships, and lose all his comrades, but would return unrecognized by all after twenty years' " (β 174-176).

The reason why Homer prefers the direct to the indirect speech becomes clearer if we compare the indirect soliloquy[25] with the monologue.[26] There are about a score of each in the two poems. If one compares the two forms one sees that it is largely the situation which determines the poet's choice of one or the other. If the facts in the hero's mind are of chief importance, the poet presents them in the condensed and indirect form. But if the moment is fraught with emotion, and especially if there is no opportunity for dialogue, we hear the character "think aloud." Thus Menelaus, balked of his vengeance (Γ 365-368), and Asius, discovering the disastrous result of bringing his chariot to the attack on the Greek wall (M 164-172), express their feelings in direct speech. Hector's debate with himself before the Scaean Gate and his final determination to win glory by his death (X 99-130, 297-305) must be given dramatically, or we do not share in the hero's emotion. In the account of the voyage from Ogygia to Scheria (ε 269-474) there is no opportunity for dialogue; there are six direct, and no indirect, soliloquies, and these include two self-debates. But when Penelope, descending the stairs to meet Odysseus after the Slaughter, debates with herself whether to believe the words of Eurycleia that the stranger is Odysseus, or to test him further, the poet's indirect summary of what is passing in her mind is sufficient, for the dialogue which is to follow will adequately present the emotions of this recognition scene.

As the self-debate may be presented both directly and indirectly, so all the forms of the direct single speech, that is, the speech outside of the dialogue, are also to be found in Homer in condensed, indirect form. The indirect form is preferred in (1) digressions, (2) subordinate incidents, or (3) where the situation is not suited to the use of direct speech. Homer refuses to dramatize undramatic material: *quae desperat tractata nitescere posse, relinquit.*

A typical use of such interpositions is at the end of an episode, especially when no change of scene follows. By this the poet gently withdraws attention from the action itself, so that the new episode is less liable to blurring by conflict with the vivid impression of what precedes. The sharp outlines of the latter action fade, as it were, from the mind, giving place to the contemplation of its general aspect or of its emotional implications. The episodes of Helen on the Tower and of Glaucus and Diomede end in this way. Helen closes the first with a reference to her brothers, Castor and

Polydeuces, whom she does not see among the Greek heroes on the field. " 'Either they did not come with the other leaders, or else they are unwilling to enter the fighting, dreading to hear the scornful reproaches—and they are many—of me.' Thus Helen spoke, but [the poet adds] the lifegiving earth already held those brothers in its embrace at home in Lacedaemon, in their own native land" (Γ 239 ff.). At the end of the dialogue between Glaucus and Diomede the two heroes greet each other as family friends and exchange arms. The poet adds, "Then the son of Cronus robbed Glaucus of his wits; he exchanged his armor for that of Diomede, gold for bronze, the value of a hundred oxen for the value of nine" (Z 234-236). Both times, the poet's intrusion makes less abrupt the transition to another thread of the narrative. So in the *Odyssey* at the end of Book XX. The long series of insults which Odysseus has endured from the suitors, Antinous, Eurymachus, and Ctesippus, and even from his own slaves, Melanthius and Melantho, has now come to an end. The metabasis to the Vengeance is about to begin with the Contest of the Bow. Penelope, sitting on a stool at the top of the great stairway, is listening to every word of the men in the great hall below. At this point the poet interposes: "For those men had been jovial when they prepared the dinner; it was a gladsome feast, and all that the heart could desire, for in sooth they had butchered many cattle. But there could not be a sorrier supper than was to follow—what the goddess and the mighty hero were to set before them, for they had begun the quarrel by their unseemly deeds of iniquity."

Journeys and all movements from one place to another are "flat spaces," and rarely permit the dialogue. If they are emotionally unimportant they are described by the objective narration. But there are two places where the narrative alone will not suffice. In each of these the poet gives not an objective picture, but a subjective impression.

The voyage of the Phaeacian ship bearing Odysseus to Ithaca (ν 78-115) is the most important in Homer, for it brings home after twenty years of hardship the most famous wanderer in Greek literature. But it is without incident and has no place for speech. Therefore the poet devotes to the action only seven verses, less than one-fifth of the passage: the rowers dipped their oars; Odysseus fell asleep; the poop of the ship lifted, the waves roared astern; the ship flew steadily on; and when dawn came, it drew near the island, and the sailors rowed it ashore. With the rest of the verses the poet creates an impression of the voyage, giving it emotional content and allowing time for the hearer to dwell upon it. He uses four similes, describes, in the present tense, the day star and the harbor of Phorcys, and makes his own famous comment: (The ship speeds on, swift as a bird, cleaving the billows)

> Bearing a man who in wisdom and counsel was like the immortals,
> One that erstwhile had known in his heart much distress and much sorrow,
> Both in the battles of men and in cleaving a path through the billows.
> Now he was peacefully slumb'ring forgetful of all he had suffered.

Even more impressionistic is the account of the pursuit of Hector by Achilles around the walls of Troy (X 136-214).[27] The episode is thrilling in interest, but it is only the prelude to the combat which ends with the death of Hector; hence it must not be filled with incident. The poet is therefore confronted by a "flat space," which, like the voyage of the Phaeacian ship, is of great emotional importance, yet has no place for the dramatic element. Here again only a small part of the passage—less than one-fourth—is given to the simple account of the action. The start and the finish are described, and the length of time consumed in the chase, thrice around the city walls, is masked by two Olympian scenes. The poet generalizes: "Every time that Hector made for the walls, Achilles would head him off"; or summarizes: "Thus thrice around the walls they sped." At different stages similes—six in all—are used to suggest different aspects of the race. One of these is the most subjective in either poem: as in a dream one can neither overtake a runner nor escape from a pursuer, so Hector could not increase his lead nor Achilles lessen it. The poet describes the two springs, where the death of Hector is to take place (see above, p. 35), again in the present tense, and adds a pathetic reference to their joyous use by the wives and daughters of the Trojans, in the days of peace, "before the coming of the Achaeans." He makes two personal comments on the pursuit: a goodly hero was the pursued, but there followed him a far mightier. "[Fast they ran,] for it was no footrace for a cow or an oxhide, that are today prizes for the swift-footed, no, the stake in this race was the life of Hector." The poet even resorts to one of his rare rhetorical questions: "How *could* Hector have kept out of reach of death, save that Apollo gave him strength—for the last and final time?" Finally the poet gives us a glimpse into the mind of both the heroes. Hector hoped that he could lure Achilles within bowshot of the defenders on the walls; Achilles' gesture to the Greeks forbidding their interference was made in the fear that he should be robbed of (both his vengeance and) the glory of slaying Hector.

The Pursuit of Hector is the longest account of important action, unrelieved by speeches, in either poem. It is also one of the most subjective passages in Homer. The nature of his material forces the poet to use the impressionistic method. The same method is needed in describing the movements of armies. This cannot be dramatized by speeches, nor can masses of men be pictured graphically in a swiftly moving oral narrative. The poet gives a few sensuous features: the bristling of the spears, the flashing of bronze and the gleam of the helmets, shields, and breastplates; the clouds of dust, whitening the soldiers; the shouting in a charge or at a rally; the cries of exultation and the groans of the dying; the loud snorting of frightened horses and the roar of their labored breath in mad retreat; the crash of overturned chariots, and the general din of battle. "The earth ran with blood, and the dead lay in multitudes, side by side in the dust." Quite as frequent is the poet's account of what was passing in the minds of the soldiers: eagerness and confidence in an advance; intrepidity and sudden panic. "They bethought themselves of flight and forgot their valor." "Duty and a sense of shame restrained them." And the poet again and again interposes to deepen the impression of the moment. He piles simile on simile; he personifies the spirits of battle. He marks crises by telling what might, or might not, have happened, or what was just about to happen. He even addresses his listener directly. The cloud over a part of the battlefield was so black, "you would not think there was a sun or a moon in the world." "Neither Ares nor Athena could fail to be satisfied with this fighting." "If a man could pass through the line of battle, protected from the missiles by Athena, he could find naught lacking in the fierceness of the struggle."

To illustrate the impressionistic treatment of armies in battle, let us take the accounts of the first hostile onset (Δ 422-456) and of the last retreat of the Greeks (P 722-761).

At the end of the Epipolesis, Diomede leaps from his chariot with his arms to the ground. "And terrible was the rattle of the prince's bronze armor as he sprang. 'Twould have daunted e'en the very stout heart"—the poet often thus passes from the sensuous to the emotional, and from the objective to the subjective, when, as here, an impressionistic passage is to follow. The onset of the two armies ensues. The poet gives us few facts. The Greeks advanced in gleaming armor, with their leaders, line after line in disciplined silence, broken only by the officers' commands. As the Trojans came on, cries broke out at every point in their vast army. The demons of war inspired both Trojans and Greeks. The two armies met with a clash of shields and spears, and fought hand to hand. Loud was the din. Cries of agony and of triumph followed, and the earth ran with blood. They fought fiercely and with loud shouts.

To these facts—which, however, Homer's richer language fills with life—are added impressions. The "primitive" Dionysus in the *Frogs* could not describe his feelings, but could tell what they were *like*. So Homer uses the simile for what baffles description. The orderly succession of countless lines of Greeks is like wave after wave breaking on a sandy beach. The moblike outcries of the advancing Trojans suggests the bleating of innumerable ewes at milking-time, when their lambs are calling them; and the din of battle, the roar of swollen mountain torrents pouring their waters together in a deep gorge.

The poet also addresses his listener: (The Greek lines advanced so silently that) "you would say not a single common soldier possessed the power of speech." The undisciplined outcries of the Trojans prompt him to explain: They were not of one language and one speech; it was a babel of tongues, for they came from many alien lands. Finally, he allegorizes the undertone of hatred which war provokes. The spirits of war were Terror and Panic and "Discord, whose fury rageth ever, sister and comrade of man-slaying Ares. She is but a puny creature when she first raiseth her crest, but anon she walketh the earth and her head toucheth the heavens. She it was who now [τότε, to return to our story] inspired the two armies to mutual strife, as she went through the throng, increasing the sorrows of men."

The account of the Greek retreat with the body of Patroclus (P 722-761) is of about the same length. Menelaus and

Meriones carry the body on their shoulders. Behind them the two Ajaxes repel the attacks of the Trojans, led by Aeneas and Hector. We have thus three central groups and the two armies. The picture of this retreat is one of the best illustrations of the amazing art with which Homer in few words conveys an impression, fraught with intense emotion, of a scene which baffles precise description. Atmosphere and tone are given by the picture at the beginning and at the end of the account, the Trojans attacking, and the Greeks retiring in panic, throwing away their arms. The five units in the entire picture are separated from each other by four similes, each suggesting some emotional aspect of the preceding group. The roar of the oncoming Trojan chariots is likened to the conflagration of a town on a windy night; the bearers of Patroclus' body, to a pair of mules struggling and sweating as they drag a huge timber over a crooked, rocky path in the mountains. The two Ajaxes keep back the attackers as a wooded ridge of rock turns aside the mighty swollen torrents from the mountains, "and with all the force of their current they cannot break through." The repeated assaults of Aeneas and Hector terrify the Greek army like hawks swooping at a flock of small birds. "So they forgot the joy of battle, and many were the fair pieces of armor that fell round about the trench. *But they could find no respite from the fighting.*"

The extent to which the poet interposes in the account of the third battle of the *Iliad* has given offense to critics both ancient and modern, and it probably diminishes the interest of the modern reader. For reading, the interpositions are not well adapted: they are too brief, and are confined to variations of a comparatively few general patterns. But in oral narrative it is different—as one can prove by reading the subjective passages aloud and *con espressione*. The attention of an audience is best held by action and speeches of the characters. The listener would be wearied by lengthy comments. But the poet's brief subjective contributions to the tale, if they were rendered by the reciter with the emotion of the poet, which they imply, would be a tonic to the attention, rather than a burden. The fact that so many of Homer's interpositions are very brief, from a half-verse to two verses in length, is one of the many evidences of the poet's constant thought for the mental comfort and ease of his audience. We consider this in our next chapter.

CHAPTER FIVE

THE POET AND HIS AUDIENCE

We have been considering the Homeric poems as a picture of Human Life Writ Large presented by a threefold partnership. The Voice of the Past is responsible for the facts and for the action, the *dramatis personae* by their words reveal the effect of the action upon their lives, and the poet supplies in the first person what neither the account of the action nor the words of the characters can give. There is a fourth member of the firm, a silent partner—the listening audience.

In the drama the contribution of this silent partner is recognized. Some years ago Christopher Morley, finding the modern theater audience blasé and passive, revived the nineteenth-century melodrama. Within five months 150,000 persons came to the Rialto Theater in Hoboken to see *The Dark Hour*. Agnes Repplier says this play succeeded because "there was real creative unity between actors and house."[1] The Greeks knew how important the audience was in the orator's success. Demosthenes says, "In most arts a man is reasonably independent, but the art of oratory fails if the audience does not help the speaker."[2] This principle applies to poetry. The written epic may at times forget the immediate presence of its audience, and still succeed; the oral epic, never. To the oral epic poet the audience is the instrument on which he plays. Both instrument and player are partners in producing the music.[3] If a book fails to interest us at the first reading it can be laid aside and taken up again later. Emerson records in his *Journal* his reply to a young man who found nothing of interest in a book Emerson had recommended: "Perhaps it was not *your hour*." To Homer's audience the moment of recitation was always its

---
[1] Superior figures refer to notes which will be found on pp. 251–252.

hour, for the winged word does not return. The oral recitation, like the oration of Demosthenes, succeeded or failed at its delivery. Hence the attention of the listener is the poet's first desideratum. He must not only catch it; he must hold it by preventing it from straying. Above all, he must in every possible way relieve the listener of undue mental effort, or his fatigued mind is no longer receptive.

I

When we examine Homer's manner, if we remember that his audience never read, or even thought of the possibility of reading the poems, we are struck by the great variety of ways in which it conserves the listener's attention. Many of these are apt to be dismissed by the modern critic with the epithet "primitive." The primitive mind is the mind of a listener, not a reader. But the amazing and almost universal appeal of the Homeric poems, long after they ceased to be recited, when they were always read, is evidence that the poet's manner, the final result of a long development of primitive narration, may come nearest to perfection of the narrator's art. It may even offer suggestions for the improvement of the modern story.

The most primitive feature of Homer's manner is the tendency to repeat incidents, motifs, patterns, formulae, and epithets. This seems to have been accepted without remark in ancient times, if we may judge by the silence of Aristotle, the rhetoricians, and Horace. In Alexandrian criticism of the text, repetition plays some part, and the modern Dissectors made it a chief counter. Milman Parry used it for a new theory of Homeric style, but contributed nothing to its evaluation. Professor Calhoun has given a positive value to Parry's work. He has already established three points: (1) the element of pleasure in the familiar, (2) the countless variations with which the larger formulae are used, (3) the probability that Homer selected his formulae with far more reference to their immediate context than scholars have recognized.[4] Professor Drerup's study of the Homeric triad is along the same line. Again and again the poet uses the same expression or incident or feature, three times *and no more*. This is both primitive and in accord with reason. There is a certain completeness in the triad. To beginning and end it adds a middle, thus making an Aristotelian "whole." "When I say it three times it is so," is clever nonsense,—Aristophanes used it (*Frogs* 369),—but it makes sense when addressed to an audience containing many child minds. The undisciplined intellect fails to grasp the full meaning of many utterances of a speaker, until repetition makes it clear. In the universal experience of the race the thrice-told tale is accepted, but more than this is "damnable iteration."

Parry thought that because some Homeric epithets often repeated were not understood by later Greeks, the formulae had lost much of their content even for Homer's audience. This cannot be proved, but the underlying principle is sound. The least responsive minds might interpret a familiar phrase as the mere symbol for a fact, with little attention to its content and atmosphere. This would be especially true of the formulae for the preparation and eating of meals, for retiring at night and rising in the morning. Even the keenest listener would feel his attention eased at these points. This relief could not fail to freshen the mind for the reception of the new incidents which followed.

The Homeric repetition is based on the principle which governs the acquisition of all our knowledge of the external world. We must observe the same object again and again in order to know it well. Furthermore, as views of an object from different angles give it perspective, so the slight changes in Homer's repeated phrases and passages imperceptibly give depth and add content to the mental picture. Hence the formula, in its widest sense, no matter to what degree it developed because of the convenience of the bards themselves, in its use by Homer reveals an equal consideration for the listener.

Still more consideration is shown by telling the hearer in advance how the action is to issue,[5] for it recognizes the audience as a partner who has the right to share in all the knowledge which concerns the partnership. Homer's loyalty to his silent partner, and at the same time his realism, is seen when a new character enters the action. In real life, when one brings a stranger into a group, courtesy demands that he be presented at once and by name. Few writers observe this requirement of good breeding as consistently as Homer does. In the *Aeneid* Sinon enters at II, 57; we first learn his name at verse 79. We do not learn the identity of Ulysses' comrade, left on the Cyclops' isle, until 20 verses after his first appearance. Dante postpones, sometimes for a page or more, the names of many of the chief sufferers in the *Inferno*.[6] But Homer, with a single exception,[7] introduces the newcomer at once by name. We may illustrate by contrasting Homer with Vergil in the comparison of Nausicaa and Dido, respectively, to Artemis. Since Vergil is here using the Homeric passage, the difference is all the more pertinent. Homer says (ζ 102-108): "As Artemis moves, on the mountains, in her hunting, either on Taygetus exceeding high or Erymanthus," etc.; Vergil (I, 498-502): "As on Eurotas' banks or on the top of Cynthus moves Diana with her band." To the reader this order gives no difficulty. But imagine the words of the two poets to come to the ear one word after another, each word exciting the imagination and the perceptive process to paint a picture or construct an idea, and we see the greater courtesy of the Greek poet. The latter, as one might say, introduces us to the lady, and we walk with her in the country; Vergil takes us to the country, without telling us why. This may pique our curiosity, but it is not, as we have said, the highest art. Homer in his similes, so often that we may say he does it regularly, gives us the theme before describing the place and the time, for this is his way of presenting details. He is rather analytic than synthetic. He proceeds from the general, which we all know, to the particulars, which may be new.

Homer shows his economy of the hearer's attention also in his choice of minor characters, again in contrast to Vergil. Iopas, who sings at Dido's feast, and Bitias, who receives from her the wine cup, have no other connection with the story, and Vergil describes neither. Without a formal introduction their sudden entrance in an oral narrative would turn aside the listener's attention to wonder who they were. At least they would interest him less than Demodocus when he sings of the Wooden Horse, for Homer has carefully groomed the Phaeacian bard for his part. In a long story with a very large cast of characters, the interest is maintained and increased if the minor characters are in some way related to others whom we know. We instantly and unconsciously identify the new by its relation to the old and familiar. The *Iliad* supplies an interesting illustration of Homer's use of this principle.

At the beginning of the Teichoscopia the eight Elders of Troy are introduced by name: Priam, Panthous, Thymoetes, Lampus, Clytius, Hicetaon, Ucalegon, and Antenor. If van Leeuwen is right in thinking that Ucalegon is a punning name "Jemenmoque," for Antimachus, the royal council represents four of the five Trojan families prominent in the *Iliad*: Priam and his four brothers (if Thymoetes is included), Panthous the seer, and Antimachus and Antenor, leaders, respectively, of the pro- and anti-Paris parties. Anchises alone is absent; rightly, for he belongs to the party opposed to Priam. These five Trojan families, with their servants and friends, provide seventy-five of the Iliad's *dramatis personae*, more than are found in the longest novel of Dickens. The relationship thus established is one of the numerous minor threads in the pattern of the *Iliad*. We pass over the families of Anchises, Antimachus, and Panthous, to consider those of Priam and Antenor.

These two families supply threescore characters of the poem. Eleven sons of Antenor and twenty-two of Priam are mentioned by name—numbers out of all proportion to the progeny of any Greek hero in the poem, even Nestor. Priam has fifty sons and twelve daughters. These are round numbers, without claim to factual precision or historical accuracy. They have led scholars to emphasize the Greek scorn for the polygamous Priam. Finsler (*Homer*, I, 210) refers to "Priam's harem." Neither Homer nor his Greek heroes give evidence of this. The poet does not picture the Trojans as βάρβαροι; Achilles mentions Priam's sons along with his wealth as tokens of great prosperity (Ω 546). The size of Priam's family is explained by Homer's poetic economy. In every episode of battle in which Trojans are slain, except M and Ξ, that is, in Δ-Z, Θ, Λ, N, O-P, T-X, at least one warrior falls who is connected with the family of Priam. These include eleven sons, two prospective sons-in-law, five nephews, and two intimate friends (besides two charioteers) of Hector. The numerous offspring of Priam—carefully, although casually provided for by the description of his palace (Z 244-250)—and of Antenor are invented mostly to provide heroic *Kannonenfutter* which is linked with the chief Trojan characters already familiar to the listener.

II

Homer's economy of the listener's attention, and his unceasing care to keep it from straying, is best shown by the arrangement of his thought. We have spoken of the continuum of time and place in Homer. The continuity of ideas is quite as carefully observed. Bougot called the underlying principle "the law of affinity,"[8] but overlooked its most typical application.

In the Homeric narrative the last person to retire at night is the first to rise the next morning. The assembly is "dismissed" by the last speaker or the last persons mentioned.[9] The divinity who sends the fair wind, Apollo, Athena, Calypso, or Circe, is the one who is *uppermost in the mind of the listener*. It follows that when two persons, objects, or ideas have been mentioned, it is the second which is uppermost in the mind. In the Catalogues the Greek forces are described, then the Trojans; in the episode immediately following (Γ 2, 8), the Trojans advance first, then the Greeks. But in the second onset of the two armies (Δ 427, 433) the Greeks are the first to move forward because our attention has been centered on them. This principle—which is almost a law in Homer—may be stated thus: When two or more coördinate ideas are repeated, the order, *ceteris paribus*, is inverted: ab ba.

Aristarchus seems to have been the discoverer of the principle, and the Romans were familiar with it, but it has been ignored by modern scholars.

At the end of the Greek Catalogue the poet asks and answers two questions: Who [a] was the best fighter? Whose [b] horses were the best? The horses [b] of Eumelus, [a] Ajax. The scholiast[10] quotes the reply of Aristarchus to the objection of a certain Praxiphanes, "It is a peculiar habit of the poet always, as here, to recur to the latter point first." Cicero, writing to Atticus, says that he will answer his two questions ὕστερον πρότερον Ὁμηρικῶς. He answers the second, and then the first.[11] Scholars explain the phrase as referring either to the figure hysteron proteron—which, however, all *Greek* grammarians called prothysteron or hysterologia—or to the inversion of the order of events in the *Odyssey* by which the Wanderings are described later. But Aristarchus makes perfectly clear the meaning of the Homeric hysteron proteron. The scholia contain at least twenty-five references to the πρὸς τὸ δεύτερον πρότερον ἀπάντησις. Aristarchus says that Homer uses it "always," or "habitually," or "generally"; his failure to use it is "contrary to his wont"; one use of the natural, rather than the inverted, order is used as an argument for rejecting a passage (Schol. A on O 56).

Unfortunately the scholia fail to give Aristarchus' explanation of Homer's reason for preferring the inverted order, but Eustathius seems to have known it. He notices the inversion, pointed out by Aristarchus, in the answers to the two questions in the Catalogue (B 763), and says it is made to keep the *continuity of the thought* (διὰ τὸ συνεχὲς τοῦ λόγου, 339, 24).

Most of the inversions noted in the scholia are simple and obvious, like the following (not noted by Aristarchus) at the beginning of the *Iliad*. Chryses besought *all the Achaeans* and the *two sons of Atreus:* "*Sons of Atreus* and ye *other Achaeans.*" . . . Then *all the other Achaeans* approved, but *Agamemnon* rejected the plea. The order is: ab ba ab.

More interesting is the inverted order in the answers to questions.[12] Two of these are particularly interesting. Odysseus asks the shade of his mother (a) of her own death, whether she died (b) of disease, or (c) by the gentle darts of Artemis; (d) of Laertes; (e) of Telemachus; (f) whether another has taken possession of his estate and royal power; and (g) of Penelope. Anticleia answers these seven questions in exactly the opposite order: "Penelope remains in thy halls [g]; no one has taken thy kingship [f]; Telemachus is master of thine estate [e]; thy father dwells in the fields [d]; and I died, not by the gentle darts of Artemis [c], nor by disease [b], but of grief for thee [a]." The other instance bears on the Higher Criticism. The cornerstone of Kirchhoff's *Nostos-theorie* was the failure of Odysseus to tell his name to Arete (η 238 ff.). The Queen asks him three questions: (1) Who are you? (2) Who gave you those garments? (3) Did you not say you came hither wandering over the sea? Odysseus answers the last question first and at some length, and at the end of his tale answers the second question. "I came ashore on your land naked; your daughter had pity on me and gave me this raiment." Arete has now learned what she wanted to know; and the question about his identity can be ignored, as the story requires.

In the carrying out of two commands or purposes Homer often inverts the order.[13] When Zeus wakes on Mount Ida he bids Hera summon Iris and Apollo (O 55); she calls Apollo, then Iris (vss. 143 f.). They go to Zeus, who dispatches first Iris, then Apollo (vss. 157, 221). The latter is given a twofold command, (1) to take the aegis and with it to put the Achaeans to flight, and (2) to go to Hector and rouse his strength (vss. 229-232). Apollo goes first to Hector's aid, and it is not until verse 308 that we hear of the aegis, with which at verse 322 he makes the Achaeans forget their prowess. This fourfold inversion cannot be accidental. The poet must invert intentionally. The recognition of this intention removes another difficulty of the Higher Critics, arising from the twofold plan of Athena in the *Odyssey* (α 84 ff.). Hermes is to go to Calypso and bid her send Odysseus home, and Athena is to prepare Telemachus for the return of his father. The failure of the poet to mention the first part of the plan again until Book V offered a major problem to the Higher Critics of the last century. The problem vanishes as soon as the Homeric hysteron proteron is understood. Athena has briefly mentioned the errand of Hermes, but has described her own at length. This errand is now uppermost in the mind and Hermes is forgotten, as was the first question of Arete.

In description we find the same principle governing the succession of ideas. Odysseus describes Wild Goat Island thus (ι 116-141): (a) It was near the land of the Cyclopes; (b) it was the home of countless wild goats; (c) it had a harbor where sailors were safe from all winds. Odysseus then narrates: "We sailed into the harbor [c]; we hunted the wild goats [b], and we looked off at the land of the Cyclopes [a]."

In the picture of the lions attacking the bull on the shield of Achilles (Σ 577-586), both herdsmen and dogs are mentioned three times, in this order: (a) herdsmen and dogs, (b) dogs and herdsmen, (a) herdsmen and dogs. Here the inversions are natural ones; the dogs are the first to detect the presence of the lion, and to rush to the spot, but in the presence of the lion the herdsmen would urge the dogs to the attack. But this reason for inversion does not hold for the Ambush (vss. 524-529). The two scouts watch for the approach of the sheep (a) and the cows (b); these soon come in sight, and with them two herdsmen (b). The men in ambush attack, and quickly cut off the herds (b) and the flocks (a), and slay the shepherds (a). In this passage there is not only inversion—sheep, cows: herds, flocks—but also the choice between herdsmen (νομῆες) and shepherds (μηλοβοτῆρες) is determined by the kind of animals last mentioned. Even in small details like this, Homer preserves the continuity of thought by relating the new idea to the one last mentioned. His speech is λέξις εἰρομένη in the most literal and best sense. It is "threaded speech" because each thought is linked to the next by the juxtaposition of associated ideas.

Two speeches are often thus linked together. In the Quarrel, Agamemnon threatens to take Briseis from Achilles, and closes his speech with the suggestion that Achilles command the ship which is to return Chryseis to her father (A 138, 146). Achilles replies: "How shall any Achaean eagerly obey thy command... *to go on a journey?*" (150 f.). A recognition of the Homeric hysteron proteron would have prevented many commentators from missing the point of the italicized words. Later in the same speech Achilles says (159), "We came to win *honor* for thee," and concludes his speech (169), "So[14] I'll *go back* to Phthia." Agamemnon replies, "*Flee* by all means; I have others here to do me *honor*."

The speeches of the Embassy were to the ancients models of rhetoric. They form a debate with three speeches on either side. In one respect they are in striking contrast to the forensic speeches of the tragic Agon. In the latter the second speaker when rebutting his opponent's arguments usually follows the same order.[15] In the dispute about the arms of Achilles in Quintus Smyrnaeus, who was strongly influenced by Euripides, the second speaker, Odysseus, follows the order of his rival Ajax.[16] In the Embassy, however, it is quite the reverse. Achilles takes up first an argument made by Odysseus near the close of his speech (I 315 ff. = 300 ff.). Phoenix begins his plea with a reference to the last two verses of Achilles' speech (434 ff. = 428 f.). In Achilles' reply his words echo the last words of the old man (608 = 603, 605), and Ajax begins the last of the three pleas,"Let us be going" (625), words which are suggested by "These men shall go," almost at the end of the preceding speech of Achilles.

Such is the "threaded speech" of Homer, the true λέξις εἰρομένη, because it continuously carries on the thought (Ar. *Rhet.*, 3, 9, 2). Its opposite is the λέξις κατεστραμμένη of the orator, which gives an end to each small unit of thought (*Rhet.* 3, 9, 3). The rhetorician watches for antitheses, carefully balancing one colon against another; Homer marks the antitheses in continuous life by giving equal continuity to the thought. The orator, like Gorgias, is an exhibitionist; he always thinks of the form of his speech. Homer thinks only of its function, to transfer the picture in his own mind to the minds of his audience. The Homeric hysteron proteron is not a rhetorical figure, but the unstudied, intuitive expression of intimate human discourse.

Unfortunately, the rhetoricians denied this. Aristarchus, who discovered the hysteron proteron, said, "Let Homer speak for himself." His rival Crates, head of the Stoic School at Pergamum, said: "Let Homer speak for rhetoric. The

Homeric hysteron proteron is nothing but chiasmus."[17] The *locus classicus* for this claim is in Eustathius, who was steeped in rhetoric.[18]

In the Truce, Menelaus says, "Bring two lambs, one white, the other *black*, for *Earth* and Sun." This is the Homeric hysteron proteron: the black lamb is associated in thought with Earth; hence the order, white and black for Earth and Sun, is intuitive and natural. The order, white and black for Sun and Earth, implies a certain reflection, which recognizes and emphasizes the contrast. But Eustathius thought differently. His comments are, in brief, as follows:

This is a novel order. It is *chiastic*. The *ordo quadrata* [Eustathius seems to know that the periodic sentence is the *sermo quadrata*] would be "white and black for Sun and Earth." The latter is the natural order. Homer's order results in a lack of clearness: He has arranged the four words, not in the "square" order [Eustathius gives a diagram to explain this], but like the letter X. This is artificial and contorted. The poet has imitated the mind of a man whose mind is confused, and one who is not at home in arranging words *naturally*. A similar striving for effect is seen in "*Achilles* was chosen polemarch, and the *princes* tarried by the ships. *They* were to keep the Trojans within the walls, while *he* ravaged the country round about." This order is ornate because of the inversion of the thought.[19]

These comments of Eustathius show that by the twelfth century the discovery of Aristarchus had been forgotten. To Eustathius the Homeric hysteron proteron is nothing more than chiasmus, an ornate, artificial figure of rhetoric. And such it has been to the present day. We have given evidence to the contrary from Homer himself. This finds a certain corroboration in Plato.

Plato, like Homer, presented his characters personally, by dialogue to which he imparted the impression of life. Plato avoided rhetoric himself, and despised it in others. And more than any other Greek author except Homer[20] he inverts the order when he repeats parallel ideas. We find this Homeric inversion in the most colloquial and informal parts of the dialogues. "Socrates, whither bound? Where have you been?" "In the Academy, and I'm bound straight for the Lyceum."[21] In the *Republic*, except in the discussions which are purely logical, the inverted order is slightly more common than the antithetic. On the contrary, when Socrates apes the rhetorical orator, the inversions are few. In the *Menexenus*, Socrates again and again uses the antithetic order in pairs of ideas which he elsewhere inverts. The Sophists, Hippias and Prodicus, in the *Protagoras* avoid inversions; so does Lysias in his essay on Love in the *Phaedrus*.[22] But the *Apology*, which passes as the impromptu and therefore unstudied utterance of Socrates, contains a score of inversions.

Aristotle is known to have avoided the rhetorical. In his treatises he uses the inverted order almost as much as Plato does.[23] Herodotus and Thucydides employ it occasionally, but in the Attic orators and in Greek prose writers in general after the fourth century the occurrences of the Homeric hysteron proteron are negligible, except where there is a logical reason for the inversion.

Why did Aristotle and Plato and Homer so often prefer the inverted order, which to us, as to Eustathius and Cicero and Pliny, seems the opposite of the natural order?[24] We should not be content to follow most commentators of Plato, and when we find the inverted order, say, "Note the chiasmus." We ought rather to ask ourselves, "Why did Plato prefer the inverted order?"

Comparative literature may help us to answer this question. Early Hebrew literature abounds in the Homeric hysteron proteron. Everyone knows that Bishop Robert Lowth in his lectures on Hebrew poetry, given in 1743, is the modern discoverer of the formal principle of Hebrew poetry, the parallelism of thought. But few scholars today are aware that in 1820 John Jebb, Bishop of Limerick, pointed out by numerous examples from many parts of the Bible that to the Hebrew writer the inverted order was a natural arrangement of parallel ideas.[25] Bishop Jebb called this "introverted parallelism" or "epanodos," which is closer to Aristarchus' usual phrase, πρὸς τὸ δεύτερον πρότερον ἀπαντᾷ. By epanodos Bishop Jebb understood the recurrence to the second, or to the last-mentioned thought, whether or not the first in the series received later mention. During the generation following, Biblical students carried on the work of Jebb. Then his discovery was in large part forgotten until 1930. In that year Professor Nils W. Lund, of North Park College, Chicago, began to publish the results of his intensive studies of inversions in Biblical writers. The result of all these researches which bears directly on the Homeric hysteron proteron is that the inverted order in Hebrew literature is not confined to poetry; it is found in the unstudied utterances of Jesus, and—what is more to our purpose—in simple historical statements in the more primitive books of the Old Testament. Exodus 9:31,"and the flax and the barley was smitten; for the barley was in the ear, and the flax was bolled." II Samuel 3:1,"Now there was long war between the house of Saul and the house of David, but David waxed stronger and stronger, and the house of Saul waxed weaker and weaker." The tenth chapter of Genesis records the descendants of Shem, Ham, and Japheth (vs. 1), but in the account which follows the order is reversed, Japheth (vss. 2-19), Ham (vs. 20), Shem (vss. 21-31).[26] Apparently, no matter how much Hebrew poets used the inverted order to give form to their couplets and to larger architectural units, the tendency to inversion is inherent in the ancient Hebrew speech and literature.

It cannot be due to chance that the earliest Hebrew and the earliest Greek literatures show the same inclination to arrange ideas in the order which seems to us as it did to

Eustathius to be unnatural. There seem to be but two possible explanations. The first is that Homer and his predecessors were influenced by Asiatic peoples. This does not seem impossible. The Orient is the native soil of the *raconteur*; Ionia must have had some contact with the peoples of southwestern Asia and Mesopotamia. Some scholars find parallels between Homer and the Gilgamesh epic. But until we have more knowledge of the channels by which this influence could have reached the bards before Homer, another explanation commends itself more strongly.

The recurrence to the last idea is to be expected in all primitive speech. The psychological law of the association of ideas will tend to prevail until reflection modifies or to some extent supersedes it. After the reason has abstracted from concrete facts their logical relation, the balanced or antithetic order becomes the natural order. But even in the highest cultures the primitive mind is found, especially in popular audiences. Hence, even after the reasoning process has been developed, creative poetry may use the primitive way of thinking for the purposes of its art. Hebrew poetry made of the "introverted parallelism" a formative principle. But Homer, in using the deuteron proteron, was seeking, not formal beauty, but an unbroken succession of ideas, by which he lightened the burden of his listener's attention, and thus with more nearly accomplished perfection imparted his own thought to the minds of his audience.[27]

III

The best efforts of the poet may fail if the listener does not contribute his share in the telling of the tale. This is a willing participation in the poet's purpose. If the most attentive audience is adversely critical, the speaker's words lose part of their effectiveness. No wonder that Aeschylus was not at his best in reciting from his tragedies in the *Frogs*; he knew that Euripides was "watching for the faults" (Ar. *Frogs*,

1151). Socrates, in his quest for truth, demanded first of all the loyal, hearty coöperation of another mind. So Homer seems to have expected willing assistance from his silent partner, the audience. There is evidence in the Homeric poems that the poet relied on his listeners to supply for themselves certain explanations which, if given by the poet, would needlessly interrupt the narrative and break the illusion.

The success of a narrative in achieving verisimilitude depends somewhat on the degree to which the acts and words of the characters appear natural and reasonable. The demand for this motivation is felt more strongly as the listener abandons the receptive attitude of mind for the critical. But superfluous rationalization, like the centipede's attempt to decide "which leg comes after which," interferes with the action. The eager listener or reader, bent on entering the life of the tale, largely ignores the lack of it, and no great storyteller succeeds in providing it always, except by deliberate and cold-blooded revision.[28] The intensity of the moment may lead both poet and listener to ignore the lack of motivation. For example, neither Homer nor any of his critics seem to have seen any need for explaining the elaborate headdress of Andromache when she suddenly left her weaving and rushed away to the Tower "like a mad woman" (X 440-472). As, from the Tower, her straining eyes caught sight of Hector's body dragging behind the chariot of Achilles, she fainted, "and far from her head she flung her shining headgear, diadem, and snood and woven kerchief, and her veil," the wedding gift of Aphrodite. Even Hera, who in the Tricking of Zeus makes the most splendid toilet in Homer, wears on her head only a veil. And Andromache, like a dutiful wife, had obeyed Hector's bidding to mind her household tasks, that is, to remain at home, where she had no occasion to wear at least the veil. The slight irrationality here is at once strong testimony to Homer's gift of narration—since even the critics have not noticed it—and a hint of his technique of motivation. Homer's rule is this: in the nexus of important actions, to make the most careful preparations and the most convincing explanations; but in details, especially where these merely heighten the effect of an otherwise impressive moment, to neglect motivation and often to omit it altogether. This is a wise procedure, for often the explanation would waste the hearer's attention and turn it away from the action. Instead of doing this, Homer *makes the listener supply the motivation.*

The discovery of this important feature of Homer's narrative technique was not made until within the last generation. The Alexandrian critics were often troubled to explain how one of Homer's characters could know this or that. For example, in the Doloneia, at the end of the long dialogue between Dolon and his captors, Diomede calls him by name, "Think not, Dolon, that thou shalt escape" (K 447). How can Diomede know Dolon's name? The scholiast (BT; cf. Eustathius 938, 31) rationalizes: Dolon, son of a herald, must have accompanied his father on missions to the Greek camp. Aristarchus reduces this explanation to a schema, which he frequently used; for example (schol. H on ρ 501), "How could Penelope know except κατὰ τὸ σιωπώμενον?"[29] By this Aristarchus meant that there was some way in which Penelope had learned what Antinous had said, but that the poet passed over this in silence. This is rationalism in another form. We have one ancient comment, however, which gives a less rational but still unsatisfactory explanation. How could Patroclus know that it was Apollo who had disarmed him? Aristarchus replies, "The poet endows his heroic characters with the knowledge which he himself possesses."[30] This is no more than saying that Homer fails to explain how Patroclus knew; it implies a defect in narrative technique.

In modern times Carl Rothe was the first to discuss the principle, but he did not recognize its importance or state the principle clearly.[31] This was done at last by Fraccaroli (*op. cit.* 397, 400): "The poet's relations with the characters whom he puts on the stage are purely imaginative and transitory; only his relation to the reader is real and permanent. Therefore one should not be surprised that he gives more attention to the latter relation than to the logic of his tale.[32] ... The knowledge [that the truce has been arranged, Γ 250 ff.] the *reader possesses and, as it were, has communicated this knowledge to the characters* [the Elders on the Tower]." We may put the principle in this way: In matters of slight importance what the listener knows, because the poet has told him in the preceding narrative, the character may be assumed to know.

This principle of narrative technique is one of the best illustrations in literature of close partnership between the poet and his audience. Homer uses it continually. Fraccaroli, Rothe, and van Leeuwen (on K 447) have together pointed out about a score of examples, but actually they are far more numerous. The writer has collected nearly one hundred from the two poems, and there must be many more. As Fraccaroli remarks, they may be found *a ogni passo*. Since these not only illustrate a distinct feature of Homer's manner, but concern the criticism and interpretation of certain passages, and bear on a chorizontic argument, we shall discuss some of them, especially those which have hitherto escaped notice.

The simplest instances arise from the numerous personal combats of the *Iliad*. The two opponents invariably know each other, except where one of them immediately gives his family history at some length (Glaucus to Diomede, Asteropaeus to Achilles). Their knowledge is to be explained by the fact that the poet has just imparted it *to the listener*. This is Homer's way of avoiding an unnecessary interposition to explain how Sthenelus knew Pandarus (E 246, cf. 168) and Diomede knew Dolon (K 447); how Odysseus and

Acamas knew the names of Socus and Promachus (Λ 450, cf. 440; Ξ 482, cf. 476); and how Ajax and Menelaus knew the identity of Archelochus and Euphorbus (Ξ 472, cf. 464; P 23-28). Hector, wounded and faint, knows that it is a god who speaks to him because the hearer is aware that it is Apollo (O 247). Achilles calls Iris by name (Σ 182) since we have just learned from the narrative that Hera sent her to him (vss. 166-168). Sometimes the hero knows more than the name of his opponent. Idomeneus and Achilles in their exultations over the slain Othryoneus and Iphition show that they know the facts about these heroes which the poet has just described (N 374-376, cf. 364-369; T 389-392, cf. 382-385).

A more developed use of the principle is found where the words or the acts of a character reveal knowledge which he has had no chance to gain. Achilles could not have known that Chryses prayed to Apollo (A 380, cf. 35). Diomede could not have known that Achilles might not carry out his threat to sail home the following day;[33] Odysseus had reported to the council that he would do so (I 682), but the listener remembers what Achilles said to Ajax (vss. 650-655). Patroclus could not have known that Sarpedon made the first successful attack on the Greek wall (Π 558, cf. M 397 ff.), or that Apollo had disarmed him. The reader knows that Patroclus was wearing the armor of Achilles and that it was Patroclus who slew Sarpedon: hence no one asks how Hector[34] and Glaucus knew (Π 543). Ajax fears that Patroclus' body will be thrown to the dogs: the poet has just told us that such was Hector's intention (P 241, cf. 126 ff.). Priam thinks that Achilles has slain Lycaon and Polydorus (X 46). Nine sons of Priam have been slain. Why does he select these two? Because the hearer remembers that they are the only two sons of Priam slain by Achilles in the preceding account.

Homer uses this principle to explain the knowledge and the acts of his divinities. Even the gods, who are omniscient only when the poet so wills,[35] often owe their knowledge to the better information of the audience. Ares knows that Athena had beguiled Diomede to wound him (E 881), in spite of the fact that she had donned the cap of Hades, which made her invisible even to gods (vs. 845). Calypso instructs Odysseus to build a raft. This was what Zeus had told Hermes to command her to do, but Hermes had omitted this part of his message (ε 33, 112).

The most interesting illustration of motivation-by-the-audience in the account of divinities occurs just after the Tricking of Zeus. When Hera returns from Mount Ida to Olympus, thoroughly terrified, and on a distasteful errand, Themis correctly infers the cause of her panic: "Hera, ... you seem to be frightened out of your wits! Upon my word, I believe the son of Cronus has been threatening you!"[36] Now Hera had told no one that she was going to Mount Ida; to Aphrodite she had said that she was to visit Oceanus and Tethys. But to the hearer, who has just witnessed the stormy scene on Mount Gargarus, the words of Themis must have seemed entirely reasonable—as they have to the critics ever since. The same is true of the two following illustrations.

It is impossible that Eupeithes knew that Odysseus had gone to the farm of Laertes (ω 437 ff.). Penelope alone could have told him this, and she is *incommunicado*. "Rumor" was not the source of his knowledge, for Athena had hidden Odysseus and his companions in a mist when they left the palace. Still more impossible is Hector's knowledge that Paris is at home (Z 280). Paris had mysteriously disappeared from the lists, and no Trojan knew where he was. But both these facts have been made so clear to the reader of the previous narrative that even the Higher Critics noticed no "inconsistency." Yet numerous difficulties which they did find disappear as soon as our principle is applied to them. Kirchhoff objected to the guess of Melanthius that the arms had been carried to the armory, and that Odysseus, seeing Penelope after twenty years' absence, could have known that she was deceiving the Suitors by suggesting wooers' gifts.[37] The hearer's information justifies the knowledge of both Melanthius and Odysseus.[38]

Wilamowitz accepts[39] the ancient rejection of ν 320-323 (Odysseus says to Athena, "Thou didst lead me to the city"), because Odysseus had not recognized that his guide was the goddess (η 19-78). But the audience, as the poet intended, knew it at the time!

Even Rothe (*Odyssee als Dichtung*, 91) calls it "a slight inadvertence of the poet" to make Anticleia and Agamemnon in the lower world refer to Telemachus as a man grown, when at the time they were speaking he could not have been more than thirteen or fourteen years old (λ 185-187, 449). If Rothe is right, it was a wise oversight for an oral poet. To the audience Telemachus was a man, not a boy. If the two shades had described him as a boy, the hearers must have queried, Why was he so young? They would have answered this query by reflecting that Anticleia and Agamemnon had died years before. All this would have turned the attention of the listeners away from the scene which the poet was describing—and all for a slight detail! Homer is extremely careful to explain the causes of the main action and the great crises of emotion. It is reasonable to assume that for the explanation of minor matters he deliberately relied on the information which he had given his audience.

Our principle—which we should like to call the σχῆμα κατὰ τὸ ἤδη εἰρημένον, or the λύσις ἐκ τοῦ ἀκροατοῦ—not only solves minor "difficulties"; it explains major cruces.

(1) When Hector on his visit to the city finds Paris at home with Helen, he says to him, "Man! you do ill to cherish *this resentment* against the Trojans," etc. (Z 326). "Der Groll des Paris" once formed the basis of a widely accepted theory of an "original Iliad" in which the proposal of Ante-

nor (that Helen be returned to the Greeks in accordance with the terms of the truce), which now comes after the words of Hector (H 348 ff.), was the cause of the "grudge of Paris."A mere man of straw! Hector's visit to Paris and Helen recalls the last mention of Helen at the end of Book III, and the poet's words which then followed, "The Trojans would have given Paris up to the Greeks if they could have found him, for he was hated by them all like grim death" (Γ 454). Hatred begets resentment. Paris, after all, had done his best in the combat with Menelaus—after his first moment of panic. It was not to be expected that he would be eager to reënter the fighting if he knew the Trojans at this moment hated him bitterly. Since the listener knows of this hatred, Paris may be assumed to know it.[40]

(2) A still more famous crux. Why does Eumaeus tell Penelope that the Beggar had spent "three days and three nights" at his steading, when he had actually spent four? The poet's partnership with his audience suggests the reason. The hearer remembers three days and nights spent at the Swineherd's hut, for the account of them had been packed with interest (ξ, ο, π); on the fourth nothing happened there; Telemachus was driving from Sparta to Pylus, and broke the journey at Pherae. "Three days and three nights" would pass muster with the listener; "four" would have given him pause.

The poet's reliance on the coöperation of his silent partner is seen also in a species of Sophoclean irony by which the listener's superior knowledge gives added point to the words of a character. In the commonest examples a character ascribes failure, or success, or some act, to divine intervention which the narrative has just described. Eurycleia tells Odysseus that "some god put Penelope to sleep" during the Slaughter (χ 429); the poet has told us that "brighteyed Athena caused sweet sleep to fall upon her eyelids" (φ 357 f.). This dramatic irony is very common in the *Iliad*.

In the aristeia of Diomede we know from the beginning that Athena is helping the hero; Pandarus says to Aeneas, "Some god stands by him" (E 185 f.). Antilochus, while the chariot race is on, says that Athena is on the side of a rival (Ψ 405 f.), and Ajax, after he has lost the footrace, complains that she has likewise been the cause of his defeat (Ψ 782 f.). Hector's helmet, "which Apollo gave him," deflects the spear of Diomede; the latter cries, "Apollo saved you" (Λ 352 f., 363). Achilles says, "Apollo saved you again," when the god has snatched Hector away in safety (Υ 441 ff.). Hector tells the Greeks that Zeus broke the truce (H 69); the hearer knows from a previous Olympian scene that this is literally true (Δ 70 ff.). After Patroclus has slain Sarpedon, Glaucus says that Zeus has refused to save his own son; the listener knows that this is literally true (Π 522; cf. 431-458).

Sometimes the use of this irony is very subtle but none the less effective. Diomede taunts the wounded Aphrodite, "Is it not enough for thee to *beguile weak women?*" In the previous narrative the listener had last seen Aphrodite when she was beguiling the weak-willed Helen, and had heard Helen say to the Goddess, "Why art thou so eager to beguile me?"[41]

The best illustration of epic irony is in Achilles' reply to Odysseus in the Embassy, in which he rejects Agamemnon's offer of the hand of one of his daughters: "And a daughter of Agamemnon I will not wed, not even if she vies with Aphrodite in beauty and with Athena in accomplishments. Let him choose some other Achaean, one that befits *him, one that is more kingly.*" Let us recall the scene in Agamemnon's quarters. Nestor advised the appeasement of Achilles' wrath "by kindly gifts and soft words" (I 113). Agamemnon offered munificent gifts, but, instead of the soft word, had said, "And let him admit how much more kingly I am" (vs. 160).[42] The king admits the wrong done in taking away Briseis; he repeats the insult which caused the wrath,[43] by refusing him the honor due the "noblest of the Achaeans." The word βασιλεύτερος, used by Agamemnon—for the first time in the *Iliad*—and grimly repeated by Achilles, clearly marks the essential point of the quarrel. But it is the knowledge of the listener, not of Achilles, which makes this repetition natural.

The advantage which the oral narrative gains by ignoring unessential explanation when the previous narrative has prepared the listener to overlook slight inconsistencies, is seen in Homer's one exception to his rule. In the Apologue, Odysseus describes the Olympic scene between the Sun God and Zeus, which resulted in the loss of his ship and his comrades. Then he adds,"This I heard from Calypso; she said Hermes told her" (μ 389 f.). This is the greatest blemish in the whole narrative art of Homer. It breaks the illusion at a critical point, and it breaks it badly for a listening audience. The reader is less disturbed, but the hearer's attention is diverted to the situation described many episodes before. Questions might suggest themselves: How did Odysseus know that Hermes had visited Calypso? When, after the visit of Hermes, did Calypso have occasion to speak with Odysseus on the subject? (Hermes rarely went to Ogygia, perhaps never. The Phaeacian audience had no reason to know that he ever went there before.) Even if the listener were so naïve that these questions would not suggest themselves, his attention has been turned away to matters which have nothing to do with the loss of the comrades. But the poet was in a dilemma: if he did not thus break the illusion, he must omit the scene between the Sun God and Zeus, and thereby the vivid and dramatic motivation of the climax of the Wanderings. He chose the lesser evil.

This passage was used by van Leeuwen as evidence in his argument for different authorship of the *Odyssey*. Since this argument is given much weight by the chorizont Wilhelm Schmid,[44] let us quote it in full: (Calypso recognized

Hermes, "for gods know one another full well") "ut hoc loco, sic et alibi passim poeta insignem et multo majorem quam solet poeta Iliadis dedit operam, ut probabilia sibi et audientibus redderet quae narraret.... Cf. α 320, δ 802, ε 197, 199, θ 448, ι 163-165, 338 sq., 428, 508-510, κ 73-76, 222 sq., 330-332, 569-574, μ 389 sq., ν 113, π 161, 208-212, 356 sq., 456-458, ρ 10, τ 27 sq., 287, 360, 478 sq., υ 187 sq., φ 95, χ 491."[45]

Most of the poet's explanations which van Leeuwen cites from the *Odyssey* are slightly different from those we have been considering: they answer a possible question, How can this be true? not, How can he know this? Yet even the poet's answer to the latter question van Leeuwen finds more common in the *Odyssey*.[46] Of course the irrational knowledge of another's identity is more common in the *Iliad*, because two armies are opposed to each other, and single encounters are so numerous that much must be taken for granted. Furthermore, the divine element is treated differently in the two poems. In the *Iliad* a large number of gods are *dramatis personae*. These move freely among mortals. But in the *Odyssey* divine intervention is centered largely in Athena. Again, the *Odyssey*, a tale of adventure and intrigue, requires a slightly different technique to make the narrative convincing. For this reason at least eight[47] of the passages cited by van Leeuwen can have no parallel in the *Iliad*. All the others can be more or less closely paralleled in the *Iliad*.

(1) Nectar and ambrosia is served to Calypso, while Odysseus eats the food of mortals (ε 197 ff.). This has an exact parallel at E 340-342—which van Leeuwen rejects as the work of Homer because it shows the technique of the Odyssey!

(2) Penelope could not notice the recognition of Odysseus by Eurycleia, "for Athena turned her attention to other things" (τ 478 f.). In the *Iliad* there are two similar explanations. Aeneas returns to the fray, his wound healed by Leto and Artemis. His comrades ask no questions, "for the

THE POET AND HIS AUDIENCE

toil of battle prevented" (E 514 ff.). Again, Athena turned the attack of Odysseus towards the Lycian common soldiers, "for it was not fated that he slay Sarpedon" (E 674 f.).

(3) Athena once more transforms Odysseus into an old beggar, "for fear Eumaeus may recognize him" (π 456 ff.). This is exactly like E 845: Athena dons the cap of Hades, "for fear Ares may see her."

(4) ζ 42 ff. we have discussed. Van Leeuwen rejects as late two of the parallels in the *Iliad*, but leaves T 96 and 416.

(5) ν 113. The Phaeacian sailors found the entrance to Phorcys' harbor, "having knowledge" of the harbor (πρὶν εἰδότες). This is closely paralleled by Ξ 475. Ajax says that he thinks Archelochus, whom he has slain, is a brother or son of Antenor. The poet continues ἦ ῥ' εὖ γιγνώσκων.

(6) ε 79 (Calypso recognized Hermes) "for gods know each other, no matter how far apart they dwell." The only parallel situation in the *Iliad* is Ψ 201: Iris visits the home of Zephyrus, where the winds are. The poet does not say Iris was recognized, so there is no occasion for the Odyssean explanation; but by the latter interposition it seems much more probable that the poet was merely directing attention to the remoteness of Ogygia, for in both poems *ex hypothesi* the gods, at the will of the poet, may be omniscient.

(7) θ 448, "the knot that Circe taught him" is a cross reference, of which the *Iliad* contains many; for example, Ψ 291, 560, 783. It is unique in Homer only in being a reference by the poet himself to an incident yet to be described.

(8) φ 95. Antinous says, "for I remember how Odysseus looked though I was but a child." This explanation is no more ingenious or careful than many in the *Iliad*; for example, that of Nestor which gives the reason for his fighting against the Centaurs (A 270), "for the Lapiths summoned me."

(9) υ 187. Ferrymen brought the neat cattle from Elis, "men whose business it is to carry men across the water."

This, according to van Leeuwen, shows the poet's attention to the probability that Philoetius could have brought from Elis some of Odysseus' cattle for the Suitors' banquet. It is hardly different from H 467 f.: the Greeks had wine for their feast after completing the wall; "Ships brought it from Lemnos."

(10) Van Leeuwen sees a greater realism in the *Odyssey* in the disappearing of divinities, dreams, and so forth. Penelope's Dream slips away through the keyhole. Spirits must vanish in some mysterious way, which cannot be reduced to formula. The shade of Patroclus "sank gibbering into the earth like a mist" (Ψ 100 f. Perhaps the passage means rather, departed gibbering for the underworld, vanishing like a mist). But Athena could not have disappeared, as van Leeuwen thinks, through the clerestory of the hall at Ithaca (a 320). After her departure Telemachus rejoins —or joins—the Suitors. He had no occasion to change his seat in the hall; he must have accompanied Mentes at least to the door of the hall.

We may grant that the *Odyssey* shows in some respects a better technique than the *Iliad*; Lowell's remark that it "reads of itself" indicates this. Improved technique is to be expected in the later work of the same poet. It does not weaken the hypothesis that a great poet had succeeded in creating a unified tragic plot, using material which was more or less the common stock of bards, and that then he had taken a new theme in which selection of incident could take the place of coördination and adjustment, and the reduction of the number of *dramatis personae* could permit a more careful attention to each. The mastery of plot, and the *Kleinmeisterschaft* in details, is essentially the same in both poems.

CHAPTER SIX

THE POET AS SINGER

POIESIS BEGAN by being *aoide*. It was music that made poetry forever distinct from prose. And the fundamental principle of music is number. All music, from the beating of the tom-tom to Beethoven's Fifth Symphony, shows a never-failing subordination of sound to measure. In early Greece, the song, the dance which often accompanied it, and the recited verse which succeeded song, possessed in common the element of rhythm. Rhythm, measure, number, was the sovereign principle, the One which determined the arrangement of the myriad many, as Aristotle said of nature.[1] In the beauty of nature the One, which is "Law," is a vital principle, not a code of ordinances. A tree is beautiful because in color, outline, and mass of leaves, branches, and trunk, a myriad of chaotic elements have been harmoniously ordered by the law of form. But pure form is never beautiful; it is neither natural nor living. It is the infinite minute variations within the law of form which give beauty both to nature and to the greatest art.[2]

I

In the whole realm of Western epic poetry Homer's verse most closely follows nature. It approaches most nearly to the perfect adjustment of the many elements of speech to the one principle of form. The dactylic hexameter was used by poets for a millennium and a half after Homer, but no poet, Greek or Roman, equaled him, or came near it, in the balance between freedom and law. Homer never for long blurs or dims the basic form of his measure, yet neither does he permit this form to intrude itself upon the attention. In the freedom with which he gives variety to verse of a single pattern he is without a peer.

---

[1] Superior figures refer to notes which will be found on pp. 253–254.

The dactylic hexameter permits either a dactyl or a spondee in each of the first five feet. A simple mathematical operation shows that there are thus thirty-two possible arrangements of dactyls and spondees. Homer uses every one of them; yet his measure remains dactylic. In the *Aeneid* the verse containing five dactyls, *quadrupedante putrem sonitu quatit ungula campum*, is rare; in Homer it is common. In Andromache's excited speech to her handmaids (X 450-459) half of the ten verses are of this kind.

The adjustment of the words to the feet shows the same freedom. The hexameter, as pure form, is a frame of six compartments. If its Law were strictly enforced, each verse would consist of a single sentence of six words, each word exactly filling a foot. Homer has one verse[3] which by a very slight change would illustrate this slavish obedience to the law of the verse, ὕβριος/εἵνεκα/ταύτης/ἴσχεο/εἴκων/ἡμῖν ("As for this outrageous insult, restrain your rage in compliance with our will"). Such an arrangement of words is impossible because of the nature of language; it is also utterly repugnant to our sense of beauty because it transgresses the fundamental principle of art and nature alike, that form should not be openly revealed, but should rather be felt as a molding principle. Hence arises the conflict between form and language, which above all distinguishes recitative verse from prose.[4] Each word must not exactly fill a foot, yet each must begin and end within it. This conflict makes possible an infinite variety in the selection and arrangement of the words. In the hexameter there are seventeen places where a word may end; Homer makes a word end at every one of these places.

A third kind of variety depends on the length of the words. Why does Tennyson, who knew his Homer, call Vergil's hexameter the "stateliest measure ever moulded by the lips of man"? Partly, no doubt, because of its numerous spondees, which give solemnity; but also because Latin has few small particles, and Greek, many. These "grace notes" of speech impart to Homer's language a quality of life, and make it intimately personal. ἤτοι ὅ γ' ὣς εἰπὼν κατ' ἄρ' ἕζετο, ἦ, τοι, ἄρα, and possibly γε, what are these but the equivalents of the personal interest which the modern Greek expresses by physical gestures? To translate them is not only ridiculous, but at times sacrilege. The honest endeavor of many a schoolboy under a grammarian teacher has cost Homer and Greek many a friend, and gave Stephen Leacock a chance for ribald laughter. In Homer these particles lighten the verse. But they put into it no tone of levity. For Homer, too, is stately. Against the little particles he sets whole verses of great rolling words.

Λ 427, αὐτοκασίγνητον ἐυηφενέος Σώκοιο.

More than 430 verses, one verse in every 65 in Homer, contain no more than four words.[5] On the other hand, one verse (ρ 466 = σ 110) contains 14 words, an instance of *polymeria*[6] unequaled, I think, elsewhere in Greek or Latin poetry; even the passionate bourgeoise Simaetha (Theocr. II, 124) does not use so many short words in a single verse. Vergil has few verses made up of very many or very few words. In this respect Homer's verse is better suited to changing moods and is far more varied.

The last way in which Homer varies his verse, which we mention here, is by abandoning and then restoring its rhythm. A pause required by the sense of some among the first words may change the rhythm of the rest of the verse. Thus in Milton (*Paradise Lost* I, 272),

And him Beelzebub
Thus answered: "Leader of those armies bright ..."

the pause after "answered" makes Beelzebub's speech begin the trochaic rhythm. In a similar way Homer often changes from the dactylic to another rhythm, but he does this reasonably, and without forsaking his pattern. The dactylic rhythm is the *genos ison*, or, as we say, in 2/4 time (— ᴜ ᴜ or — —). The anapaestic rhythm belongs to the same *genos*. If a pause in sense occurs in the middle of a dactylic foot, the following clause begins in the anapaestic rhythm, and continues thus until another pause restores the dactylic. Homer makes a pause in the thought frequently in the middle of every one of the first four feet of his hexameter,

(1) Κ 454, ἦ, καὶ ὁ μέν μιν ἔμελλε γενείου χειρὶ παχείῃ—
(2) β 58, μαψιδίως· τὰ δὲ πολλὰ κατάνεται· οὐ γὰρ ἔπ' ἀνὴρ—
(3) Β 268, σκήπτρου ὕπο χρυσέου· ὁ δ' ἄρ' ἔζετο τάρβησέν τε.
(4) Β 204, οὐκ ἀγαθὸν πολυκοιρανίη· εἷς κοίρανος ἔστω.

I have selected these examples because in each verse a decided pause in thought (2) and (3), or a slight one in the phrasing (1) and (4) at the bucolic diaeresis, restores the dactylic rhythm. The ancients recognized that (2) and (3) resulted in a change to the anapaestic rhythm. Hermogenes (περὶ ἰδεῶν, p. 394, 21 Rabe) says of Α 4, ἀναπαιστικόν πώς ἐστι γενομένης ἀναπαύσεως ἐν τῷ 'ἡρώων', and the second half of (3) was called the paroemiac verse as used frequently in anapaestic passages of Attic tragedy. The other possible change in the rhythm is to the trochaic, by making a pause in sense between the short syllables of a dactyl. But the trochaic rhythm belongs to the *genos anison* or 3/8 time; the rest of the verse cannot be continued in this rhythm, and Homer is sparing of his pauses here, except in the first and third feet. So much for the change in rhythm. As for variety, it is possible to make a pause in sense in any one of the seventeen places where a word may end. Of these there are only two, the end of the third foot and between the two short syllables of the fourth foot, at which Homer does not permit a pause sufficient for a mark of punctuation. If some mathematician would compute the possible number of combinations of all the ways of varying the verse which we have mentioned, the thirty-two schemata, the words too short or too long exactly to fill a foot, the word ends and the pauses in sense at most of the possible places in the verse, the word "infinite" applied to the variations of Homer's verse would seem but a slight exaggeration. Their effect is to make Homer's verse what his poetry was to Plutarch, "ever new,"[7] because of its freedom within the law.

II

This freedom has been limited and circumscribed by modern scholars, who, accepting imperfectly transmitted and therefore inconsistent dogmas of ancient grammarians, have shackled Homer's verse with the caesura. They demand (1) that in every verse of Homer there must be one main pause, and (2) that this must be made within the third foot, if possible, otherwise within the fourth foot—a very few scholars permitting the main pause at the end of the fourth foot. The harm which Homer's marvelous verse has thereby suffered is so great that I ask the forbearance of the reader for digressing, to the extent of the present section, in order to give briefly some reasons why Homer's hexameter should not thus be fettered.[8]

Let us first consider the external, that is, the "historical," evidence.

(1) No attention was paid in ancient times to the general phenomenon of caesura until after the beginning of the Christian era. Neither Aristotle[9] nor any of the great Alexandrian critics ever mention or refer to it. This is of extreme importance. The rhapsodic recital of Homer had not ceased in the fourth century. Boys still learned Homer from dictation. If a pause was made in the third foot of the hexameter without regard to the thought, it is almost unthinkable that Aristotle made no reference whatsoever to this fact. Varro is the first extant authority who mentions the importance of a

word end in the verse (in the third foot), and he seems to have made the discovery for himself (*obseruasse sese*, Aulus Gellius, XVIII, 15). Not much later than Varro, Dionysius of Halicarnassus, although he pays much attention to the variety of rhythms produced in Homer's verse by clauses of different length, and differently placed (*De comp. verb.*, Ch. 26), does not mention caesura. But by about 150 A.D. the doctrine was fully established, for Hermogenes (περὶ ἰδεῶν, 390, 21, Rabe) mentions the different "caesurae" without comment. The silence of all the extant writers on poetry during the great period of Greek criticism is strong evidence that caesura, as the word is generally understood today, was not practiced in the oral delivery of Homer—certainly at least after his poetry became popular at Athens in the sixth century.

(2) It seems likely that the origin of "caesura" is to be found in the work of Heliodorus, a famous metrician of the first century A.D., who studied the cola of melic verse and published a colometric edition of Aristophanes. At any rate, it is certain that the doctrine of "caesura" arose in the Derivationist school of metricians, who found in the Homeric hexameter certain dactylic cola of melic poetry. This fact is not open to doubt. Both the names and the choice of the τομαί or "caesurae" prove it unmistakably. The names are Greek, πενθημιμερές, ἑφθημιμερές, τρίτος τροχαῖος, τέσσαρες δάκτυλοι, or τετράμετρον (the bucolic diaeresis). These are names not of places in the verse, but of segments cut off by a word end, and they are all dactylic cola of Greek lyric poetry. "If you double the πενθημιμερές," says one grammarian, "you make the pentameter." The Derivationists paid no attention to the sense, and therefore did not make a pause at the end of these cola. This is clear from the examples they give of the "caesurae." The Latin grammarians use the first verse of the *Aeneid* to illustrate three "caesurae,"

Arma virumque cano∧Trojae∧qui∧primus ab oris.

A Greek treatise uses a single verse of Homer to illustrate all the four τομαί,

Δ 350, Ἀτρεΐδη, ποῖόν∧σε∧ἔπος∧φύγεν∧ἕρκος ὀδόντων ;

It is clear, therefore, that "the caesura," as first defined, was not a pause.

(3) The doctrine that "caesura" was a pause seems to have been the result of the grammatical and rhetorical study of Homer. It is not necessary to give the evidence. The pauses in thought were found to coincide with the places of the four "caesurae," and to these pauses the term caesura was given. Our best ancient definition of caesura in this sense was given by an unknown writer in early Byzantine times: "Caesura is the place in the middle of the verse where the thought is sufficiently complete to admit a mark of punctuation."[10] This writer has applied the Derivationist's term, "caesura," which meant merely the place where word ends are found, to pauses due to the phrasing of the thought, and was therefore compelled to restrict the important pauses to the third and fourth feet.

The ancient theory of caesura, as it has come down to us, confuses two different matters, the conflict between the metrical pattern and the length and position of the words, and a different conflict, which is between the rhythmical pattern and the units of thought. The former deals with the technique of verse making; it is of interest chiefly to the specialist. The latter determines the swing of the verse, the matchless rhythm of Homer. Why "mark the caesura"? And why call a pause in thought in Homer a "caesura"? Only because the dead hands of ancient pedants are upon us.

Let us turn from the dry-as-dust grammarians to Homer himself, and see whether it is likely that the poet in reciting his verses made a pause in the third or fourth foot and at the end of every verse—for the latter stands or falls with the "main caesura." Certainly in Shakespeare there is no evidence for these two pauses. Take Hamlet's soliloquy (Act IV, sc. 4):

>   What is a man,
> If his chief good and market of his time
> Be but to sleep and feed? a beast, no more.
> Sure, He that made us with such large discourse,
> Looking before and after, gave us not
> That capability and godlike reason
> To fust in us unused.

Different actors may pay different degrees of attention to pauses within and at the end of the verse. But the player who cares only to express the thought and feeling of Hamlet forgets the existence of middles and ends of lines, and phrases the words to suit the meaning. To the lover of poetry verse is not a set of rules; it is the daughter of Song, whose quickening spirit gives a varied rhythmic beauty to the dance of words.

In this spirit let us test a passage from Homer, the speech of Andromache to her maids when she hears Hecuba's sudden outburst of grief at the death of Hector (X 450-459). We shall mark the place of the "main caesura" by a single slanting line, and the end of the verse by two slants. But since Homer's listeners could not see where each verse ended, as we can, we shall print the passage as prose. The pauses in sense are indicated by the punctuation. We first give the thought in simple English:

"Come, two of you go with me/; I will see what has happened//. My husband's mother's/was the voice I heard, and in my own//breast my heart leaps/to my mouth. My knees under me//are numbed. 'Tis some ill fate has come/to the sons of Priam//. O, may that word ne'er come/to *my* ears! But a terrible//fear possesses me. Perhaps my bold Hector/—Achilles//may have cut him off from the rest—alone by himself/—outside of the city—and may have chased him to the plain//and may have put a stop forever/to that cursed gallantry//that always

THE POET AS SINGER 149

possessed him; he never/would keep back in the ruck;//he always ran far out in front/; he never admitted that any man was his better!"//

δεῦτε, δύω μοι ἔπεσθον,/ἴδωμ' ὅτιν' ἔργα τέτυκται.//αἰδοίης ἐκυρῆς/ ὀπὸς ἔκλυον, ἐν δ' ἐμοὶ αὐτῇ//στήθεσι πάλλεται ἦτορ/ἀνὰ στόμα, νέρθε δὲ γοῦνα//πήγνυται·ἐγγὺς δή τι/κακὸν Πριάμοιο τέκεσσιν.//αἲ γὰρ ἀπ' οὔατος εἴη/ἐμεῦ ἔπος·ἀλλὰ μάλ' αἰνῶς//δείδω, μὴ δή μοι/θρασὺν Ἕκτορα δῖος Ἀχιλλεὺς//μοῦνον ἀποτμήξας/πόλιος πεδίονδε δίηται,//καὶ δή μιν καταπαύσῃ/ἀγηνορίης ἀλεγεινῆς,//ἥ μιν ἔχεσκ', ἐπεὶ οὔ ποτ'/ἐνὶ πληθυῖ μένεν ἀνδρῶν,//ἀλλὰ πολὺ προθέεσκε,/τὸ ὃν μένος οὐδενὶ εἴκων.//

In these ten verses there is no pause at the end of four, and none at the "main caesura" in eight, but there are seven or eight pauses elsewhere within the verse: two after the first foot and three after the fourth; one in the middle of the second foot and possibly of the fourth, and one between the two short syllables of the first foot. To disregard these pauses in favor of the "main caesura" and of the verse end would be as absurd as to read Milton with a pause at the end of every verse. Milton himself warns us against doing the latter. But Homer, too, takes a "true musical delight" in "the sense variously drawn out from one verse to another," and from one half-verse to another, especially when, as in the passage we have selected, he is characterizing a personality[11] or marking a mood.

III

The passage just cited illustrates a third conflict, between the whole verse and the units of thought. It is generally supposed that in this conflict the verse usually prevails, for everyone notices Homer's fondness for exactly filling a verse with a complete thought. But how far, and in what sense, this impression is correct we cannot say, for this is one of the numerous minor problems of Homer's poetry which still await solution.[12]

The tendency to avoid this kind of conflict is usually explained by the method of composition of early bards, much of whose lays was improvised. Parry used this tendency as an argument for his theory of traditional formulae.[13] How far this is true cannot be known, but there is evidence that another influence contributed. This is offered by the arrangement of thought within the verse itself.

Thomas Day Seymour in reading Homer always made a pause at the end of every verse and another in the third foot unless no word ended there. This led him to study these pauses. He showed by numerous examples that often in Homer these pauses divided thought-units in the same way.[14] But the other two preferred pauses in sense after the second dipody, the hephthemimeral and the bucolic, do the same.[15] The inference is that the chief pauses in thought in certain respects are treated alike, no matter where they occur. The end of the verse is the chief pause of all, but its function in separating units of thought does not differ in kind from that of the other chief pauses. We may go farther, and say that the frequency of pauses in sense both within and at the end of the verse is evidence that the poet tended to think and to express his thoughts in short and distinct units; so his thought pauses at the end of the verse more often than that of poets whose expression is more complex.

Herein is one of Homer's charms. His poetry presents a living, moving picture, and his expression corresponds to the natural way of observing life.

Suppose the picture is of a normal occurrence at sea, like the voyage home from Chryse (A 478-483):

They put to sea; the wind rose fair; they stepped the mast and spread the sail; the wind filled it, and the ship took a bone in her teeth; the voyage was soon over.

The essential facts, which might be observed on any voyage, are given without comment or explanation, in the order of their occurrence, and each one just fills a verse or a half-verse, with a single exception (481 f.).

Next let us take the brief account of Odysseus' stay with Aeolus (κ 13-27). One or two statements just fill each of twelve of the fifteen verses. Each fact is stated simply in its natural order: arrival, hospitality; questions and answers about the Trojan War; request of Odysseus for safe escort; making of the "bottle"; the confining of the winds within it, and the tying of its neck; the sending of the west wind—simple statements, connected by "and" or "but," except verse 17, which marks the time when Odysseus can make his request. But, since this visit has a particular result, a few explanations and comments are included: Aeolus was steward of the winds; the bag was tied tight to keep adverse winds from blowing; Aeolus sent Zephyrus to carry the ship home; but the folly of the comrades thwarted his kindly purpose!

The same natural order is seen in other arrangements of Homer's thoughts. A deer hunter, catching sight of a strange object at the edge of a forest, first decides whether it is a deer, next whether it is a buck or a doe, and not till then does he think of the distance, the wind, and so forth. So the scientist observes, first genus, then species, and after that other related facts. This is in principle Homer's normal method of exposition. His two proems are well-known examples: first the theme, the Wrath, the Man; next, its peculiar quality, "ruinous," "ever ready of wit," and, finally, some concrete facts which illustrate this quality.

The essential idea with which Homer begins is always the one which is new. In the last chapter we had some illustrations, but the principle is so universal, both in Homer and in the normal human acquisition of ideas, that we shall give two more examples.

In a sentence the new idea is usually a thing or a person. Hence it almost always comes first, as in the proems. But if it is already in the mind of the listener, it gives place to some newer idea. This is seen in formulaic verses and tags.

We commonly think of the proper-name-epithet tag, as used largely in formulaic verses, especially those which introduce a speech: "To him in reply spoke white-armed Hera," or "bright-eyed Athena," or "swift-footed Achilles." But verses of this type are not normally used unless the speaker can be easily identified from the preceding narrative. Otherwise either the new speaker is first described and the formula, "This man with kindly intent addressed them and said" (A 253, *et passim*) is used, or a formula is used in which the proper name comes first. Thus when Antenor breaks into the conversation on the Tower unannounced, the words which introduce his speech are, "To her Antenor the prudent made answer."[16] This is the rule, although of course there are exceptions and *Verszwang* may have its influence.

Similarly with things. At dawn on the day of the Slaughter, Odysseus prays for a sign from Zeus and for a "chance word" from some mortal within the palace. When these are described, the two ideas come first in their sentences. But when the narrative describes the gladness of Odysseus because of the answer to his prayer, his joy is the new idea and takes precedence: "He rejoiced at the 'chance word' and at the thunder of Zeus" (υ 103, 105, 120 f.).

This precedence of the new and the essential is seen in the arrangement of two thought units in a single verse, the first giving the fact, the second adding details for ornament or emotional content, or merely amplifying or repeating the first. There are many passages in which the bare narrative is complete if we read only the first segment of successive verses.[17] Thus κ 310-320 (we know that Odysseus is on his way to Circe's palace):

> I stopped at the door (of the fair-tressed goddess).
> Standing there I called (and the goddess heard my voice).
> Quickly she came forth (throwing wide the shining doors),
> And invited me to enter (and I followed her, anxious at heart).
> She led me in and seated me (on a silver-studded throne,

A wondrous work of the craftman's art, with a footrest).
She made for me a posset (in a cup of gold: I was to drink it);
In it she put a drug (—her heart was bent on evil!).
And when she had given it to me and I had drained the
    draught (—but it failed to bewitch me),
She touched me with her wand and spoke (with these words):
"Off to the sty! (Join thy comrades!)"

The words in parentheses are segments of the verse formed by one or another of the pauses in thought, or else whole verses. Omit them, and the narrative runs thus:

I stopped at the door; standing there I called. Quickly she came forth and invited me to enter. She led me in and seated me. She made for me a posset; in it she put a drug. And when she had given it to me, and I had drained the draught, she touched me with her wand, and spoke: "Off to the sty!"

This arrangement is not only natural; it is crystal clear, because the thought is simple, an account of action which we need not visualize in all its details. But suppose the poet wishes to express the words of a character suffering from brain storm. Like Odysseus, when Polyphemus roars at him the question, "Who are ye?"

"We—you must understand—from Troy—driven out of our course—Achaeans—adverse winds driving us all over the wide seas—trying to head for home—it was a different course—different courses, that brought us here" (ι 259-262).

This is one of the few occasions in either poem where Odysseus loses his *sang-froid*. His momentary confusion is reflected in the sentence—more than three verses long, and with its single finite verb placed at the very end.

Mood or emotion is one reason for "the sense variously drawn out from verse to verse" in Homer. Another is his fondness for the bucolic diaeresis. This pause, because it repeats the rhythm of the beginning of the verse, permits after it the beginning of a sentence or even of a paragraph. This makes it necessary to continue the thought into the next verse, unbroken by the verse end. Other pauses have a similar effect, but to a lesser degree. The desire for variety of rhythms also operates. The total result is that in Homer enjambement is not avoided, but is kept duly subordinate to the pattern of the verse. But even in enjambement the same principle on which Homer arranges his thoughts holds as elsewhere.

Scholars today deny this. They try to force upon Homer the modern principle of emphasis, forgetting that, as the Hon. Stanley Baldwin has reminded us,[18] the Greeks did not need artificial stress on words. Modern scholars assert that a single word at the beginning of a verse, which is also the last word of a sentence which runs over the verse end, is "emphatic by position"; for example (A 52),

αὐτὰρ ἔπειτ' αὐτοῖσι βέλος ἐχεπευκὲς ἐφιεὶς
βάλλ'.

"The position of βάλλ' is the most emphatic possible" (Leaf).

In Homer there are nearly 3000 single runover words in this position in the verse and at the end of their clause. A careful examination of all these words[19] showed three reasons why such words are not emphatic: (1) the runover word is often unimportant and might have been omitted; (2) it is often implied in the preceding thought; (3) it is often found in exactly the same word complex, but in the least "emphatic position" in the verse.

This study of one feature of Homeric enjambement made clearer four outstanding characteristics of Homer's order of thought, which we have already touched upon:

(1) Naturalness. Homer's thought accords with the order of nature as man observes it; with the normal human order of selecting and relating simple thoughts, and with the greater complexity of arrangement caused by emotion or purposeful thinking. In all these respects Homer's speech is κατὰ φύσιν, the *oratio naturalis*.

(2) Clarity. This is the quality for which French writers are famous: "Ce qui n'est pas clair n'est pas français." This clearness of French expression is due to what Bossuet called its "civilité."[20] It is the quality of Chesterfield's gentleman, who thinks less of his own rights than of the feelings of others, and less of his own feelings than of others' rights. It is the courtesy of the aristocrat of style, the true gentleman of art. A recent writer comments thus on Bernard Berenson's view of art: "A work of art is a kind of reservoir of energy discharging itself into our nervous system, exciting our activity and putting us into a state of mind which the artist wishes to express. We enjoy a vigor and a feeling of superior sensibility *without any sense of effort*, and this exercise of unused faculties is the greatest of all pleasures." The phrase which I have italicized describes Homer's *civilité*. Other writers, both of prose and verse, demand of us a greater mental effort. They may give equal pleasure, but it is not the pure pleasure of art. "The artist through his picture enters our body and plays on it like an instrument." Homer with unsurpassed poetic courtesy forgets himself and thinks only of his listener, the instrument on which he is playing. By his courtesy he minimizes the listener's mental effort, and leaves his soul free to find a purely artistic pleasure in his poetry.

(3) Fluidity. The interlacing of Homer's ideas is so nearly perfect, and at the same time so unobtrusive, that no part of the hearer's attention is lost by the effort to bridge over even a slight chasm of thought. The Homeric epic has been compared to a river; no matter how different are the scenes through which it flows, or how varying the speed of the current, the narrative flows, and flows continuously.

(4) Variety. Homer molds his thought upon one verse pattern for nearly 30,000 verses. He repeats one-third of these verses, or parts of them, at least once, and some of them many times. And Parry was convinced that all but a

very few of Homer's phrases had been worn threadbare by previous bards for generations untold. But no "scourge of Homer," from Xenophanes to Stephen Leacock, has ever, so far as I know, included among the poetic misdemeanors charged against "The Poet" the crime of monotonousness.

The tonal quality of Homer's verse must have helped to make the hearer feel that his verse was "ever new." The verse was unusually melodious because the Homeric dialect is rich in vowels. In many verses these outnumber the consonants. No law governing their melody has ever been discovered. "Barbarous ages," which invented rhyme and alliteration, were still in the future. Homer rhymes and alliterates, but not according to any pattern. But we can be sure that his ear was attuned to melody and discord because of the rare verses where the sounds of the syllables agree in pleasantness or unpleasantness with the moment which the verse describes. The offensive stench of the sealskins under which Menelaus and his comrades lay in wait for Proteus, the "ocean-nurtured seals' most loathesome odor," is described by a verse in which the long o-sound predominates,

δ 442, φωκάων ἁλιοτρεφέων ὁλοώτατος ὀδμή.

That this tonal quality suggests a joyless moment we may infer from Creon's lyric outburst in the Exodos of the *Antigone* (vss. 1228-1233), in which there are ten omegas in forty-one syllables. The pleasurable momentary experiences which stir Homer to melody have not received much attention. No one seems to have looked for his most beautiful verse. I propose for this honor a verse from the picture of the herd on the shield of Achilles, Σ 576. The lowing cows were hurrying from the barnyard to their pasture,

By the river murmuring ever, by the slender, waving reeds,
πὰρ ποταμὸν κελάδοντα, παρὰ ῥοδανὸν δονακῆα.

Formally considered, the second half-verse almost repeats the first, as we see if we write the halves independently,

πάρ ποταμὸν κελάδοντα,   ao ao εα oα
παρὰ ῥοδανὸν δονακῆα.   a ao ao oα ηα

Much of the formal beauty depends on the word "almost." παρά almost repeats πάρ. Both verses are made up of three words, each longer than the preceding, but only the second is a perfect ῥόπαλον of 2 + 3 + 4 syllables. The vowels *a* and *o* alternate throughout each verse—almost, but not quite—and the order is inverted after the first pair of alternations. Thus the most "vocal" articulate sound, *a*, is placed in the opening and closing syllables. There are no harsh-sounding consonants, and only one sonant mute, δ, occurring thrice. Of the twenty consonants, ten are liquids. (But this is to anatomize beauty!) The verse is otherwise pure poetry. It is quite unnecessary for the action, which is given in the previous verse. It is rather the overflowing of the poet's feeling. The asyndeton shows this: how much the verse would lose if the conjunction ἰδέ were read in place of παρά! The poet calls upon the ear to hear the river murmuring, and then on the eye to see the slender reeds waving; both "murmuring" and "waving" give life to the picture. The selection of two universal characteristics gives the picture a lyric quality, but without sentimentality. Finally, the poet does not attempt to catalogue the features of the scene; he stops where we should be glad to have him continue.

This verse and the one that precedes it bring again to our attention the peculiarity of Homer's manner which we observed in the arrangement of two units of thought in some of the single verses. In Homer there is at times a certain separation between the simple facts of the tale and the illumination of these facts—we might almost say, between the pure narrative and pure poetry.

Today, because serious poetry is chiefly lyric, we expect

to find in it something more than thoughts presented in verse and in the festal garb of speech which has not been worn threadbare by daily use. It must include also certain transformations of familiar ideas and, above all, additions not required for the understanding of the meaning, but of themselves stirring in us a certain delight, and bathing our souls in a sea of beauty. The latter qualities we do not find at all points in Homer's epics.

Homer is sublime chiefly because he saw life exalted. His chief concern seems to have been to present his exalted vision true to the life which all human beings live. But in the round of life there are times when the deeper emotions are at rest, especially when the hour is filled with normal occupations. In passages describing these there is little occasion for the imaginative stimulation which we associate with lyric poetry. Yet, even in such passages, Homer succeeds in imparting beauty to simple narrative of simple and normal action. This is seen in the account of the journey from Pylus to Pherae (γ 478-488). The horses are harnessed; the chief maidservant puts into the chariot a luncheon of bread, wine, and cold meat, "the fare of gentry." The two princes mount the chariot. Pisistratus takes the reins, and touches the horses with the lash. The horses speed eagerly down to the plain, soon leaving the city far behind. All day long they "shake the yoke on their necks" (within a generation we should have said, they never slackened the traces). The sun goes down, shadows fall deep on the road, and they reach Pherae.

This account has made the journey seem real; it has not endowed it with imaginative beauty. It contains, however, one feature which is not needed to make the narrative clear: the gentry are "Zeus-nurtured"; the chariot, "exceeding beautiful" and "curiously wrought"; the cloistered courtyard, "echoing," and so forth. It is the epithet which, more than any other single element, poetizes the epic narrative.

The adjective is particularly at home in the long verse. Many stanzas of Gray's *Elegy* can be written in shorter measure merely by omitting the adjectives.

> Now fades the (glimmering) landscape on the sight,
> And (all) the air a (solemn) stillness holds,
> Save where the beetle wheels his (droning) flight,
> And (drowsy) tinklings lull the (distant) folds.

Without the epithets this becomes,

> Now fades the landscape on the sight,
> The air a stillness holds,
> Save where the beetle wheels his flight,
> And tinklings lull the folds.

More than half the lines of Tennyson's "To Virgil" can be reduced to the ordinary tetrameter by the omission of an adjective. In the same poet's "Break, Break, Break," the adjectives are confined to the beginning and the end, "thy cold, grey stones," and "the tender grace of a day that is dead." The fisherman's lad and his sister, the sailor boy and his boat, the ships and their haven under the hill, all lack the epithets which Homer would have given to all, or to most of them—chiefly, perhaps, because Tennyson is using a short verse. The long hexameter, if it did not suggest, at least permitted the free use of the epithet which is not needed to make the thought clear, yet makes, more than any of the other parts of speech, a poetic addition.

This is shown by the position of the adjective in the verse. We have seen the tendency of the second part of the verse to give picturesqueness and to add emotional content to the simple fact expressed in the first part. The adjective is placed in the latter half of the verse at least three or four times as often as in the first half. Every reader of Homer is familiar with the typical verses containing two or three nouns of which only the last is qualified by an adjective: "Alexander and Ares-beloved Menelaus" (Γ 136); "the hillside and the shady copse" (ε 470); "whip and shining reins" (ϛ 81); "back and broad shoulders" (ϛ 225); "Dulichium and Same and wooded Zacynthus" (α 246); "geese and cranes and long-necked swans" (B 460); "alder and poplar and sweet-smelling cypress" (ε 64).[21]

This preference of the adjective for the second part of the verse has been explained by the convenience of the improvising bard; noun and epithet form a tag that easily completes the verse. We cannot accept this explanation *in toto*. Some of the epithets in the second part of the verse precede both the noun and its verb. Furthermore, the adjective is not the only way of completing the verse, except perhaps in the formulas which precede the speeches—where the *Kalevala* also uses the epithet. Finally, even if we grant the sufficiency of this reason, we are still in the dark about the function of the epithet.

Aside from *Verszwang*, there are yet many reasons why Homer used epithets so frequently. "Ornate alias," which avoids the repetition of a proper name, was foreign to the Greek idiom. Homer never says of Telemachus that "the young hero," or "the young prince," or even "the young man," called the assembly, or spoke to Eurycleia. He always uses one of the two names of a character, his own or his patronymic. This may be owing to courtliness; at any rate, it makes perfectly clear to the hearer the identity of the person concerned. Again, when Homer refers to things, he calls a spade a spade. He is sparing of metaphor, particularly in simple narrative. Penelope says that ships are "the steeds of the sea" (δ 708), but this is exceptional. Homer does not use the kenning, although this may be found in Hesiod and the Old Testament, and is common in the Edda.[22] Perhaps it smacked too much of the common speech. The poet's language, unlike our own, was free from words directly borrowed from other tongues. Finally, differentiation of nomenclature according to slightly different kinds of the same thing had not gone far in his time. Every vessel in Homer's narrative except the raft of Odysseus is a νηῦς. Even the merchant ship is mentioned only in similes (ε 250, ι 323). Now since Homer always uses the name of a person and avoids metaphors and synonyms in mentioning a thing, there is danger of monotony unless an adjective is added to give variety.

The epithets of the horse are a good example. In the Chariot Race (Ψ 262-652) the horse is mentioned sixty-five times, always as ἵππος. No adjective is used thirty-eight times, always when our attention is on the action more than on the horse itself. Even here there is variety, for the word stands in ten of the possible twelve places in the verse. An adjective particularizes the horse about half a dozen times. Otherwise the epithets are general, and nearly half of them are placed elsewhere than in the final clausula.

In the two poems Homer applies nearly a score of generalizing epithets to the horse.[23] Taken together they suggest that the Homeric epithet has a function beyond the convenience of the improvising bard, and even beyond the "lingering look" which it causes us to bestow upon an object.[24] This is to supply the lack of description of a familiar object which the poet does not wish to particularize. The epithets taken together enable us to describe Homer's horse as follows. His hoofs are strong; he lifts them lightly; they seem eager for action and bear him swiftly, often with mighty leaps. He has a lovely mane and coat, and the frontlet of his bridle is of gold. He arches his strong neck and snorts.[25] One sees him usually in a span, drawing the chariot and responding instantly to the lash. He is very swift as he springs forward to the prize. This has little of the fire of the Ode to the Horse in Job (39:19-25), because where these epithets are used the horse is a detail in the action. When he holds the center of the stage (Θ 185-197, P 456-462, T 400-424), the poet has other ways of giving him importance.

The Homeric ship, too, is described by its numerous epithets. We mark its shape: it is hollow, curved, symmetrical, with prow and stern rising to a point; its color, black or blue-black, but red towards the prow; its parts, oars (long and well made—and well made, too, its many thwarts and rowers' seats), decks, and stern. Good workmanship went into its making, and it is a thing of beauty. It is fleet and swift as it moves over its course on the sea.

From the epithets of the horse and the ship we may, I think, draw some conclusions about Homer's use of the ornamental adjectives.

Homer can describe both a horse (Ψ 453-455) and a ship (the raft of Odysseus, ε 244-261), just as he describes Thersites. He does this when the horse or the person for the moment is important, and when these do not appear from time to time in the whole story. It may be forcing the evidence, but the fact remains that the poet never gives Thersites an epithet—although Odysseus does—and that although the raft is mentioned nine times after it has been described, it has an epithet only twice (ε 33, η 264, πολυδέσμου). I think this corroborates the view that the epithet in some measure takes the place of description. We have seen that what Homer describes is of interest in itself because it is new or exceptional or else because the description has some function in the action. Yet a thing entirely undescribed, or without any characterization, is only a fact. It is not a component of a picture of life. Therefore by an epithet Homer marks some easily recognized feature of a familiar object, and thus deepens the impression that it is real. To particularize the object by drawing attention to some unusual characteristic would defeat the object of the epithet, by calling upon the hearer for undue attention to it. For the same reason Homer does not tell us whether Nestor was bald, or whether Helen was svelte.

The adjective in Homer, as in Pindar and Vergil, often

adds a splendor and glory to life. When Homer uses a standing epithet of things that are universal in human experience, like sleep, the dawn, the sky, he gives to them a value which we ourselves feel only in unusual moods.[26] In Homer the dawn does not "come up like thunder," nor do "the woods against a stormy sky their giant branches" toss. Sleep is "sweet," not troubled, although it follows the exhaustion of weeping Penelope (α 364). It is still "sweet" when it brings disaster to Odysseus (κ 31, μ 338).

Homer has been called naïve because of some of his standing epithets; for example, when Nausicaa and the women of Troy wash "shining" raiment. This view is hardly logical for those who have "white" flannels cleaned, or an "evening" shirt laundered, when the latter could by no means be worn in the evening in the condition in which it is sent to the laundry. The sky which is "starry" in the daytime can be seen today on the ceiling of the Grand Central Station in New York City. If one remembers that the epic is "more philosophical" than history, one need not be supercilious about any of Homer's epithets. By selecting an aspect universally familiar he makes an object real to the imagination; he poetizes it. Pindar himself could find no better epithet for milk than "white" (*N.* III, 78: Frg. 166). The poetic quality of this epithet shines brighter when it is compared with Euripides' "rivulets from hill-grazing heifers" (*Iph. T.* 162).

Homer's epithets need a new and a complete examination. There are many questions about them which are still to be answered. These are important both in discovering the secret of Homer's charm and for a knowledge of the essence of poetry. For in his use of the epithet Homer reached a peak which no later Greek poet attained. Pindar and Aeschylus perhaps achieved an equally great effect, but it was at the expense of naturalness and spontaneity. One feels their effort, and this feeling robs us of the mental ease that

Homer gives[27] while at the same time he makes us feel at home in the new world into which he irresistibly draws us.

IV

The ornamental epithet is common to all poetic expression; the simile is Homer's gift to poetry. In the early literature of other nations it is rare or nonexistent, but the author of every long narrative poem directly or indirectly influenced by Homer uses it often and in more or less the same pattern that Homer gave it. The attacks upon its poetic excellence during the *Querelle* and the innumerable and divergent attempts to explain its *raison d'être*, not to mention its parody in *Tom Jones*, mark it as perhaps the most unique poetic feature of the Homeric poems.

The simple comparison, like the metaphor, is a universal means of expressing thought. It is idle to ask which is the more primitive. The use of one or the other seems to be determined by the mood. The directness of the metaphor suits it to a moment of emotion. It identifies, with a total neglect of differences. The simile, with its more deliberate and limited application, is chosen by a calmer mood. A small child that had been suddenly confronted by a panther, while it was still sobbing with fright would call the beast "a big cat." Later, after it had forgotten its terror, it would be likely to say,"It was like a cat, only bigger." In the heat of anger one would not say,"You remind me of a cur," but "You cur!" Both the metaphor and the comparison by their concreteness relieve and supplement the effort of the reason. Both appeal to experience, but while the metaphor fuses the known with the unknown, the comparison keeps the two separate and thus gives the mind time to relate them to each other. The illustrative example of public speakers, the parables of Jesus, the "pack-asses" and the "cobblers" of Socrates, and the fables of Aesop, all of which are comparisons, enable the hearer to appropriate a new idea by the simple process of noting its resemblance to familiar experience. For this process the metaphor gives no time. Hence in literature the metaphor is par excellence the expression of the lyric mood, whether of Pindar and Aeschylus or of Demosthenes in impassioned moments (*De cor.* 299 f.). The comparison, on the other hand, is peculiarly suited to narrative. The Messenger in Attic tragedy often uses it.[28] It is found frequently in Kipling's *Plain Tales*, in Richard Harding Davis, and in Conan Doyle. There are a dozen simple comparisons in the tale of Tennyson's Northern Cobbler. It is common in Homer, but in this form it is not the Homeric simile.

The simile *à queue longue*, as Perrault called it, the unique form of poetic expression which Homer gave to all future poets, begins as a comparison, but immediately transcends its function, and presents a little picture for its own sake. If the longer Homeric similes had been gathered by themselves, the Alexandrians might have called them *eidyllia*, for they are "little poems." The two Homeric poems contain 240 of these "idyls," varying in length from two to nine verses, with one of thirteen. Together they amount to nearly eight hundred verses, a body of poetry comparable in length with the Hesiodic *Works and Days*.

An ancient commentator describes the Homeric simile thus: "The added details of the simile contribute nothing to the comparison, but have their place as poetic ornament (ποιητικὸs κόσμοs)."[29] No better explanation of the function of the Homeric simile has ever been given, as far as it goes. It fails to tell us what kind of poetic ornament. To determine this we must notice the common poetic qualities of the similes without regard to their context. Let us begin with one of the most familiar similes, The Pygmies and the Cranes (Γ 3-7):

"As when the clamor of cranes pours forth up in the sky, when they have left winter behind, and never-ceasing rain, and with clamor they direct their flight towards the stream of Oceanus, bringing death and destruction to the Pygmies, for early in the morning they challenge [the Pygmies] to bitter combat."

In spite of the repetition of the word "clamor" the impression which the lines leave with us is of the battle between the Cranes and the Pygmies. These have no connection with the Trojan War. They are pictured for their own sakes, just as they are on the foot of the François Vase.

The detachment of the similes has long been noticed. Pierre Gin in 1786 compared the *Iliad* to a great picture gallery. The large canvases are the battle scenes, and scattered among them are the similes, "charming pictures taken chiefly from nature, which permit the visitor to rest from the fatigue of examining the elaborate paintings."[30] About the same time (1792; Finsler, *op. cit.* 251), Madame Roland writes to Lavater that his letters, coming to her in the midst of a life constantly threatened by the Jacobins, seem like the splendid little pictures that Homer scatters among his battles.

This detachment of the "long-tailed" simile from its context was used against Homer in the *Querelle*. Saint-Évremond (*Sur les Poèmes des Anciens*; Finsler, *op. cit.* 200) made the point that it often caused the reader to forget the scene it was supposed to illustrate. He failed to see, however, that after the brief distraction the attention returns to the narrative renewed and invigorated. This refreshment is the greater because the similes offer a complete change from the life which the narrative pictures.

The similes recalled Homer's listener from the remote Heroic past with all its myths and legends, to his own time and the life with which he was familiar.[31] The scenes on the shield of Achilles, as we have seen, imply that both the poet and his audience were commoners, at least that their chief interest was not in the life of the nobles. So it is the life of the common people which furnishes the stuff for most of the similes in which man appears. The only direct reference to popular superstitions about the chthonic powers of evil is in a simile: an evil "demon"[32] causes the illness of a father (ε 394 ff.). Most of the similes are taken from peace, and the few from war—hardly more than half a dozen—picture forays rather than an organized campaign. The similes take us for the moment far away from the Trojan plain and Olympus to the sky, the hill, the lowland; to forest or the sea; to the sheepfold and the tilled fields of men—rarely to a city. In the narrative, man holds our attention, but in the similes he plays a minor rôle. Even when they picture a contest between man and beast our sympathy is often with the latter, as it is with the tall poplar that grew in the lowlands."But a chariot maker felled it with the gleaming iron, to fashion from it a felloe. And it lies, till it be seasoned, on the river bank" (Δ 483-487). Often with the poet we forget both man and beast and watch the forces of nature at war or at peace, and we return to the narrative, feeling with Byron,"I love not man the less but nature more/From these our interviews."

The greatest contrast between similes and narrative is between the kinds of emotion aroused by each. Addison says that Milton never quits his simile "till he has raised out of it some glorious image or sentiment proper to inflame the mind of the reader, and to give it that sublime kind of entertainment, which is suitable to the nature of an heroic poem."[33] Here Milton's epic differs fundamentally from Homer's. The latter's similes are not "heroic." Wordsworth's description of his own *Lyrical Ballads* fits the Homeric similes better than Addison's words, just quoted. "The principal object, then, ... was to choose incidents and situations from common life. ... Humble and rustic life was chosen because, in that condition, the essential passions of the heart find a better soil in which they can attain their maturity ... because in that condition the passions of men are incorporated with the beautiful and permanent forms of nature." In their attitude towards nature Wordsworth and Homer are much alike. Principal Shairp's essay on Wordsworth is a good commentary on Homer's similes: In his treatment of nature there is no exhaustive enumeration of details. Only one or two essentials are given, and from these Wordsworth passes "to the sentiment, the genius of the place." So Homer first gives the theme, then the place of the little episode (nearly 150 times); more rarely the time (in about ten similes), then a few details, and not infrequently the sentiment. For example: ". . . and the shepherd is afraid, and drives his flock into a cave" (Δ 279). The mist on the mountains is "not loved by the shepherd, but better for the thief than the night" (Γ 11). "The shepherd is glad in his heart . . . when the moon shines bright amid the stars on a clear night, when the wind is still," for he can scan "every hilltop and jutting cliff and valley" for the sheepstealer (Θ 555-559); or when the ram leads the flock "from the pasture to drink" (N 492 f.). A mighty, rushing wave, "wind-nurtured under a cloudy sky," breaks over a ship, burying her under its foaming waters, while the gale roars against the sail: "the sailors tremble in their hearts. They have good reason to fear; they are passing but a little way from death" (O 624-628). Mischievous boys, teasing the wasps whose nest is by the roadside, are "a common nuisance to many" (Π 260-265). "Wordsworth loved the mountains." Homer in his similes refers to the mountains more often than to any other feature of nature, once in every four or five of the similes of the *Iliad*. "Wordsworth was familiar with all the moods of nature." In the poet's account of the main action of the *Iliad*, and of the *Odyssey* with a single exception,[34] it never rains or snows, and the moon and stars never shine; winds, clouds, thunder, and lightning appear only by divine intervention and for a particular purpose. We know only by inference that the Wrath runs its course during the summer months, and that Odysseus returns at the end of autumn or beginning of winter. But seasons and stormy winds, snow and rain, clouds and thunder, and the moon and stars often contribute to the pictures of the similes. Finally (says Principal Shairp), when Wordsworth took for his theme man, it was not from the cities, but from the cottage or farm; it was "the shepherd on his hills, or the vagrant on lonely roads."[35]

This comparison with Wordsworth's shorter poems makes clear the greatest contrast between the similes and the narrative of Homer. The similes arouse the lyric emotions; they are pure lyrics. It makes no difference that they lack the direct personal reference, the "I" and the "You." The lyric, in essence, is "the purest, most typical form of poetry."[36] This is measured rather by the depth and genuineness of the emotion expressed through sensuous images than by the machinery which is employed. There are many lyrics, both ancient and modern, in which the image is not directly referred to either the poet or the listener. "Some whole poems," says Shairp of Keble's lyrics, "are little more than descriptions of some scene in nature."[37] Wordsworth's "Airey-Force Valley" contains no personal reference; "A Night-piece" and the "Song for the Wandering Jew," none save the last four lines, in which the poet applies the description to himself or to the thoughts of the impersonal reader. In the description itself, both in these three poems and in every simile of Homer, the formal subjective element is the present tense: the picture belongs neither to the past nor to the story; it is entirely the affair of the poet and his listeners—the artist and his audience.

It is in the use which he makes of the similes, and not in the pictures themselves, that Homer diverges from lyric poetry. The similes must be cast in the meter of the epic, and they must be carefully articulated with the narrative.

In all other respects, in brevity, detachment, theme, treatment, and feeling, they are lyrics.

Let us test this conclusion by comparing a few of them with similar pictures in poems unquestionably lyric. Let us take, first, three descriptions, one from each of the three poetic genres, of the continual succession of waves.

A (from Matthew Arnold's "Dover Beach"):

> ... from the long line of spray
> Where the sea meets the moon-blanch'd land,
> Listen! You hear the grating roar
> Of pebbles which the waves draw back, and fling,
> At their return, up the high strand,
> Begin, and cease, and then again begin,
> With tremulous cadence slow ...

The only personal interposition, "Listen! You hear," is quite unnecessary.

B (from the second stasimon of Sophocles' *Antigone*, vss. 586-592):

The swollen billows, when, driven by the fierce breath of the sea winds from Thrace, they run o'er the darkness of the deep, and roll up the black sands from the depths, and the buffeted headlands, lashed by the wind, roar mournfully.

C (from the *Iliad*, Δ 422-426):

When on a loud-roaring shore the sea billows rush on, ever more closely following each other, when Zephyrus hath begun to blow; first a billow raiseth its crest out at sea and then it breaketh on the land with loud thunder; it archeth itself and pileth upon the banks, and spitteth forth the froth of the sea.

In lyric quality we think few will rank the last passage third. It matters not that its note is not melancholy or mournful, like that of the first and the second. Gladness, no less than sadness, may cause the soul to burst forth into song. The paean can be as lyric as the dirge.

Next let us compare Homer with Sappho, the most lyric of all Greek poets.

Sappho, Frg. 116 D:

The sweet apple, reddening on the end of a branch, on the highest twig at the top of the tree, overlooked by the apple-pickers—nay, not overlooked, they could not reach it.

Iliad, Δ 141-145:

Ivory, stained by Maeonian or Carian woman to be the cheek-piece of a bridle. It is kept stored away in a treasury. Full many a man hath ardently desired to have it. But a man of wealth keepeth it among his treasures, both as a gaud for his steed and to be the glory of its driver.

This pair of miniatures, in vividness of color and in expressing both the desirability and the unattainableness of the object, are strikingly alike. If Homer is here slightly less lyric, it is because he has departed from his custom, and has taken his theme from the life of nobles.

Again, let us place together, since their likeness of tone has been challenged,[38] two pictures of nature asleep.

Alcman, Frag. 60 (Mackail's translation):

The crests and clefts of the hills are asleep, and the headlands and ravines, and foliage and all moving things that the dark earth nourishes, wild hill-haunting beasts and the race of bees and the creatures in the depths of the dark-gleaming ocean, and asleep are the tribes of long-winged birds.

Iliad, E 522-526:

Clouds which Cronion sets motionless on the mountaintops, on a day when no air stirreth; while sleeps the might of Boreas and the other fierce-blowing winds, that with their blowing drive asunder the shadowy clouds with their shrill blasts.

Professor Mackail sees in Alcman something that is "almost like a deliberate challenge to the old by the new poetry."

But is not Homer the better poet? "The emotional effect of the landscape [we quote again from Winchester, *op. cit.* 131] does not, in strictness, proceed from the details we see, but from the spiritual or imaginative influence of the whole. The poet, therefore, will seek to interpret rather than to describe. Perceiving in what particulars the spiritual power of the scene resides, he will care only for these. He knows that the part is better than the whole." Homer with a single adverb (ἀτρέμας), a noun (νηνεμίη), and the contrast between Boreas slumbering and awake, has interpreted the effect of nature's forces asleep far better, we think, than Alcman has done with all his enumeration.

Finally, let us turn to Wordsworth, and compare a Homeric simile with the first stanza of his "Song for the Wandering Jew,"

>Though the torrents from their fountains
> Roar down many a craggy steep,
>Yet they find among the mountains
> Resting-places calm and deep.

Iliad, N 137-142:

A huge boulder from a cliff, set free by the swollen torrents that with their mighty waters have loosened the bonds of the shameless rock. High it leaps as it bounds along, crashing through the woods. But they hinder it not; on and on it bounds—till it reaches the plain: then it rolls no more, for all its eagerness!

Wordsworth calls his little poem a "Song." In his similes Homer, too, is a singer.

CHAPTER SEVEN

HOMER THE POETIC DEMIURGE
PLOT AND CHARACTERS

THE HOMERIC POEMS give us our closest approach to an authentic picture of the Heroic Age of Greece in its highest human aspects. This picture is authentic so far as it is due to the full flowering of long poetic tradition, uninfluenced by any revolution of thought or new advance in culture. The quiescent mood of the Greek spirit, which seems to have prevailed in Homer's time, was admirably suited to clarify and purify the tradition of the great past. In this mood, with the past still overshadowing the present, poets naturally overlooked the imperfections and blemishes of their theme; only its grandeur caught their fancy. So Homer's picture differs from what the spade has revealed, much as fifth-century Attic potsherds differ from Keats's *Ode on a Grecian Urn*. It is neither fragmentary nor photographic. No more is it historical. It is a supreme poet's conception of human life at one of its peaks. Out of the tradition he created a new cosmos.

Aristotle's comparison of a creation of this kind to "a thing of life, of unity, of completeness" (*Poetics* 23, 1459a 20, ὥσπερ ζῷον ἓν ὅλον), has never been equaled. We have considered the first of these qualities in Homer's poetry. It remains to discuss the unity and completeness of the poems.

I

Unity is an abstract term. In literary criticism it defies precise definition. The work of creative imagination cannot be reduced to a formula. The lover's philosophy,

> Nothing in the world is single;
> All things by a law divine
> In one another's being mingle,

is also true of the poetic relation between the One and the Many, but this relation differs in all great works of creative art. Again, literary unity is best seen in the finished product. Homer's method of composition is likely to have been by episodes, with a slow growth of the final plan of either poem. Plato's *Republic* seems to have grown in a similar way. This introduces a rivalry of unities which is not found in a poem like *Paradise Lost*. Even in the "clear bird's-eye view" of the story, which Aristotle demands, the single pattern could not have been as clear to listeners as it is to scholars. Therefore we should regard the literary unity of the poems as a vital and organic principle which makes each incident in the tales perform some function in the Human Life Writ Large.

The third quality in Aristotle's comparison, completeness, is quite as important. Completion of a single human life, as the Hebrew Psalmist reminds us, comes when the tale is told. In Homer this point is reached when the characters who embody the virtues of the age that is past have lived a complete and significant portion of their lives, in which they have worked out their own destinies. Furthermore, since the emotional experience of the listener must also be complete, the picture of this portion of life must adequately awaken, sustain, bring to a climax, and then satisfy the feelings appropriate to the greatness of the theme. In the Homeric poems there are varying degrees and different kinds of completeness: one of the episodes, another of each poem, and a third of the two poems taken together.

In the unity and completeness of the epic story Aristotle makes character of secondary importance; plot is the determining element, and plot is defined as "the organic relation of incidents" (ἡ τῶν πραγμάτων σύστασις, *Poetics* 1450a 16). Yet both Attic tragedy and the Homeric poems show clearly that action is only, as it were, the skeleton of the organism, whose life is most deeply revealed by the effect of the incidents upon the persons. In Attic tragedy we witness only the psychological "reaction" to off-scene occurrences. In Homer,"father of tragedy," it is less the actions than their dramatized effect upon the persons which makes the deepest impression of the finality of great lives: the laments for Patroclus and Hector, of which the dirges of Attic tragedy are the lineal descendants, are sufficient evidence. This impression springs from the psychical blends and the motives and standards of conduct which determine the lives of the persons. Therefore, we shall make character the basis of our examination of both the oneness and the completeness of the poems.

The *Iliad* alone gives but a fragmentary picture of the Age of the Heroes; at the end of the *Odyssey* their tale is told. The story of Troy is complete when the *Iliad* ends: with the breaking of the truce and much more with the death of Hector, the city is doomed. Hence only two Trojans are named in the *Odyssey*—Cassandra, slave of Agamemnon, and her father Priam, king of the sacked city; Hector is not mentioned. But every prominent Greek whose story was left unfinished in the *Iliad* finds a place either in the Telemachy or in one of the two Necyias.

The last words of a Greek in the *Iliad* are Helen's (Ω 773-775): "So I weep for thee and for myself no less. My heart is breaking. I have no kind and gentle friend left in broad Troyland; everyone shudders at the thought of me." As Aeschylus did not leave the Curse of the Atridae until he had removed it in the *Eumenides*, so Homer, so tender to Helen in the *Iliad*, heals her broken heart in the Telemachy. In the *Iliad*, Agamemnon, the cause of the Wrath, is contrasted with the hero of the poem in countless ways (see below); the completion of Agamemnon's story in the *Odyssey* makes of him and his family the recognized foils to the family of the hero. At the Games (Ψ 890-897) Agamemnon fails to respond to Achilles' final words of reconciliation, and nowhere in the poem has he admitted the hero's claim to superior honor—only his fighting power. But in the Second Necyia the shade of Agamemnon makes the final amend (ω 93-95): "Thus not even in death didst thou lose thy fair name. Nay, thy goodly renown shall be everlasting over all the world. But as for me, what joy have I in the winning of the war?"

Aristotle classes the *Odyssey* with tragedies ending happily. It also ends with finality. Of the four prominent sons of heroes, Neoptolemus and Orestes have not appeared as *dramatis personae*, and Telemachus and Pisistratus offer no problem that suggests a sequel. In contrast to the *Iliad* the *Odyssey* concludes the tale of the Trojan heroes as Sophocles ends the Theban story in the *Oedipus at Colonus*, and as Aeschylus completes the tales of Agamemnon and of Prometheus.[1] The *Iliad* looks forward. It ends with a truce, and the last verbs in the poem are in the imperfect tense. The last verse of the *Odyssey* denotes finality: Athena made peace between them. The rest is silence.

The completeness of either poem is like that of a drama in a trilogy. The adjectives applied to the two themes at the outset include both the nature of the tale and its scope. The "deadliness" of the Wrath hints at a story of passion ending tragically. The Wrath, as Homer tells its tale, not only brings death to Patroclus and Hector and countless minor heroes; it results in the fall of Troy (cf. Ω 499), and the early death of Achilles (cf. Σ 96, Ω 85, where Thetis is already in mourning for her son). The "tale" of the Wrath is not "told" when Hector falls. The account of the games not only includes the indispensable funeral of Patroclus, but also permits the congé of the greater heroes. More than this, it shows the restoration of Achilles' good will towards the leaders against whom he had become embittered in the Quarrel. The wrath against Hector is still vehement at the beginning of Book XXIV and continues even after Achilles has consented to permit

---

[1] Superior figures refer to notes which will be found on pp. 255-256.

the ransom of Hector's body. It ends at verse 589: the maids have bathed and anointed the body, and have wrapped it in tunic and cloak, "And Achilles himself lifted the body and placed it on the bier." Only after this act is Achilles at peace. The burial of Hector is owed both to the story and to the audience, it is true, but equally to the theme. The Wrath had made Achilles say repeatedly that he would not permit the burial of Hector. The latter's funeral is therefore the last event in the tale of the Wrath.

In the *Odyssey* the "ready wit" of the hero, announced in the first verse, determines both the story and its end. Reason takes the place of passion as the mainspring of action. There is no passion on Olympus. Athena has her way, and she is "wit" personified. She never loses her temper, as she does in the *Iliad*. On earth neither the "patient" and "resourceful" Odysseus, nor the "prudent" Penelope, nor the "wise" Telemachus awakens the affection inspired by the passionate Achilles, Hector, Helen, and Andromache, because the passions of these three characters always obey the reason.

The reward of Odysseus completely satisfies the requirements of the theme. Resourcefulness, put to the test in countless ways at home and abroad, on land and sea, demands an end of the ordeal: a green old age, amid a happy people, and a gentle death "away from the sea";[2] not fame—for he has already won this (ι 20),—but peace.

The story of Penelope, too, is admirably completed. Her part in the poem is one of forced inactivity—we never see her at her loom, as we do Helen and Andromache,— loneliness, and agonized waiting. She must wait not only for the return of Odysseus. Days elapse before she learns that her son has sailed for Pylus (δ 701). Eurycleia postpones sending word of this to Laertes, as the Queen desires (δ 754, cf. π 142). She must ask Telemachus twice before he will tell her of his journey (π 44, 101), and Eumaeus three times before he goes to fetch the Beggar (ρ 507, 529, 544). Even then she is compelled to wait till evening before the Beggar comes to her (ρ 582), and must ask him twice for his name (τ 105, 162). It is true that she turns the tables on husband and son and the old nurse in the recognition scene (ψ 20, 62, 83, 105, 174). Yet in her last appearance she is again inactive, alone in the palace and anxiously waiting (ψ 364 f.). But her reward is great. In the Second Necyia the shade of Agamemnon bestows it (ω 194-198): "How excellent was the heart of blameless Penelope! . . . Therefore the fame of her goodness shall never die, but the immortals will make for the dwellers on earth a lovely song to the glory of loyal Penelope."

The endings of the two Homeric poems are in no sense epilogues; they are organic members of the whole. The characters themselves, by their actions and words, weave to an end the chief threads of the tale. For this reason the conclusions are deliberate and extended. In sharp contrast are the beginnings. The induction into the action is a transition from the present to the past and from the real to the ideal. In it the poet himself must speak, and must do three things: he must justify his tale, present his theme so as to awaken interest, and then link the theme with the action.

There may be two reasons for a narrative. The first is its moral. This is the aim of most narratives in the speeches of the *Iliad*. Zeus uses narrative to inspire confidence in his threats; Nestor, to give weight to his advice. The narratives of Phoenix, Agamemnon, Andromache, Priam, and Athena are of this kind. In all these the motive is outside the story itself; it is an ulterior motive of the speaker. The other reason is the interest which the story has for another. Such are most of the speaker's narratives in the *Odyssey* and all the Messenger's rheses in Attic tragedy. Homer is therefore true to his conception of epic as both dramatic and of interest for its own sake, when he invokes the Muse. Vergil's greater theme justifies the first person, "cano." Milton combines an address to the Muse with an explanation of his own purpose.

The epic theme may be announced in two ways. In one, a broad and well-known field is narrowed to the theme; in the other, the theme, mentioned at the outset, is briefly enlarged. The first method is used in the *Nibelungenlied* and *Beowulf* and the *Kalevala*. The second is that of Homer and of the Old Testament: "In the beginning God created the heaven and the earth." "There was a man in the land of Uz, whose name was Job." This may be primitive, or it may be Oriental; but is clearly better suited to oral narrative, for it instantly awakens the interest of the hearer. Its superiority has been recognized by writers under the influence of Homer.

The interest of the listener demands some expansion of the theme. The poet must give a "sample" of the way in which the theme is to be treated, "that the listener's mind may not be kept in suspense, for vagueness causes the attention to stray."[3] This should not resemble a table of contents, for that overloads the attention. Neither *Iliad* nor *Odyssey* refers at the beginning to the second part of the story, neither to the wrath against Hector nor to the situation at Ithaca.[4]

The transition to the beginning of the action may also be made in two ways. The first describes the characters and the setting. In any tale, oral or written, this is an egregious error: it burdens the mind with matters which are not yet pertinent. The Teutonic epics make this mistake, and so does Apollonius. In general, as the personality of the poet assumes greater importance, the induction grows longer and more complex. The induction of the *Iliad* is easily the greatest in its field, for it introduces the action with directness, simplicity, and fullness, and with a remarkable continuity of thought within a dozen verses.

> Goddess, thy theme be the Wrath of Achilles, whose father was Peleus.
> Ruin it brought; beyond number the woes of the Greeks it engendered.

Many the valorous souls it sped on their way unto Hades,
Souls of the warriors of old; their bodies the dogs made their booty;
Vultures surfeited on them. But Zeus brought his plan to fulfillment.
All this began on the day when two heroes parted in anger,
One, Agamemnon, wide-ruling; the other, the godlike Achilles.
What god brought them together in angry strife and defiance?
Leto's and Zeus's son. Agamemnon roused him to anger.
Pestilence dire he brought to the camp and death to the soldiers.
Atreus' son had insulted Chryses, priest of Apollo.
        [*The action begins*]
Chryses came to the ships of the Greeks to ransom his daughter.

The theme is as germinal as the acorn from which springs a mighty oak. Its tragic import is given by a single adjective, "ruinous." The woes "past numbering" and the "many" souls sent to Hades give it largeness; "the treasure trove of the dogs and the feast for the vultures" give it quality in the imagination. The fulfillment of the "plan of Zeus" introduces the second part of all epic (ἔργ' ἀνδρῶν τε θεῶν τε). The time is made sufficiently clear and is closely linked to the theme, in two verses: "the tragedy of the Wrath began when two heroes parted after a quarrel," Agamemnon and Achilles, one wide-ruling, the other godlike. The tragedy is thus due to a conflict between power and superiority of personal excellence. "Parting after a quarrel" makes the hearer curious about the cause of the quarrel; since Zeus caused the wrath to be ruinous, the quarrel, too, is likely to have originated in a divinity. The question, "What god brought the pair together in a quarrel?" bridges the gap which always threatens in the transition from proem to the beginning of the action, by a neat chiastic antithesis, διαστήτην ἐρίσαντε /ἔριδι ξυνέηκε (vss. 6, 8). With the answer,"Apollo," and a triple summary of the reason, the steps from cause to quarrel are briefly retraced: Apollo, angered at Agamemnon, sent a plague; the king had insulted Apollo's priest, Chryses; the latter came to the ships to ransom his daughter—and the action has begun. One hardly knows whether to admire more the choice of the theme or the skill with which this theme is packed with interest, and time, place, circumstances, and the actors in the first scene are introduced, all within a dozen verses. Not a word is wasted. Even ἡρώων (vs. 4) is likely to be no mere ornate alias for "Achaeans," but to include the Trojans. Finally, if the mention of Agamemnon and Achilles does not clearly suggest the Trojan War, the reference of Chryses to "Priam's city" (vs. 19) removes all doubt.

The focal nature of the *Iliad's* theme makes the beginning of the action grow out of it. The theme of the *Odyssey* is both more indefinite and more comprehensive. The tale of Sir Readywit is limited only at one end: it does not include any part of the war itself. And it includes the tale of the heroes linked with him in the *Iliad*. Hence the beginning of the action is arbitrary; in its choice lies the chief literary invention of the author. But the transition from theme to beginning is exactly the same as in the earlier poem, a sudden antithesis, which association of ideas makes effective. "Begin the tale at any point," "At this point all the other surviving heroes were at home"—which indicates the inclusion of the other heroes in the story. The same divine guidance of the action as in the *Iliad* is provided for. "All the gods except Poseidon pitied the hero"—which points to the happy ending. The singling out of Poseidon leads naturally to the opening scene, and the divine plan. This is less simple, less original, and less effective than the beginning of the action of the *Iliad*, but it is in accord with the Homeric principle of divine interference, to bring an impasse to an end. Both the *Odyssey* and the last book of the *Iliad* begin with this impasse, and with the pity of the majority of the Olympians. The poet risks failure to captivate attention at the start, as perhaps Dante does in the *Divine Comedy* when he makes a prologue of the first Canto. But both Homer and Dante use a new literary invention: the structure of the plot is made to depend largely, or solely, on the narrative in the first person. More is gained than is lost. Sophocles presents *Oedipus Rex* in the same way.

Between the beginning and the end of the story, Aristotle places the "middle" (μέσον). This implies both the "means" and the "medium." It is the actions and the reactions of the characters which together present a complete portion of life.

The "plot" of a story is an abstraction. Aristotle's term, μῦθος, is better, for a "myth" is a picture of life. A true estimate of the harmony and vitality of a picture of human life cannot be based solely on an examination of the "plot" of the "story." The consistency and meaning of any complete portion of significant human life depend on the experiences of the persons. These experiences depend partly on actions and events, but still more on individual blends of motives and will, of capabilities and weaknesses. Hence the organic harmony of the Human Life Writ Large is best seen in the characters of the heroes, and in the relations between their characters and their experiences.

In the *Iliad* there are three persons, Achilles, Hector, and Zeus, who by reason of their character and actions determined by it, by their weakness and their strength, and by their conduct in the face of obstacles, which include the inevitable, together effect the tragic outcome of the Wrath. These three have enemies—and two of them have friends—varying in degrees of importance. They also have surrogates, who at times rival them in the interest of the audience. The three are alike in being creatures of feeling rather than of calm reason; they differ in the kind of feeling which guides their action. The ruling passion of Achilles is preeminence in all the qualities of manhood displayed in war, in greatness of spirit, and above all, honor, which was the reward of this preëminence. Hector looks for the same reward, but through devotion to country and family. Zeus is portrayed as a being in whom passion has almost burnt itself out—a striking contrast to the "new god" of the *Prometheus Bound*. In Homer's Zeus the springs of action have run dry. His rigid control of heaven and earth by violent measures, and his amours, are alike things of the past. If this were not so, the events of the *Iliad* would have been impossible. On Olympus, Zeus threatens and acts secretly or by subterfuge, never by force. On earth, he is both loathe to act and indolent in action, even in executing the decrees of Fate. In both *Iliad* and *Odyssey*[5] he is a blasé, "middle-aged" individual, and one of the *chef d'œuvres* of Homer's invention.

The importance of Zeus in the action is clearly foreshadowed in the proem: "But [in the baneful results of the Wrath] the plan of Zeus was carried to fulfillment."[6] Both the character of Zeus and the organic function of his plan, in determining the progress and the variety of the action, are seen in the definite steps in the fulfillment of his promise to Thetis. Through this promise the plan becomes the immediate or ultimate cause of all the fighting in the *Iliad*. We are told repeatedly that previously there had been no pitched battle between the entire forces. The length of the war is brought to our attention only in Book II, and then in round numbers[7] and for a special purpose.

The promise of Zeus to Thetis is made in secret: Zeus confidently, and somewhat pompously, implies this in his first words to Hera.[8] But Hera at once undeceives him, thereby scoring the first trick.[9] Hence the first step, arraying the armies for a pitched battle, is taken while Hera sleeps. A general engagement is necessary if the Greeks are to be driven to the ships. For this purpose the armies must be marshaled and the Catalogues introduced. The single combat between Menelaus and Paris is altogether natural, even in the tenth year of the war, if the armies have never met before. The outcome of this duel apparently means the end of the war, and the thwarting of the plan of Zeus. This is prevented by a second step, the masterpiece of Zeus's otherwise rather clumsy strategy. By a "casual remark" (παραβλήδην ἀγορεύων, Δ 6) he makes sure that Hera and Athena will be in the mood to suggest and carry out the breaking of the truce. His subterfuge serves a threefold purpose. It creates for the hearer the certainty that Troy is doomed, which forecasts the close of the war, and still does not prolong the war after the end of the Wrath. After the bowshot of Pandarus no character, Greek, Trojan, or Olympian, has any doubt of the ultimate destruction of Troy. Secondly, it provides for the success of the Greeks in the first battle. Finally, it squares the contest of wits between Zeus and Hera, and leaves the former free to show his hand, and to use sterner measures. The spirit of former years, called back with difficulty to fulfill his promise to Thetis, is at last aroused.

At the beginning of the second day of fighting, Zeus openly declares his intention to act as he will, and threatens dire chastisement on the divinity who interferes. Hera and Athena challenge his threat, but are convinced by Iris that he is in earnest. At the close of the day, he promises to them the execution of his plan on the morrow. Night brings the failure of the embassy, the success of which would have thwarted the plan, and an exploit which heartens the Greeks for the next day's battle. Book XI marks three important points in the action: Zeus reveals to Hector—and to the hearer—the term and limit of the Trojan success: till Hector reach the ships and night come on. Diomede, surrogate for Achilles in the fighting hitherto, retires wounded—which makes the success of Hector less painful to the Greek audience,— and the sending of Patroclus to Nestor's quarters initiates the movement which is to transfer the Wrath to Hector. Hera and Athena salute Agamemnon as he prepares for the fray, but otherwise remain quiescent, certain that Zeus is roused to action. In Book XII, no gods interfere with the operations of Zeus, who brings Hector beyond the Greek wall. Then the "middle age" of Zeus reasserts itself; once more he relapses into inactivity, and Poseidon restores the battle. It is at this juncture that the mood of Hera, caused by her failure to "call the bluff" of Zeus in Book VIII, produces one of the most pleasing diversions in any tale of war, and almost wrecks the plan (Ξ). Book XV tells of the end both of the plan and of the battle between Zeus and Hera; and Zeus wins a clear-cut victory: Hera, for the only time in the poem, is deadly pale with fright, and Hector is at the ships, calling for fire. But Patroclus is already hurrying back to Achilles, and the plan of Zeus, apart from leaving Hector at the ships "when night comes on" (cf. P 206, with Λ 194), is no longer needed to bring the Wrath to its tragic ending.

Hector seems to have been invented by the poet,[10] in the first place, to be the human instrument by which the plan of Zeus is carried out. Until the plan begins to take definite shape he is not prominent in the fighting, but is, as it were, groomed for his rôle. In the Quarrel, Achilles mentions him as the enemy's most dreaded champion. We see him in Book II; in III we hear him speak, but Paris holds the center of the stage. In the first battle his rôle is still secondary: Aeneas and Sarpedon are more prominent. He does not as general exhort his army as so often in the later battles. It is Apollo who does this (Δ 509-513). The Argives are routed by Ares and Hector in Book V, but in Book XV by Hector and Apollo: the order is significant. It is Ares against whom

Hera and Athena enter the battle, and Hector is ignored in the outcome. But as the first battle draws to an end, and the plan of Zeus can begin to assume definiteness, Hector also assumes a leading part. He is presented to us in his intimate family relations, with Hecuba, Helen, and his wife and infant son (Z), and then in two capacities as a fighter. In Book VII he is the dreaded single champion, courteous and great as a fighter, but not quite so good as Ajax; in Book VIII he is a "bold charioteer" (vs. 89, a dramatic entrance). Now, when both stage and leading actor are ready, Hector receives specific instructions to carry out the plan (Λ).

As long as the plan of Zeus determines the action, Hector is little more than an instrument. Nominally commander-in-chief, he is ignored in making the truce (Γ 105-108) and is silent in the debate on the return of Helen (H 347-378). As general he must be roused and advised by others.[11] The only two plans of action which he makes without suggestion from others accord with the words of Zeus.[12] His achievements as single champion belie his repute among the Greeks as the most dreaded enemy.[13] Sarpedon is the better fighter. Without him the Trojans would not have forced the Greek wall (M 290 ff.). Sarpedon rallies his men and faces the victorious Patroclus; Hector takes to flight, in advance of his army, not protecting its retreat (Π 419-427, 712-714). Finally, Hector alone of all the heroes is helped by Zeus directly at the two climaxes of his success (M 450, O 694 f.).

The plan of Zeus and Hector as its instrument are used by the poet to determine the action during the absence of Achilles. Two things are gained thereby: the picture of the Heroic leaders in the first great war of Greece against Asiatics is made more complete, and two stories of wrath are welded together into one tragedy. The *Odyssey* has a similar architectural principle. The plan of Athena and its instrument Telemachus, which unite the stories of the Return and the Vengeance, make possible a more complete account of the great heroes of the *Iliad*. In both poems, plan and instrument cease to function as such when the *desis* nears completion; for example, after Book XV. But in the *Odyssey* the plan is fully revealed in the first scene, and the instrument fails to grow into a character which rivals in importance the hero himself.[14] This is not due to flagging power in the same poet, much less to imitation by another. For the *Odyssey* a new theme has been discovered, and a new organic principle has been developed to give the story life. On these Homer spends his creative effort: the device already once used he employs merely for convenience, and without enthusiasm.

In the *Iliad* the plan and the instrument together furnish the lifeblood of the tale of "ruinous wrath." Through them it proceeds inevitably and "of necessity" to a tragic failure of the two noblest ideals of manhood in war which tradition offered to the poet's mind. Hector is the embodiment of devotion to country and family; Achilles, of the faultless and high-minded conduct of a hero who is preëminent in manly qualities. The plan, which carried out the purpose of Achilles, apparently succeeds for both Hector and Achilles.[15] But, for both, its success utterly defeats their aims because of a very human "mistake" (ἁμαρτία)—not a moral delinquency—which springs from their respective guiding principles of conduct. The tragedy of the *Iliad* begins to emerge from the epic tale only after the plan has served its purpose and Hector, no longer an instrument, thinks and acts entirely for himself.

The genius of Homer presented Hector and his fate so poignantly that for most readers he overshadows the hero of the poem. Hence its due meed of recognition has been withheld from Homer's masterpiece, Achilles, and from the significance of the tragedy of his wrath. There are many reasons for this.

In the first place, the poet perhaps too apparently holds

Achilles up to be admired by concentrating in him the highest qualities of heroic manhood, which Hector lacks. Achilles is the handsomest, the strongest, the swiftest; he is the best fighter, and the bravest, inspiring fear in every enemy, fearing no mortal. Hector often shows fear. Achilles is a leader of men: he calls and first addresses the only two assemblies in which he takes part, and he assures Priam that there will be no fighting until Hector is buried. Hector, as we have seen, is neither a good leader nor a good general. Odysseus and Diomede deceive Dolon, but Achilles asserts his loathing of the lie, and all his utterances, except when he banters Patroclus (Π 7-19), are direct and sincere. Confident in himself, he is not given to boasting—as Hector is. The latter says of Patroclus, "Whom I slew," although he had but given the *coup de grâce* to a disarmed and disabled man. Achilles, after slaying Hector, says, "*We* have slain Hector." He is courteous to a fault: witness his words to the heralds of Agamemnon (A 334-336), and his last words, at the Games, to Agamemnon himself (Ψ 890-894). Hector is often lacking in courtesy, as the ancient commentators remarked and as the modern verb derived from his name testifies.[16] Achilles is not cruel: until Patroclus is slain, he shows more mercy in battle than is recorded of any other hero, Greek or Trojan. He is punctiliously religious: the account of the solemn ceremony preceding his prayer to Pelasgian Zeus for the safe return of Patroclus (Π 221-232) reveals a finer reverence for divinity than one can find elsewhere in Homer, even in the portrait of the pious Swineherd (ξ 420-446). In short, Achilles' unquestioned and manifold superiority to all other heroes of the poem may make him too good for human nature's daily food. Even his passionate disposition is excused by his youth, for he is younger than all the other leaders, not as old as Patroclus, and apparently about the same age as Antilochus, younger son of Nestor.

HOMER THE POETIC DEMIURGE 189

A second reason for Hector's greater claim on our affection is the contrast in the situations of the two heroes, in their relations with other human beings and in their respective motives of action. The poet makes this threefold contrast with great clearness.

There are two essential qualities of the true knight:

His plume like a pennon streams on the wanton summer wind.
At the *call of duty* still that white plume shalt thou find.
No *fear* in his heart must dwell but the *dread* that *shame* may throw
One *spot* upon that blade so bright, *one stain* on that plume of snow.

Hector possesses the first quality, but lacks the second. He never falters in his duty to country and family, but through fear of Ajax (P 166 f., 230-232) he brings a stain upon his honor by boasting of a victory and by assuming the *spolia opima*, to neither of which he had a just claim: he had not slain his foe in a fair fight, nor had he, as Zeus sadly comments (P 205 f.), "taken the armor duly (κατὰ κόσμον) from the head and shoulders" of Patroclus.[17] Achilles is guided rather by the second quality of the knight,

A soldier must with *honor* live, or at once with honor die.

This motive seems less generous[18] than that of Hector, but it springs inevitably from the situation. The goal of Achilles resulted from a choice which was like the Choice of Heracles in the allegory of Prodicus, between a long life of ease and a brief youth of heroic effort leading to glory immortal. Glory implies a just estimate and recognition of proven worth, that is, *timé*, honor. The situation prevented this from being a selfish motive. As Homer represents this, it laid no other responsibilities on Achilles. His father had willingly sent him to the war; no enemy threatened his own country, and no feeling of Greek national unity claimed his services. His mother was a goddess; his wife is never mentioned, and for his son he expected Patroclus to provide. He thus gave up all that makes life worth living, in order that, as it were, he might be to future ages the *beau idéal* of young manhood.

The most marked contrast between the two heroes is in their relations to other human beings. Achilles is separated from father and infant son; his mother is a goddess. The quarrel isolates him from his friends, Ajax, Antilochus, and Odysseus. Even Phoenix, in the only meeting which we witness, fails to understand him. So he is one of the loneliest figures in literature; in the midst of the choicest men of his day, yet alone, except for Patroclus—whom he must lose! What a contrast to Hector, whom all the dwellers in Troy "greet as a god"; whose body the whole city goes forth to meet! "No one was left in the city, either man or woman" (Ω 707 f.). To Priam Hector was "the best son I had" (Ω 499); "Let Achilles slay me once I have clasped my son in my arms" (Ω 226 f.); to Helen he was the only one who was "kind and a friend—all [the others] shudder at me," and to Andromache, "Hector, thou art to me father and mother and brother, and thou art my splendid husband." Our feeling for a character in a story is influenced by the emotions he inspires in others; grief for Hector expressed by Priam, by Hecuba, by Helen, by Andromache, and by the whole city, because of their love for him, enters our own hearts.

Again, there may be at times in a hero of decisive character—which Hector lacks—a certain hardness, which repels affection. A weaker character, Menelaus, for example, often inspires greater love. Hector, more often than Achilles, shows tenderness,[19] but his heart goes out rather towards the weak. In his exhortations to his army he more than once refers to the women and children of Troy.[20] When he goes to the city on the first day of battle (Z 237-240), the wives and daughters of the Trojans gather about him, asking for news of their men."And he bade them all in turn to pray to the gods." Helen speaks of his "gentleness and his gentle words," but there is little gentleness in his spontaneous utterances to men, and he shows an utter lack of the intimacy and affection for a male friend or a kinsman which exists between Sarpedon and Glaucus, between Agamemnon and Menelaus, and between Idomeneus and Meriones.

Achilles, unlike Hector, is a man's man. In the *Iliad* he never speaks to a mortal woman. Even Briseis on her return has words only for the dead Patroclus. In the brief references to his life in Phthia, men, not women, are prominent. We are told what Peleus said to him, what care Phoenix bestowed upon him, what Chiron taught him. He was an only son, and his mother was a goddess; he never expresses his affection for her. All the love of his passionate soul went out to Patroclus, who entered the life of the lonely boy and became, as it were, the "big brother," and the idol of his heart, even after the older boy became less "big" and himself needed protection. The only two prayers in the *Iliad* for a loved one are those of Hector and Achilles: the former prays for his child, the latter for Patroclus. Hector and Achilles are the only heroes, except in the chariot race, who address their steeds; Hector bids them repay the care which Andromache had lavished upon them; Achilles rebukes his horses for deserting the dead Patroclus. It is by such means that Homer reveals the souls of his characters. Hector's tender love for all the weak is centered in wife and child; Achilles' absorbing love for one idolized friend dwarfs all his other affections: "Now thou liest slain, and my heart, for lack of thee, refuses food and drink. The cruelest loss that could be mine, even if I should hear that my father was dead ... or my dear son, the child in Scyrus" (T 319-326). The long life which Achilles had renounced for honor was to be enjoyed by the loved friend; in him Achilles was, as it were, to live on (cf. T 331-333). There was no conflict between this love and the love of honor. Achilles is not selfish when he cautions Patroclus, "Be not too eager to fight the Trojans. Thou wilt make mine honor less" (Π 89 f.). This was the reason most likely to keep his friend from risking the death that actually was to befall him (cf. Schol. BT on Π 83). The poet never permits us to see the counter-affection of Patroclus. He prefers to make the loneliness of his hero still greater by confining his friend's words, like those of Phoenix, to a gentle rebuke. The love lavished on Hector and the love withheld from Achilles—by all except his mother—have robbed the hero of the reader's affection.

But the chief reason for our sympathy with Hector rather than with Achilles perhaps lies still deeper. The fate of Homer's hero is made tragic in the Sophoclean way. In the *Antigone* the heroine is not the chief bearer of the tragic emotion; she is not even mentioned in the final scene. In the *Oedipus Rex* Jocasta cannot fail to awaken pity, but Oedipus is the chief tragic character. One reason for this is that death pays all debts. Both Creon and Oedipus live on —with nothing to live for! This is the tragedy of Achilles, and one must search long in the world's literature to find a more perfect one. The germ of the tragedy is not in a Curse, an inherited duty, or Fate, but in the hero himself. Hector dies; *de mortuis nihil nisi bonum*. Hector's unlovely qualities are forgotten. We remember only his virtues and the love that he inspired.

In the poet's affection for Hector, as interpreted in modern times, lies a paradox. The ancient commentators recognized that Homer was *philachilleus*: Achilles was Homer's hero and his most loved character. It is not possible that he placed an enemy above Achilles, whom his poem made the ideal of manhood for later Greeks. The paradox disappears if we notice two poetic reasons for Homer's presentation of Hector.

Homer, as we have remarked, does not describe his chief characters (except by epithets). We enter their lives and know them as we do our friends and unfriends, by familiar acquaintance with what they are and do. Achilles, like Helen, needs no description. He is what he is, the peerless hero, head and shoulders above all others. But Hector is by no means "the gallant knight" until death is close upon him. Only then is he loved by all the Trojans, by Zeus, and by the poet himself. It is only after his death that his physical beauty is mentioned. "The Achaeans gazed in admiration at his stature and his wondrous beauty" (X 370). When his body drags in the dust we first see his raven locks: "His fair black hair flowed out on either side, and all his head, *once so beautiful*, lay in the dust" (X 401-403). The beauty and the lovable qualities of Hector are brought to our attention because the situation and the characters have made his death the supremely pathetic moment of the poem. The death of Achilles, with which Wilamowitz thought the *Iliad* originally ended, would have been an anticlimax. Achilles would have died "of the fifth act." There would have been no tragic motive for the single combat with Penthesilea—a woman!—nor in the slaying of Achilles by Apollo and Paris, nor in the mourning for Achilles by heroes who had rarely shown affection for him, nor in a new picture of Thetis, in funereal garb and sorrowing for her son (cf. Ω 90-94). This ending would have turned a great tragedy into a mere chronicle.

The greatness of this tragedy and of its determining element, the character of Achilles, has been obscured partly by the influence of the *Aeneid*, in which Hector is the friend and *immitis Achilles* the enemy, but still more by the failure to place the hero of the *Iliad* in his milieu and to judge him by the standards of the Greek Heroic Age. Andrew Lang sees in him "a touch of the Maori or Iroquois," and in the *Iliad* a "moral tragedy," with its basic idea the "corruptio optimi, the ruin of a noble spirit." Bowra says of him: "He is not a 'preux chevalier'—Roland would never have acted as Achilles acted, from injured pride." These opinions are extreme, but the authority with which their authors speak gives them weight; they represent a very general tendency to find in Homer's hero defects of character and errors in conduct inconsistent alike with the admiration for Achilles which the ancients found in the *Iliad*, and with the Greek tradition of this hero. In modern times Achilles is accused of partial, though minor, responsibility for the quarrel itself; of selfish persistence in nursing an injured pride, in refusing the pleas of the envoys from Agamemnon in spite of Agamemnon's "ample atonement," and of savage brutality in his treatment of Hector's body. It is even held that the poet himself does not regard Achilles as the embodiment of all the knightly virtues of the Heroic Age, because he is victorious over Hector through "the treacherous interference of Athena, at once so revolting and so needless," and because the poet himself passes a moral judgment on his alleged brutality. To accept all, or any, of these charges is, we think, to misread Homer. We shall therefore present briefly the evidence against them.

In the Quarrel, the wrath of Agamemnon precedes and causes that of Achilles. It breaks out first against Calchas, but is transferred to Achilles because of a fancied intentional slight upon the king's honor. That it is altogether fancied, the poet has taken pains to show. When Achilles tells Agamemnon that it is impossible to make good the latter's loss of Chryseis until another town is sacked, he adds: "It is not seemly to require the *common soldiers* (λαούς) to return their share of spoil to be divided again" (A 126). Achilles is thus made totally unconscious of any feeling that Agamemnon's honor is affected by his return of the priest's daughter. But to Agamemnon honor is concerned with externals. He was born in the purple. The last words in the poet's description of the scepter are significant: "Thyestes left it to Agamemnon, to hold sway as ruler of many islands and all Argos" (B 107 f.). His power is inherited, not won by effort. This is characteristic of the king: he has taken no part in the previous fighting, but has received the major part of the spoils. Hence he measures honor by its material evidence. If he must give up his prize without receiving an equivalent value, his honor is diminished. Hence, judging others by his own standards, he thinks Achilles intends that he shall be humiliated.

To Achilles, on the other hand, honor consists in an attitude of mind, and is based on a true estimate of worth. Briseis, ungenerously taken from him, is only the visible token of honor. He does not obey Athena because of her promise of ample material rewards: "I must obey your word, Goddess. 'Tis better to obey: the gods hearken to the prayers of the obedient" (A 216-218). In warning Agamemnon that the latter will be helpless when Hector slays the Greeks, he closes with these significant words: "thou didst utterly fail in honoring (οὐδὲν ἔτεισας) the noblest of the Achaeans" (A 244). He does not say: "thou tookest away the prize from the noblest."

This conflict between a higher and a lower conception of honor results in the failure of the Embassy. The phrase "Achilles sulking in his tent" is unfair both to Homer and to his hero. "Raging" is the meaning of μῆνιε (A 488). A passionate, high-spirited prince who has chosen immortal fame for high emprise instead of life, cannot be said to "nurse a grievance" when the honor on which that fame depends is taken from him. It is the failure to restore that honor which fully justifies the refusal of Agamemnon's "ample atonement."

After the success of Hector in Book VIII, Nestor urges Agamemnon[21] to win back the help of Achilles "by acceptable gifts and kindly words" (I 113). Agamemnon admits his folly in slighting the honor of Achilles, but adds: "The man is worth an army."[22] He thinks of the effect of the insult, not of the insult itself; of the girl taken from Achilles, not of the generous recognition of Achilles' worth, which he had denied. Hence he offers kingly gifts, but no apology. Elsewhere in Homer there are three far less serious breaches of courtesy which are healed; for each, an apology either precedes or accompanies the material atonement.[23] But Agamemnon, far from apologizing, virtually repeats the words with which he finished the insulting speech that caused the first outburst of Achilles' wrath: (A 185 f.) "that thou mayest know how much greater I am than thou"; (I 160) "and let him submit to me, who am so much more a king than he." No wonder there is only half-praise in Nestor's comment: "The *gifts* (δῶρα μέν) thou offerest are completely satisfying." Nestor no more mentions the "gentle words."

The "penitence" of Agamemnon (Lang); the "forgiveness" for which he sued (Gilbert Murray); his "repentance," which now puts Achilles entirely in the wrong (Bowra)—these are difficult to discover in Homer's account. The princely offer of gifts is made only when Agamemnon, always a craven in defeat, sees before him the utter destruction of his army. "Skin for skin; yea, all that a man hath will he give for his life."

Homer not only refrains from all reference to a true repentance in Agamemnon; he gives positive, though indirect, evidence which forbids us to think that he would put Agamemnon in the right and Achilles in the wrong. In the *Odyssey* Agamemnon and Clytemnestra are the recognized foils to Odysseus and Penelope. In the *Iliad* Agamemnon is presented in striking contrast to Achilles in all the qualities of heroic manhood, save one: Agamemnon has a deep and sincere love for Menelaus—and Achilles has no brother. With this single exception the king has almost no good quality. To gratify his own lust he defies Apollo and the wishes of the whole army and brings on the plague, which he does nothing to remove. In the assembly he grossly insults Clytemnestra, the proudest queen in Hellas, by placing above her in physical and mental gifts the daughter of a parish priest of the enemy. As a general he loses heart at the first defeat: the only strategic measure which he proposes in the whole poem is the abandonment of the expedition.[24] It will be objected that Homer calls him "both a good king and a mighty spearman" (Γ 179). These, however, are the words not of Homer, but of Helen, Agamemnon's brother's wife, and they are spoken to Priam, king of the enemy. The national feeling of the Greek audience makes them altogether fitting from her lips on this occasion. For the same reason Homer always portrays the Greek commander-in-chief as physically every inch a king. But his heart is utterly selfish, craven, ignoble. To the army he does not admit his fault, but lays the blame on Zeus. In his *aristeia*[25] he is given no real glory: he is unnecessarily cruel and utterly forgets his debt to Antenor for hospitality to Menelaus, when he not only kills the son of Antenor, but cuts off his head. At the Games he shows himself no true sportsman and, as often, lacking in courtesy: he accepts without a contest against a younger antagonist, Meriones, the first prize for spear-throwing, and he gives no word of thanks, much less of final reconciliation, to Achilles. From his first appearance in the opening episode of the story until he takes his unkingly congé at the end of the Games (Ψ 895-897), he is clearly the villain of the tale—and a contemptible villain.

In contrast to the standards of Agamemnon, the poet has revealed, in the Embassy, Achilles' lofty ideal of honor and his delicate sensitiveness to its demands, with a dramatic skill that even Sophocles never surpasses, and only Shakespeare, perhaps, in *King Lear* equals. And he has also shown the groundlessness of a second charge against Achilles, that he erred in refusing the pleas, certainly of his friends Odysseus and Phoenix, and possibly of Ajax. It is worth while, as well as only fair to Homer, to notice the art with which, by an absolutely objective account of the action and by the words of the characters, the poet has represented his hero as consistently loyal to his conception of honor.

In the Quarrel there is a remarkable omission. In all the other assemblies of the Greeks the army in some way expresses its feelings; it shouts its approval of the request of Chryses (A 22); it approves two speeches of Odysseus, and Agamemnon's call to battle (B 271, 333, 394); it approves the speeches of Diomede (H 403-404; I 50); and at the last assembly (T 74) the poet tells us of the joy of the army at the making up of the quarrel. But in the quarrel itself the army is silent. Nor does either Odysseus or Ajax speak on behalf of Achilles when Agamemnon threatens to take the latter's prize, and not their own as he had first threatened (A 138; the choice of the heroes is significant): "either thy prize, or that of *Ajax* or *Odysseus*." Friends as dear as Odysseus and Ajax in the Embassy say they are, ought at least to rise and protest in open assembly against such an egregious outrage upon their friend Achilles! But the poet keeps the army, and Odysseus and Ajax, silent. He thus fully justifies the hero, after he has brooded for days over their desertion, in hoping that the Trojans may crowd the Greeks to the sea and slay them, "that *all* may have their fill of their king."

These "friends" for many days ignore the existence of Achilles. They fight the first general engagement of the war without him. They bury their dead, they build their wall with never a thought of Achilles. Then comes a crushing defeat. Only Achilles can save them. Now they remember him and go to his barracks. The warmth of his greeting shows both his affection and his willingness to forget their defection. But what does Odysseus, who represents Agamemnon and the army, have to offer? In brief, this: from Agamemnon munificent gifts, but no apology or recognition of Achilles' worth. "But if thou hatest him and his gifts too much, pity the sore-pressed Achaeans, who will honor thee as a god, for thou mayest slay Hector." Not a word of friendship, much less of regret for their defection, only the "honor" of slaying Hector! Among friends obligation is mutual. By what Odysseus fails to say, the poet has made Achilles' refusal absolutely necessary for this young, high-spirited prince of the Heroic Age, a millennium before sanction was given to the command, "Do good to them that despitefully use you": "I do not think that Agamemnon *or the rest of the Danaans* will move me, for it has proved that there is no gratitude for fighting the enemy without rest" (I 315-317).

The plea of Phoenix which follows, and the reply of Achilles, contain the best bits of character drawing in either poem, because the contrast between the standards of conduct of the two men is so incisively, yet so unconsciously, revealed. Phoenix is ethically a low-grade character. He tells quite frankly how he debauched the concubine of his father, and how, when his father cursed him, he entertained the thought of parricide. Hence we are not surprised that in drawing the moral of the story of Meleager he shows his inability to rise to Achilles' conception of honor: "Yield, and secure the gifts, for the Achaeans will honor thee as a god. But if [as Meleager did] thou shalt reënter the fighting later [and do not receive the gifts] thou wilt have less honor." Achilles replies: "Of such honor I have no need."

The sensitiveness of Achilles to what he feels is an obligation is exquisitely revealed in his reply to Phoenix. Phoenix began his plea by expressing his willingness to return home with Achilles, if the latter must go. He also reminded Achilles of his loving care when Achilles was a child. In recognition of the first exhibition of loyalty, Achilles consents to postpone the decision to return home. In return for the affection of Phoenix to him since childhood, he gently rebukes him for so much interest in Agamemnon, Achilles' bitterest enemy, and then offers him "half of his kingdom."

The allegory of the Prayers and the punishment for refusing to hear them is in the nature of a warning. But until the hero's honor, as Achilles defines honor, has been safeguarded—and up to this point no offer has been made, no word has been uttered, which his conception of honor can permit him to accept,—Achilles must face even the offended Litae.

Achilles has been further blamed for curtly dismissing Odysseus and Ajax after he has replied to Phoenix. It must be remembered that they came in the official capacity of envoys from Agamemnon (I 520 f.)[26] They were Achilles' personal friends, to be sure, but an envoy should always be *persona grata*. They were none the less official envoys, whose stay could be terminated at the will of their host, and Achilles had prefaced his reply to Odysseus with emphasis on its finality: he had refused all parleying.

The third plea, that of Ajax, is perhaps the masterpiece of the episode. It is, as it were, a Parthian shot. "Odysseus, we'll be going . . . Achilles has no heart; he takes no thought of friendship such as ours, which has made us honor him above all others by the ships. Cruel! Many a man has accepted wergeld from the slayer of a son or brother. . . . [*To Achilles:*] But in your breast the gods have put an unyielding and cruel heart . . . all for the sake of a girl, one girl! We offer you seven, the best that can be found, and much more besides. Be kind! Respect this roof, under which we meet, we, envoys of the Danaans, and in our hearts your nearest and dearest friends of all the Achaeans."

This plea is not only perfect in ethos; it also returns to the first and strongest point in the interview. If either the aged friend Phoenix or bluff Ajax, not Odysseus, had spoken first (cf. vs. 223, one of the fine touches of Homer), the result might have been different. When the Envoys entered, Achilles said to Patroclus, "My best friends are here, under my roof." But Odysseus made no reference to friendship or to the honor paid to Achilles by his friends, and after this omission the words of Phoenix (vss. 520-522, "Agamemnon has sent your dearest friends to plead with you") are meaningless. But now Ajax assures Achilles that his first impression was true. Yet Ajax, like Odysseus and Phoenix, cannot rise to his friend's high ideal of honor, but thinks material recompense is sufficient. So Achilles now recognizes the claim of friendship, but feels that the slight upon his honor still remains, since his best friends misunderstand the real point at issue. He is thus confronted by a momentous choice, between the claim of friendship—asserted but not proved at a crisis—and the claim of honor still unsatisfied. He wavers, and then makes the wrong decision."Ajax, I *almost* agree with all you say—but my heart swells with indignation at the public, wanton insult. Agamemnon treated me as if I were a vile outcast from society."[27] Then he promises to grant the prayer of Ajax, but not yet: the Greeks must pay for his still-unrestored honor. He will face Hector when his own ships are in danger.

This decision is fatal, but it is made as Aristotle demands of high tragedy: it springs not from "moral baseness," but from a "great error" (*Poetics* 1453a 15). His mistake was fatal in its consequences; Homer nowhere hints that it was a deviation from moral rectitude. As Homer tells the story, the Greek army, by its desertion of Achilles in the Quarrel, and by its neglect and disregard of the hero during the days that followed, merited its reverses, and Patroclus would not have lost his life if he had obeyed the command of his friend. The tragic desolation in the heart of Achilles after the death of Patroclus is due to his own interpretation of the facts. Like all noble natures, he forgets the shortcomings of others, and thinks only of what he believes to be his own.

This thought causes the utter *bouleversement* of his hopes and ambitions. Again and again in his words we hear the refrain,"Too late" [νῦν δέ]!—"Too late to keep my promise to Menoetius that Patroclus should return home [Σ 333]; too late to think of the possibility of returning home myself [Σ 88, Ψ 149-150]; or of anything but killing Hector [Σ 114] and of bringing sorrow on many Trojan women [Σ 121]; too late to care for the insult of Agamemnon [T 67], or for his gifts [T 148]; or even for food, till Hector is slain [T 203], —food, which Patroclus used to prepare quickly and deftly in the brief respites from fighting [T 315-321]; too late to spare the lives of Trojans [Φ 103], and too late to care about following up the victory and possibly capturing Ilios [X 391]." "Death is all I hope for (τεθναίην, Σ 98), but first I will meet the slayer of Patroclus" (Σ 114).

Yet this meeting with Hector, this vengeance which was the only remaining motive in life, has robbed Achilles, in the minds of many modern readers, of the honor and glory to which his brief life was devoted. Today the hero of the *Iliad* is "*immitis Achilles*," a very Berserk in his rage, oblivious of all claims of humanity in refusing Hector's plea for burial and Lycaon's for life; relapsing into savagery in outraging Hector's body and in slaying the twelve Trojan youths at the pyre of Patroclus, and winning no glory in overcoming Hector in combat, because of the "trickery of Athena."

The compassion for Hector which the poet clearly means to arouse in us from the beginning of Book XXII no doubt explains this interpretation of the interference of Athena. But there are many reasons against it. In Homer no mortal except Odysseus, and he only in the adventures which he himself describes, is allowed to achieve greatness without divine assistance. This is also the way of Aeschylus (*Pers.* 347). Furthermore, Athena's deception of Hector is only a requital for Apollo's more revolting part in the death of Patroclus. Athena always goes her opponent one better! In the Games, Apollo makes Diomede drop his whip; Athena breaks the axle of the chariot of Eumelus.[28] Again, Athena only brings to an end the impasse which the pursuit has reached;[29] she only induces Hector to face Achilles as he had originally resolved to do, and as he actually does because he thinks the combat will now be two against one. Finally, Athena's return of Achilles' spear to him influences the manner of Hector's death, but not the issue of the combat: if both heroes had continued the combat with swords, the issue could not have been changed. Athena's interference merely contributes to our compassion for Hector; it does not justify any diminution of our respect for Achilles.

The same pity for Hector has helped to give an interpretation of the poet's words which is unfavorable to Achilles. It is very generally held that the poet himself condemns Achilles of savage brutality in the treatment of Hector's body and in the slaughter of the twelve Trojan youths, by saying, "He [Achilles] devised evil [*or*, unseemly] deeds" (X 395, Ψ 24, 176). Modern scholars give too little weight to the fact that these adjectives (κακά, ἀεικέα) have both a subjective and an objective application: they may imply morally bad or outrageous conduct of the doer of the deed, or harm or insult to the victim.[30] Homer uses the terms in both ways, but far more frequently in the latter sense. I have given the evidence in full elsewhere.[31] Hence, since the poet is *philachilleus*, the passages in question cannot show that he holds his hero blameworthy, if he has justified such actions elsewhere in his poems. This, it appears, he has done. We give the evidence very summarily.

The Homeric poems show clearly[32] that it was the most solemn duty incumbent on a warrior not only to avenge the blood of a kinsman or friend by the death of the slayer and of others bound to him by the ties of blood or friendship, but also to outrage the bodies of these and to prevent their burial. This code of Heroic warfare Achilles follows in refusing the pleas of Lycaon and Hector, and in dragging the body of the latter. The death of Patroclus, the being who was dearer than father or son, gives Achilles the perfect right to push to extremes acts of vengeance which in his day had the sanction of piety. This right Homer makes clear by his accounts of the actions of other heroes.

Achilles is condemned for slaying Lycaon, half-brother of Hector, but a suppliant. Yet no one blames Odysseus for the death of the suppliant suitor, Leiodes, or Agamemnon for that of the two sons of Antimachus, also suppliants: Leiodes was one of those who plotted the death of Telemachus, and was slain in action where the code of war might be recognized. Antimachus had urged the death of Menelaus, brother of Agamemnon, and an envoy. There was more reason for sparing the life of the suppliant Adrastus, as Menelaus was ready to do; but when Agamemnon rebukes his brother, the poet approves (Z 62, αἴσιμα παρειπών), and the suppliant is slain. The words of Achilles to Lycaon (Φ 103-113) show that it is neither cruelty nor savagery, but duty to Patroclus, which denies his plea.

The modern reader is turned against Achilles for threatening to throw the body of Hector to the dogs instead of accepting Hector's proposal to give back for burial the body of the loser in the combat. But Homer shows by numerous passages that to expose to the dogs and vultures the body of one who had wronged a kinsman or friend was both a duty and an act of piety.[33] Even the gentle Menelaus, according to Nestor (γ 258-261), if he had found Aegisthus still alive on his return, would not have permitted his burial, "but the dogs and the birds of prey would have devoured him, lying on the ground far from the city." Most readers of the *Antigone* fail to see that Creon, in giving orders to treat the body of Polynices in exactly the same way, is justified according to the code of the time in which Creon lived. Sophocles, however, views Creon's decree with the eyes of a fifth-century Athenian. Bowra does the same in blaming Achilles. He says, moreover, that Hector, if victorious, would have given back the body of Achilles. Homer seems to deny this. Hector knew that Achilles had slain his half-brother, Polydorus (Υ 419); Patroclus slew Cebriones, another half-brother, and the poet tells us that Hector dragged the body of Patroclus that he might cut off the head (to fix it on the battlements, Iris says) and throw the body to the dogs. Hector, if true to his duty, could not have allowed the body of the enemy who slew Polydorus to be buried. Achilles knew of Hector's intention to throw his friend's body to the dogs. How then can he be lacking in "chivalry" in refusing Hector's request?

There remain the dragging of Hector's body and the slaughter of the twelve Trojan youths at the pyre of Patroclus. For both acts Homer is generally thought to condemn his hero by the comment, ἀεικέα μήδετο ἔργα, κακὰ δὲ φρεσὶ μήδετο ἔργα. But the very same comments are made when Achilles plans to give the body of Hector to the dogs (Ψ 24) and when he springs into the river to slay the unarmed Trojans who are trying to escape. We have seen that both these intentions were in accord with the code of war. It is therefore only fair to Homer and to Achilles to interpret the poet's comments as made to increase our sympathy with the victims. Certainly Odysseus does not condemn his slaughter of the Suitors when he says (χ 416),"Therefore they have met an unseemly death because of their outrageous conduct."[34] Nor is it possible that Homer is questioning the morality of the intention when he uses of Zeus the same phrase, κακὰ μήδετο (Η 478). In the days of the Trojan War the body of a vanquished foe belonged to the victor, to do with as he pleased. In the fighting over the body of Patroclus, Hippothous passed his baldric about the ankle of the body, and began to drag it away, "doing a service pleasing to Hector" (P 289-291). Hector, eager to throw the body to the Trojan dogs (P 272), would not have respected the body if he had succeeded in bringing it to the city. Andromache, foreboding the fate of Astyanax, says (Ω 734-737): "or some Achaean will seize thee by the arm and hurl thee from a tower, a cruel death, in anger because Hector had slain his brother or father or son." This act, which Andromache takes as probable vengeance for the death of a loved one, is far more savage than the dragging of the dead Hector, who had slain one far more beloved. The measure of the treatment of Hector's body is the measure of Achilles' love for Patroclus. But the poet uses it chiefly to move our pity for Hector and, above all, for Andromache.

Our revulsion against the slaughter of the twelve Trojan youths is natural, but the period rather than the hero should bear the brunt of it. We have seen that the code justified the killing of an unarmed suppliant enemy. If Achilles had slain the youths on the bank of the river, his justification would have been clear, because of the heat of battle. But we must remember that at the funeral the mind of Achilles is still as passionately smitten with grief as in the battle. Again the measure of his love is the measure of his action.

The passionateness of this love and the "error" of the hero, which was prompted by his high-souled ideal of conduct, explain the concluding scenes of the Wrath. After the funeral and the games, Achilles should have thrown the body of Hector to the dogs, as he promised the dead Patroclus. The genius of the poet provided a more tragic conclusion by a simple and natural invention: the anguish of Achilles persists with unallayed vehemence (Ω 3-13), even though all the last rites have been paid to the loved friend. It is this anguish which causes him to drag the body of Hector day after day, until, as in the pursuit of Hector, the action reaches an impasse, which requires the entrance of the *deus ex machina*. Homer gives no motive for this impasse other than the love for Patroclus (Ω 6-9). He does not analyze the feelings and impulses of his characters, but only makes them live and suffer, that we may suffer with them.

But there are hints of an added reason for the persistent dragging of Hector's body. Life for Achilles will soon end (Σ 96); even the days that remain are meaningless. Patroclus is dead, and Achilles, in his own generous judgment, has forfeited the claim to "honor" which was his guiding star. Achilles never forgets a duty, and never seeks an alibi, as Agamemnon does (T 86). Nothing happens to Achilles, as to Odysseus, because of neglect or untimely sleep. He says: "I failed to bring the light of deliverance to Patroclus." The inability to excuse one's own error makes the strong personality inclined to heap full vengeance upon the enemy who is also responsible for the hopeless situation. So Achilles, unable to forgive himself, vents his rage against himself upon the body of Hector. Again, as in his reply to Ajax, his defect, if he is judged by Homer, is not in the act itself, but in the extent to which it is carried. And again the excess comes from the fineness of his character. Achilles had done everything, except to give up his wrath while the stain upon his honor was still unremoved, to ensure the safety of Patroclus. The latter alone was to blame for his death. But the loftiness of Achilles' nature permits him to remember only his own shortcomings. The measure of his conception of heroic conduct was also the measure of his excess in carrying too far a course of action in itself altogether in keeping with the highest standards of manhood in the Heroic Age. His fatal error marks Homer as the first and one of the greatest tragic poets.

II

The completeness of the Homeric epics depends largely on use of the "episodic." The word ἐπεισόδιον originated in the terminology of the drama. From the time of Aristotle, in whose writings the word first occurs, it had two contradictory implications, both derived from the origin of tragedy. Dialogue, which was impossible without the entrance of an actor, disturbed the original lyric unity of the dithyramb. Hence an "episode" may mean an extraneous incident, introduced because of the personal desire of the author rather than because of the demands of his theme. But when the dialogue had grown to be the chief bearer of the tragic story, "episode" assumed an opposite meaning: it was now an integral chapter of the mythos. The word "episode" has therefore both a good and a bad connotation, the former when it meets the demands of the plot, the latter when it owes its presence rather to the author's personal purpose.

In Homeric criticism the word is used in both these senses. The Phaeacian episode is required by the plot; it is an act in the epic drama, and is described in the narrative form of action. The Boar Hunt, on the other hand, is ἔξω τοῦ μυθεύματος (Ar. *Poetics*, 1460a 29). The action pauses while the poet himself describes the origin of the telltale scar. To illustrate the completeness of the Homeric epics in the use of the episodes, and to determine whether Homer is "episodic" in the good or the bad sense, we shall select only one episode of each kind, the Catalogues and the Diomedeia.

Of episodes in which the action is suspended while the poet at some length describes matters outside of the action, there are seven in the two poems: in the *Odyssey*, the Gardens of Alcinous, the Boar Hunt, and the family history of Theoclymenus; in the *Iliad*, the later destruction of the Greek wall, and the Catalogues of Achaeans, Trojans, and Myrmidons. Each of these episodes shows one or more of the marks by which the poet differentiates the story of the action from his own comment or exposition.[35] (See above, Chap. V.)

With the origin and the historical or genealogical significance of the three Catalogues, important as these matters are, we are not concerned, but only with their function in the tale. In discussing this we shall use the Catalogue of Myrmidons only for illustration.

The Catalogues in Book II are as firmly anchored in place as is any other episode in the poem. Nestor bids Agamemnon draw up his forces "tribe by tribe" (vs. 363), and the commander himself refers to the vast numbers of his forces (vs. 120). Agamemnon further says that the Trojan allies, men from many cities (vs. 130), prevent him from taking the city; the Trojan Catalogue is chiefly of these allies. Book II must be rewritten if the Catalogues do not belong in it. Furthermore, Homer's interest in the names and the personalities of even the minor heroes precludes the possibility that he could have described the first advance to battle in the long war without at the same time giving a list of the leaders. This view is corroborated by the accounts of the five Trojan and the five Myrmidon contingents, both given before their advance.

Two chief objections to the authenticity of the Greek Catalogue are removed by careful attention to Homer's manner. It is held, first, that this catalogue was not composed for the *Iliad* because it seems to describe the rendezvous at Aulis. Now in the passage which introduces the Catalogue (B 484-493) the poet uses the first person: "I will not mention by name the common soldiers ... all who came to the siege of Ilios. But I will tell of the leaders and [the numbers of] all the ships." This shows that the Catalogue is an interposition by the poet himself. In such a digression, as we have seen, the poet is not bound to the time of the action. He may at will adopt the pluperfect or the future of this time, and he may also speak for his own day. The Catalogue in general, like most descriptions of minor characters, is in the "pluperfect." It describes the army as it "came to the siege of Ilios." Hence Pyraechmes, rather than Asteropaeus, his superior as a fighter, commands the Paeonians in the Trojan Catalogue (vs. 848): Asteropaeus arrived ten days before the last battle (Φ 155 f.). But other tenses are also used: the imperfect of the time of the action (vss. 526, 559, 568, 578-580, 587, 686-694, 699-709, 721-726); the future (the return of Achilles and Philoctetes to the fighting, and the death of two Trojan allies "in the river," 694, 724 f., 860 f., 874 f.), and the present of the poet's own day (547-551, the festival at Athens in honor of Erechtheus).

A second objection, that many heroes, mentioned in both lists, take no part in the subsequent action, is removed by noticing the fondness of the poet for new names in the episodes and various lists of heroes. Homer, as we have seen, loves to personalize the combatants.[36] He is rarely (only five times) content with giving merely the number of men slain by a hero.[37] These are in groups of 12, 20, or 27. Against these should be placed the list of names of warriors slain in groups of from six to nine by both Greek and Trojan leaders.[38] In the *Nibelungenlied* only the chief characters are named; for the other knights and ladies the poet is content with "many," or with the arithmetical count. By this means he makes a background of human integers, like the mob in a play, against which the chief actors stand out in high perspective. But this tends to remove the hearer from reality, and to give him an impression rather than an experience of the past. Homer, on the other hand, prefers a definite group of named characters, more or less familiar, and no others. There is but a single exception to this rule: only five Trojans are named of the many who protected the wounded Hector (Ξ 425-427). Otherwise Homer introduces to us by name, at least, every member of a group. No divinities descend to the plain in the Theomachy except those who are named. We know by name all the seven Trojan elders on the Tower (Γ 146-148), the nine volunteers for the combat with Hector (H 161 ff.), the seven leaders of the watch (I 81-84), the five Trojans with Asius in his attack on the wall (M 139 f.), the seven Greek leaders addressed by Poseidon in his epipolesis (N 91-93), the nine Trojan heroes who accompanied

Hector and Paris into the thick of the fight (N 790-792), the ten leaders of the allies addressed by Hector after he had donned the armor of Patroclus (P 215 ff.), and the nine sons of Priam whom the old king wrathfully commanded to make ready the wagon (Ω 249-252). These lists and other uses of names in the *Iliad* have a distinct bearing on the second objection to the authenticity of the Greek Catalogue. We find that, when the situation permits, Homer likes to combine the names of his chief heroes with those of second and of minor rank, *and that he is prone to add new names*. Priam mentions among his slain sons, besides Hector, none of the dozen whom we know have fallen, but Mestor and Troilus—new names.[39] Names are easy to invent, and the poet is not averse to the use of the same name for two or more minor characters.[40] Antiphus is the name of a leader in both Catalogues (vss. 678, 864). Three of the leaders of the five Myrmidon contingents are not elsewhere mentioned, but two of the names, Menesthius and Pisander, are given to other heroes. A large number of the 189 names of slain Trojans must have been invented. Before the awakening of the historical sense such invention was a matter of course. The tradition of the bards doubtless supplied many names, but Homer cannot have relied on tradition for all the names and for the brief biographies of minor enemy heroes.[41] When Priam upbraids his sons (Ω 249), another poet would have been content with the four familiar names, Helenus, Paris, Polites, Deiphobus. Homer, however, adds five more, four of them new. Among the seven Trojan elders the name Ucalegon does not occur again, nor that of Deisenor, one of the ten leaders of the allies addressed by Hector (P 217). There are about 1000 different proper names in the *Iliad*, including variants of the same name; more than one-half of these occur but once (543 in 973; count of Allen's index to his edition of the poem). This feature of the poet's manner satisfactorily explains why ten of the 47 Greek leaders, and ten of the 27 Trojans, all allies, do not appear again.

The two Catalogues aim at geographical completeness rather than that of personnel; in fact, the center of interest is geography. Of the ten Greek leaders not mentioned again, six belong to contingents which take no part in the fighting; three are, respectively, the second of a pair of insignificant minor heroes, and only Philoctetes, who has no part in the story, is a well-known character. On the other hand, we find no mention of important characters like Antilochus, Patroclus, and Teucer. A *Bearbeiter* who revised the Diapeira so that the Catalogues naturally follow could have changed the latter as easily into greater conformity with the rest of the poem.

These considerations lead to the conclusion that the most knowably authentic source of the Catalogues is the *Iliad* itself. That the poet of the *Iliad* at some point in the completion of the poem composed the Catalogues is a theory which is open to the fewest objections and requires the least use of hypothesis. And the poetic purpose of the Catalogues was clearly to satisfy the demands of the situation, and at the same time to present an excursus interesting for its own sake.[42]

The importance of the Boeotians,[43] at the beginning of the Greek Catalogue, is quite according to the Homeric way of describing new and insignificant heroes with greater fullness than the chief characters. But the Boeotians perform a function which is essential. The poet has already given the hearer the impression of a vast Greek army. We cannot suppose that the hearer was interested in the sum total, any more than that he used a map to find the places, or a plan of the Greek ships. In the *Odyssey* the poet has no conception of the impossibility of keeping together in a storm a fleet of twelve ships. In the *Iliad* his ignorance of the meaning of an army of 100,000 is evident. His audience, too, had not yet developed an interest in arithmetical facts. Large numbers to them meant nothing more than "many," "very many."[44] Hence the object of the poet is to deepen the impression of the enormous size of the Greek fleet and army. This he does at the outset. The Boeotians had five leaders; the soldiers came from twenty-nine towns; and each of the ships carried one hundred and twenty men. These numbers are not equaled by any other contingent, although many of the chief heroes furnish a greater number of ships. The poet has thus succeeded in his purpose: he can now introduce many other kinds of entertaining matters. (1) A superlative is applied to three mediocre characters— to Nireus in beauty, to the lesser Ajax in spearmanship, and to Menestheus in the marshaling of chariots. So the Abantes, who do not take part in the fighting except as their leader is slain (Δ 464), are praised for their warlike character. (2) Histories of legendary figures, Thamyris, Erechtheus, Tlepolemus, add interest to three contingents. (3) Three times leaders are taken from famous legends— the Calydonian Boar Hunt, the Lapiths and Centaurs, the Argonauts. (4) Three times the position of the troops in the marshaling is described—the Phocians, and the soldiers of Ajax and of Menelaus. (5) Three incidents are mentioned which occurred before the Wrath—the taking of Lyrnessus, the death of Protesilaus, and the abandonment of Philoctetes on Lemnos. (6) Famous or divine ancestry is mentioned repeatedly. The Orchomenian leaders are sons of Ares, and their begetting is described, as is that of Eudorus in the Myrmidon Catalogue (Π 179-186). Polypoetes is a grandson of Zeus; Machaon and Podaleirius, sons of Asclepius; and Tlepolemus, Pheidippus, and Antiphus (the last mentioned only here), sons of Heracles. In all these varied ways, familiar to the hearer of other parts of the poem, the Greek Catalogue is presented as if told for the pleasure of the audience.

The Trojan Catalogue is of far less poetic importance. It concerns the enemy, and particularly his allies, and it follows the more splendid description of the Greeks, when the attention is fatigued. Hence it is as brief as possible. It seems to have been planned as a two- or three-verse description of each contingent. Where it oversteps this form, with a single exception, the additional verses are found in the body of the poem.[45] This Catalogue is "owed to the story," but it is not Homeric poetry at its best. It seems clearly to have been left incomplete: the mention of Sarpedon and Glaucus seems more like the skeleton of a description than finished poetry, and at the end there is a cruder break in the narrative than perhaps elsewhere in Homer. A *Bearbeiter* who so carefully prepared for this Catalogue by the scene in which Iris appears to Priam, would hardly have scanted his work at the end. In the work of a writer of the fifth century the verdict would be, "Unfinished."

Whatever one may think of the origin of the two Catalogues, the Greek portion is Homeric poetry at its best. No one will disagree with the words of Dionysius of Halicarnassus on the beauty of the description of cities in the Boeotian section, or elsewhere. There are well-walled cities on a rock, or amid the hills, or looking down on a plain, or in a meadow; towns famous for their grapes or pigeons, or their sheep along the rivers or, like Donaueschingen, at their source; towns at the foot of a mountain or by a famous lake; towns noted for their wealth or their great Cyclopean walls, for the charm of their setting or for their wildflowers; famous for great kings, groves of gods, tombs of heroes, festivals; on crags, or a rocky shore, or by the sea, and towns near a tree-clad hill, in a quiet valley, or in the cold north—the first poetic geography. We owe to the Catalogues the handsome weakling Nireus and the dandy Amphimachus; without them we should not have had Pindar's Seventh Olympian or our knowledge of Thamyris. Later generations found in them historical documents of unchallenged authenticity, but to Homer's own audiences they must have been rather an apt and welcome introduction to the first battle.

III

The Diomedeia is "episodic" in the other sense. It is an act of the epic drama. Aside from its own intrinsic interest, it makes several important contributions to the development of the plot.

First, it provides a Greek victory at the beginning of the fighting. In two of the four battles, the second and third, the Trojans are victorious, in fulfillment of the plan of Zeus. In the fourth, the return of Achilles eclipses all the other heroes. Only the first battle is left for the outright success of the Greeks with the other leaders playing important parts. Logic requires this outcome of the first battle. The Greeks are superior in numbers and in discipline, and the Trojans have broken a solemn truce. The national feeling of the audience demands a Greek victory. The Diomedeia creates the impression that the Trojans are no match for the Greeks, even without Achilles, until Zeus "gives glory to Hector." Thus a large number of national heroes are presented under favorable circumstances.

Again, the first day of battle permits the introduction of most of the characters who appear in the sequel. How well the poet develops his pieces in the account of this day a few figures will show.

The battle itself is described in about 1100 verses (Δ 446-Z 72, with a short extension, H 1-16); it is introduced by the Epipolesis (Δ 223-445). The fighting is continuous, except for three brief Olympian scenes and Hector's visit to Troy. Of the eighteen Olympians of the *Iliad*, we miss only Poseidon, Themis, Charis, and Hermes (Hephaestus is mentioned; he appeared in A). The Catalogue names twenty-four Greek leaders who take part in at least two of the later episodes. Of these, only five, besides Achilles, take no part in the first battle: Amphimachus, Ascalaphus, Polypoetes, Leonteus, and Peneleos, all minor heroes. Machaon and Menestheus are introduced just before the battle begins, and two important heroes, Antilochus and Teucer, make their entry. The fifty Trojans are chiefly victims of Greek prowess. Helenus and Glaucus enter early in Z. Of important Trojans only Cebriones, Polydamas, and Deiphobus are reserved for later entrance. Altogether, before the end of the first battle, we have met the key personages, except Patroclus, and the greater number of secondary characters whose importance is not confined to a single episode.

The hero of the episode is the key to its function in the economy of the *Iliad*. Achilles has done "the most" of the previous fighting. In his absence Diomede is his surrogate, an invincible champion providing a central figure of interest up to the point where the plan of Zeus is matured, Patroclus is about to receive the cue for his entrance, and the Wrath portends its tragic meaning.

Diomede is never called, as Ajax is, "second to Achilles"; in a certain sense he is his rival. He is not of divine parentage, but as the greatest of the Epigonoi he represents the prime of manhood in the other great war of Greek legend. Ajax is said to be the equal of Achilles in fighting with the spear at close quarters (N 324 f.), but Diomede outpoints him in the contest of spears, just as he wins the chariot race, which Achilles would have won if he had contested. Diomede never rebukes Agamemnon for his treatment of Achilles. Unlike Ajax (H 228), he speaks somewhat coolly of Achilles, and is ready to face the victorious Trojans without him. Ajax, once at least, seems to fear Hector (H 194 f.); Diomede fears no one. He is the last to retire, and when the Greeks rally, the first to advance (Θ 253 ff.). When Nestor is in danger and Diomede calls on Odysseus for help, the latter continues to retreat (Θ 90 ff.); but when Hector is working havoc and Odysseus bids Diomede to stand by, the latter replies, "Of course I will—but Zeus wills victory to the Trojans" (Λ 317-319). Diomede is the equal of Achilles in readiness to meet any situation. Three times, although he is the youngest member of the council—he is about the age of Antilochus—he proposes a plan of action which is followed (H 399, I 696, Ξ 128). Finally, Diomede is, in the absence of Achilles, the foe most dreaded by the Trojans and Hector (Z 96, 277, 306, Θ 532).

The rôle in which Diomede is cast explains his absence from the action until the end of the Epipolesis.[46] He could not have acted in character either at the Quarrel or in the rush to the ships. Helen does not name him to Priam, because, like Patroclus, he gains in interest as a new character, suitably introduced at the beginning of his rôle. His cue is most appropriate—an insult by Agamemnon. This insult has no tragic result, because Diomede is only a surrogate. He has no single overpowering purpose, like Achilles, but only a duty, which he rarely mentions but always performs. To many he is the favorite hero of the *Iliad*, as he was to Wilamowitz. As a personality, rather than as a traditional hero, he is one of Homer's greatest creations; an altogether lovable and admirable ideal of heroic youth. But he has no tragic value: he merely holds the center of the stage while the hero is absent. Hence it is natural that he all but disappears from later tradition.

In the first battle, Hector, as we have seen, is a mute, and a subordinate actor. Aeneas and Sarpedon play more prominent parts, the former contributing to the glory of Diomede, the latter winning the only single combat for the Trojans in the *Iliad*. This mighty son of Zeus, together with his kinsman Glaucus, is used by the poet to place Hector in due perspective as the instrument of Zeus. Sarpedon is superior to Hector as a fighter, except when Zeus throws his weight on the latter's side, and in character. He is never guilty of discourtesy, much less of fear and the resulting unworthy act. He is portrayed with more sympathy than Aeneas. We know not only his ancestry, but also that he has a wife and infant son, and we learn the inherited tendency to melancholy which marks both him and his kinsman Glaucus. More than any of the other heroes except Achilles, the two Lycian princes fight for honor, and, with the same exception, no heroes on either side are portrayed in a more admirable light. They are models of the heroic virtues, from which their conduct shows no lapse. The poet's purpose seems indeed to make clear by contrast the human weaknesses of Hector, but that leaders of the enemy should be thus ennobled is strange in a poem so national in its tendency. The Glaucus-Diomede incident makes this portrayal altogether reasonable.

The old objections to the organic function of this episode (Z 119-236) vanish on careful examination of the context. Diomede's ability to recognize a divinity naturally is not permanent. With the retirement of all the gods from the field (Z 1) it would cease. When Hector rallies the Trojans, before he leaves the field for the city, the Greeks retreated: "They said that some immortal had come down from the starry heavens to aid the Trojans" (Z 108 f.). Naturally then, when Glaucus steps out from the ranks and challenges Diomede, the latter asks him whether he is a god. But the poet has been still more careful in making Glaucus unknown to Diomede. When Sarpedon is wounded in the thigh by Tlepolemus, it is not Glaucus, but "doughty Pelagon, who was his dear comrade," who pulls out the spear (E 695). Pelagon does not appear again; he is one of the few minor heroes of the enemy who is named only to be slain. By introducing Pelagon the poet avoids mention of Glaucus. When the latter confronts Diomede, the hearer has not yet seen him in the action. It therefore seems reasonable that Diomede, too, has not seen him.

The introduction of the genealogy of the two Lycian princes is commonly assigned to the poet's desire to compliment some Asiatic Greek family of his time. A better justification is found at the end of the speech of Glaucus: "My father earnestly charged me . . . to bring no shame on the race of my fathers, who were preëminent *both in Ephyra and in broad Lycia*" (Z 207-210). Glaucus and Sarpedon are Greeks by descent. Their prowess and unstained fame reflect glory on the Greek race.

The Diomedeia makes us acquainted with the heroes who captured Troy. More than any other episode it typifies the course of the Trojan War. It also prepares for the first of the three major peripeteias of the plot, the change from success to failure for the Greek forces, caused by the plan of Zeus. Finally, it is the most interesting of the four battles, if judged purely as an account of heroic fighting, and without regard to the plot. Thus it well illustrates Homer's use of the episode.

The criticism of the last century has left the impression, especially on students of literature other than Greek, that the *Iliad* is made up of episodes loosely linked together. But the careful reader finds, as Aristotle did, that this is not so. The episodes are not like beads strung on a thread. They are new figures woven into the larger pattern of the poem. These figures contain novel incidents, and usually one or two new characters, each with a speaking part. Most of these linger in the memory of the reader: Calchas, Thersites, Pandarus, Phoenix, Dolon, Euphorbus, the Sleep God, the horse Xanthus, the river Scamander, and the Olympians, Dione, Themis, Charis, and Hermes. But the familiar characters of the poem outnumber the new, and make each succeeding incident contribute to the progress of the plot towards its inevitable issue.[47]

IV

The function of the episode as an act in the epic drama and as independently interesting is seen also in the Olympic scenes of the *Iliad*. Historically considered, divine interference in all the affairs of life is as natural in Homer as in the Old Testament. Yet, as both the Embassy and the Cyclops episode prove, it is not essential in the Homeric narrative. Hence the poetic use of the gods is our chief interest.

Divinity in Homer is the poet's *raisonneur* in the presentation of a succession of situations, necessary for the development of the theme, in which the heroes work out their own destiny. When the poet takes us to Olympus, he gives us a "god's-eye" view of the ensuing action which makes the account of that action both clearer and more convincing."And God said, 'Let there be light': and there was light." Polites could have announced the approach of the Greek army as well as Iris, but when the divinity bids Hector array his forces, we know that he will instantly obey her. Odysseus of his own accord might have checked the rush to the ships: he accomplishes this without aid from Athena. But the latter's command to him assures us of his success. Achilles, as Nilsson has pointed out,[48] could not decide to kill Agamemnon. Athena's words convince us that his decision is right, and point to ultimate reconciliation."The gods know all things"—within limitations—and the listener shares in their knowledge. For a popular oral narrative this was quite an advantage, as Euripides was later to prove.

The gods also simplify the problem of causality in the succession of events. Life loses much of its complexity when the hand of God is seen in all the details of existence. The rapidity of Homer's action is often due to a shorthand use of Olympian intervention. Achilles calls the assembly when the plague rages, and Penelope decides to hold the contest

of the bow, because a goddess put it into their hearts. This
phrase, if translated into psychological terms, would fill
several pages. The plague in a modern version of the Wrath
would be caused biologically, but the ancients were con-
tent with spiritual bacteria, and Homer's account in its
concise poetic power is poetically complete. The frequent
use of divine interference when the action has reached an
impasse is the basis of the critic's definition of the proper
employment of the later god of the machine. Yet if one
tries to part Odysseus from Calypso without the aid of
Hermes, he will see clearly how much the Olympians con-
tribute to the rapidity and the continuity with which the
poet's action moves.

In thus personalizing the causes of the external world lies
the essence of all our greatest poetry, for it unites man with
that world by humanizing nature. But Homer does more
than this. He uses the Olympians as foils for mortals in the
Human Life Writ Large. The Olympic scenes of the *Iliad*
present the unlovely side of human nature which would
mar the picture of the ideal heroic man, with a fidelity
sought, but not achieved, by the Alexandrian mime.

The Olympians of the *Iliad* are masterpieces of poetic
conception, and at the same time have offered the greatest
paradox which the poems present. The poet's sources and
his own theology concern us little. It is sufficient to note
that his own expressions and those of his characters reveal
a devout religious attitude, with no trace of skepticism.

One of the most recent of the many attempts to explain
the paradox[49] makes of the gods in the *Iliad* burlesque and
comic figures: the poet speaks with his tongue in his cheek,
not seriously, much less, satirically; and his purpose is to
lighten the account of the sanguinary struggle on earth,
much as Shakespeare did with Falstaff, and, by contrast, to
make more real the historical actuality of the heroes. The
most serious objection to the gods as burlesque and comic

characters is the fallacy which this view involves. The colossal sound of Ares' fall, and his colossal appearance to Diomede as he rises to Olympus may be comic to us who are not "cradled in a creed outworn." To the Homeric Greek listener it could not have been more so than the shaking of Olympus at the nod of Zeus—which is felt as sublime even today—or of Ida and the Trojan plain at the onset of the gods (Υ 56-66). The poet exaggerates to deepen the impression of divine power.[50] Again, the humorous intent is clear in the comic treatment of divine themes by the *esprit gaulois* and in the early mystery plays in England; but the Olympic scenes of the *Iliad* are all concerned with a very serious purpose, the carrying out or the blocking of the plan of Zeus. The tale of the Loves of Ares and Aphrodite vouches for nothing more than that, as we are aware, the Greeks felt no scruple at the ludicrous presentation of their divinities. Demodocus sings this song before the Phaeacian populace, which includes, as Nausicaa has informed Odysseus, "lewd fellows of the baser sort." We may agree with Paul Friedländer[51] that Homer's gods may laugh at one another with no sacrifice of their godhead, and that when they laugh, we laugh with them: it does not follow that Homer's listener laughed *at* them because he knew they were only burlesques.

The *Iliad* contains a hint of another possible reason for the disorderly life—the life οὐ κατὰ κόσμον—on Olympus. In two speeches of his Lycian heroes is found the nearest approach to Homer's philosophy of the heroic life. Glaucus marks the brevity of a great family's fortune: after a short season of verdure its flourishing is over (Ζ 146-149). Sarpedon later draws the lesson: "Glaucus, to what end are you and I honored above all others in Lycia . . . if it is not that they may hear of our fame as single champions? Dear fellow, if we could expect no old age and no death, I would not battle in the forefront, nor would I send you into the fight. But death lurks on every side; no mortal can escape it. So on! To glory or to death!" Achilles, the poet's hero, wins glory by death. The heroic motive is not only *noblesse oblige*; it is equally *la mort oblige*. The only immortality to be won is an undying fair fame. This gives purpose, meaning, and value to the hero's living.

The gods are deathless; they live at ease, for unending existence—without the "inner check" which man has developed for himself—has little motive except the ever-present. On Olympus, life had meaning when Zeus was establishing control over the other gods and his own family, and a lesser meaning when Zeus's great son, Heracles, lived. In the *Iliad* it would have been meaningless but for the War, in which the Olympian family had become bitterly involved. When the War was over there was nothing left but immortality, without motive or meaning, of which the blasé Zeus in the opening scene of the *Odyssey* is the type and symbol. In Homer the Olympians are not spirit, but "power."[52] To mortals they must have seemed as the Grownups of Kipling and Kenneth Graham seem to children: to be respected but not understood, because their code was entirely different. Theology in heroic tradition lagged behind Homer's own ethics. If we may infer his ethical philosophy from the words of Sarpedon, it is something like this: Purpose and meaning give to human existence its supreme value; this value is possible only in the life that confronts obstacles, including insuperable death, and in meeting all obstacles this value is secured only by unfailing response to the heroic "inner check." Homer is thus the first great Humanist.

"Gods are immortal men." How immortality in Homer the Humanist robs life of the spur to decorous living is best illustrated by his portrait of Hera.

In the *Iliad*, poem of passions, Hera is the most passionate Olympian. With a single exception, her actions and words spring from a single passion, hatred. This hatred is directed, not against Paris, but against the Trojans: it is Priam and his sons and the rest of the Trojans whom she would fain "eat raw" (Δ 35). No hero prays to her, naturally, for she will sacrifice everything to her hatred. She offers the destructions of the three cities most dear to her, if by this means she may see Troy fall (Δ 51-54). Nor can she be trusted in smaller matters. The Sleep God exacts from her the most solemn oath known to Olympians before he will accept her offer of one of the Graces in return for lulling Zeus to sleep. Hera's hatred appears in perhaps its worst light—at least to modern readers—in the Tricking of Zeus. As she looks off from Olympus, the sight of Poseidon, busily helping the Greeks, gladdens her heart. Then her glance turns toward Mount Ida, and falls on Zeus, "and he was to her a hateful object" (στυγερός, Ξ 158). The last words of Zeus to her were, "I reck not of thy hatred, for thou art a creature devoid of shame." Hera now proves that her hatred is to be dreaded most because she can feel no shame. She makes the most magnificent toilet described by Homer, sweetly beguiles Aphrodite by a cock-and-bull story to lend her the magic girdle of irresistible charm. Then she presents herself to Zeus in such fashion as many great scholars as late as 1932[53] believed was derived from the sacred ritual—which we do not know was as old as Homer —of the Sacred Marriage, but which, both in intent and in manner, is that of the Dalilah more than of the bride.

Hera's hatred has transformed her into a vixen, the first scold in literature. The first words of Zeus to Thetis reveal his dread of her temper (A 518-523), and her first words after he enters the hall prove his fear well grounded. Scarcely waiting for him to take his seat, she bursts out, disdaining to use name or title, which Homeric courtesy demanded in the first words to an equal (the tone demands a colloquial rendering): "What god have you been scheming with *this time*, you sneak (δολομῆτα)! You always do things behind my back. You never have the heart to tell me any of your plans." These are the words, not of a queen of heaven inspired with a lofty and just hatred of a foe, but of a nagging wife. Hera not only knows the answer to her question, but proves the evil intent of her words by her next speech. When Zeus reproves her for prying, she replies, "I never do; you always tell me, quite of your own free will, whatever you choose to tell me." The poet's intention is clearly to depict a scolding wife, stirring up a family squabble— Hephaestus calls it a "brawl," a word used elsewhere only of "brawling" Thersites. In succeeding Olympic scenes we are not allowed to forget the shrewish temper of the Queen of Heaven. Zeus says it is chronic: "She habitually defies my every command" (Θ 407 f.); "I can do nothing with her" (E 893). When for the only time in the *Iliad* she is impotent with fright at his awful scowl and his stern threat, she vents her rage on the rest of the Olympian family (O 90-112). Themis asks her, "Has Zeus been threatening you?" Hera replies: "Don't ask me; you know yourself what a temper he has. Go on with the dinner, and I will tell the family the bad news for them. I fancy it will not please someone who is now enjoying his food." She invents some general remarks, and concludes, "So you had better each accept the evil he sends you—Ares, for example, whose son, Ascalaphus, has just been slain." After all these exhibitions of her sweet amiableness we are ready to say with Artemis that Hera is the cause of all the strife and quarreling in Heaven (Φ 513)—a remark with which the Theomachy appropriately closes!

As a study in psychology Homer's Hera is a masterpiece. Incidentally, Homer describes Hera's facial expression more picturesquely than that of any of his other female characters (O 101 f.): "A gloom fell on the Olympians. Hera laughed, but only with her lips; there was no mirth upon her forehead, above her jet-black eyebrows." This picture never inspired a Greek artist. When Zeus with a nod of his immortal head made Olympus tremble, the effect was sublime and Pheidias translated this sublimity into the greatest sculpture of an era. Olympus trembled again when Hera shook with rage at Hector's confident boast, but this Hera did not inspire the Argive Hera of Polyclitus.

CHAPTER EIGHT

THE POET AS REALIST AND AS IDEALIST

In works of the imagination "realism" is the scientific content and attitude. Pure *poiesis* beholds a vision of the mind beyond the reality of its material. In the early epic, too, the material itself was unreal. The past exists in the mind only as an idea. The epic memory views this past as one surveys a great city from a distant point of vantage. Its slums and sewers, the intimate human intercourse in its shops and dwellings, the small tragedies and comedies of its life, are little noticed. The attention is occupied rather with contours and skyline, great buildings and parks, the significant, and, above all, the beautiful. The idealist enjoys the impressions of the distant καλόν; the realist enters the city and, studying it at close range, finds also the αἰσχρόν. He differs from the idealist in his total disregard for values. Realism is thus the scientific approach in literature, as idealism is the poetic. The Alexandrian critics recognized this difference by their terms ἡρωικῶς and βιωτικῶς. Their conclusion that the *Odyssey* was closer to reality in its picture of life has been used as an argument by modern chorizonts. The truth seems to be that (1) the theme of the *Iliad* requires a more idealistic treatment; (2) in the two poems there are compensations—in certain respects the *Iliad* is more "realistic" than the *Odyssey*, in certain others the *Odyssey* is more "idealistic" than the *Iliad*; (3) qualitatively, the same kind of "realism" marks both poems.

The *Iliad* deals with matters farther removed from common human experience. War and passion are not so close to life as are peace, common sense, and the use of one's wits. Armies and heroes by the hundreds permit less realism than single families and isolated palaces and settlements. The canvases are too large for much detail: an emotional impression of these extended scenes is more in order than minute description. The national scope of the *Iliad* gives more frequent occasion for myth and legend of the remoter past than is offered in its sequel, where the past is limited to the nine or ten years since the War. On the other hand, as if to compensate for this predominance of the ideal, the *Iliad* shows a greater attention to facts which are a part of the hearer's life. The more abundant similes relate the ideal and the "heroic" to the real experience and knowledge of the audience. So do the scenes on the shield of Achilles, and the geography of the Catalogues, with its frequent use of the present tense. Even the later obliteration of the Greek wall (M 10-34) is more factual than the probable fate of the Phaeacians.[1] In a similar way the *Odyssey* offers features far less real than any in the *Iliad*. Ithaca itself lies "farthest towards the darkening west," the home of mystery. The unknown lands and seas of the Apologue were farther from reality to the Homeric audience than Troy and Olympus and Ida. Monsters and witches, and even the faery Phaeacians, were not so real as the Olympians, for the latter were parts of a living religion.

But while the isolated and less crowded scenes of the *Odyssey* permit—and require—a more realistic treatment, the kind of realism is the same in both poems. At the steading of Eumaeus the hogs squeal and grunt as they get ready for the night; on the Trojan plain the horses stand by their chariots, champing the white barley and spelt. In realistic description there is little to choose between the evening meals in the quarters of Achilles (I 205-221) and in the hut of Eumaeus (ξ 418-453). If the latter is slightly more detailed, the *Iliad* has the advantage in the two incidents of the "stirrup cup" (Ω 281-321, ο 147-181). It is the importance of the incident that determines the closeness of its approach to reality. Ethos often determines this. The child

---
[1] Superior figures refer to notes which will be found on p. 257.

Eurymachus sitting at dinner in the lap of Odysseus (π 443 f.) is not so near to life as is the infant Achilles on the knees of Phoenix, drinking from his wine cup, and drenching his tunic as he chokes in his childish helplessness. The "silly look" of Thersites, and the farmhand kick which Melanthius gives Odysseus, passing him at the Ithacan fountain, are both βιωτικά. Thersites is "unknown," since he appears only here; according to the rule of Aristotle (*Rhetoric* III, 16, 3), he must be described; the goatherd will become familiar in the sequel. This principle determines the realistic presentation of the two old kings, Priam and Laertes. Laertes appears in a single episode, and both his garb and his occupation are unkingly: wearing a dirty smock, patched and old, with shin guards of leather, and gloves, because of the briars, and a goatskin cap, he hoes his vineyard. Priam likewise is weighed down by old age: he is but a step from the end of his days (ἐπὶ γήραος οὐδῷ). He is like the cicada, *vox et praeterea nihil*. (See above, pp. 79–80.)

This realism is commonly dismissed with the epithets, "naïve," "primitive"—terms which neither explain nor evaluate, even if they are correctly applied. A narrative and manner marked by
Order, high discourse,
And decency, than which is life less dear,

is hardly primitive; it must be due to the most highly developed taste of an era. The *Nibelungenlied* is far less savage, and includes far less that is revolting, than the Volsung Saga. If this is typical of literary evolution—as Brunetière gives reason for believing,[2]—poetry after Homer showed a tendency to retrogress towards the primitive. Gresham's Law applies to literature as to economics. The public that has tasted the αἰσχρόν, like the man in Plato's *Republic* who has once eaten human flesh, becomes, if not wolfish, at least more animal in his aesthetic likings. The Laestrygonian queen fills the comrades with loathing, but Homer omits the nauseating specifications in which Swift delights. The absence of all revolting details of the plague—which Homer must have known at least by hearsay—is illuminating when compared with the scientific realism of Thucydides and with Sophocles' almost surgical description of the festering foot of Philoctetes. Sophocles permits the spurting lifeblood of Haemon to mar the whiteness of Antigone's dead face. This is not Homerically "primitive," but far less so than a Victorian version of the "heroic" slaying of a knight at the feet of his ladylove:

>   she saw him bend
> Back Robert's head, she saw him send
> The thin steel down; the blow told well,
> Right backward the knight Robert fell,
> And moaned as dogs do, being half dead,
> Unwitting, as I deem: so then
> Godmar turned grinning to his men,
> Who ran, some five or six, and beat
> His head to pieces at their feet.[3]

In Homer neither Andromache nor Hecuba sees the slaying of Hector; Penelope does not enter the great hall that has reeked with the Suitors' blood, until all signs of the carnage have been obliterated. Homer describes no cruelty for its own sake. The death of Melanthius is due punishment of a false slave in an age that knew no humanitarianism. There is no instance of prolonged physical torture in the Homeric poems. In battle the outraging of the body of an enemy does not begin till life is extinct. This failed to satisfy the less "primitive" taste of later times: in the later version Achilles dragged the living Hector.

In the action of the poems there is no matricide, parricide, fratricide, or suicide; no friend kills, or plots to kill, a comrade; no woman is ravished. These deeds occur in real life, as Homer knew. But in his picture of Human Life Writ Large they have no place. He refuses to portray the brutally animal in man. The word "primitive," therefore, may label his representation of life; it does not describe it.

"Naïve" is nearer the truth. To the child the outer world is inseparable from life. Its value is not in itself, but in its contribution to the reality of living. This value disappears when nature and fact assume an independent significance, and still more so when they are measured and their parts are related to each other by a norm which the reason abstracts from life. Homer does not count the arrows which Odysseus pours out before him on the threshold.[4] He does not even say that 116 men opposed 4 in the Slaughter; he says $52+6+24+20+12+2$. The listener would hardly have computed the sum, for numerical figures are important historically, not poetically. In seeing in the external only its emotional import in the life which he pictures, Homer reveals the child's mind. But Homer uses this kind of realism with a disciplined restraint which is far from naïve. He always keeps duly subordinate the external appearance and the setting of the larger human life which is his theme. The hundreds of human actors in the two poems are distinguished at least by names. But although Homer knew many kinds of wine (Δ 259, Λ 639, β 350) and bread (δ 56), only "bread" and "wine" are served at any Homeric dinner, whether the host is Alcinous or the Swineherd. The poet refrains from particularizing things almost as much as from generalizing human beings.

The degree of the approach to the particular in Homer depends on the poetic demands of the situation. The garb of Thersites would have had much interest for the antiquarian, but Homer mentions rather his misshapen form. The posset in Nestor's quarters, the libation of Achilles, and the harnessing of Priam's horses receive unusual attention partly because they occur in the opening scenes of momentous incidents: ἀρχὴ ἥμισυ πάντων. Usually, however, the poet is content with a single external detail which vouches for the reality of the whole: *Ab uno disce omnia.* The rim of Hector's shield knocks against his neck and ankles as he strides from the field. Later, as he enters the home of Paris, in his hand is an 11-cubit spear,[5] with its gleaming point and its ring of gold. Still later, Astyanax shrieks with terror at the sight of Hector's plumed helmet. By focusing the mind's eye on a single feature, generalized so that the experience instantly recognizes it as familiar, the object acquired a reality which was felt rather than analyzed. A similar realism is seen in the standing epithets of the sea or the ship: one familiar aspect creates the convincing impression of all the others. But the one feature is made distinct: Hector's shield has a rim of leather that runs all around its edge; his spear has a ring of gold; it is the plume nodding above the helmet which frightens Astyanax.

Homer's realism is thus less naïve than poetic. It calls upon the experience only to accept unquestionably the created picture of life. It never diverts attention from that life to an analysis or weighing of its reality. Even Homer's view of nature is more poetic than naïve. The sun, never wearied, giving delight to mortals, which *goes down*, belongs to the texture of human life, from which science's description is utterly dissevered. The scientific vision is schizopic, separating truth both from beauty and from experienced life. When Homer, like Heraclitus, "wrote the story of nature, dipping his pen into his mind," he was unaware of this dualism. Nature and man were poetically one. His men and women are real and move in a world of reality, which extends as far as the piece of leather from which Eumaeus is cutting a sandal, the salt with which Patroclus seasons the roast, and the Phaeacian servant's words, "Your bed is ready, Sir." But the mind into which Homer "dipped his pen" saw as clearly as if they were real a more beautiful world and greater men and women, which, because they have been absent from the experience of most of us, we call ideal.

THE POET: REALIST AND IDEALIST 233

This ideal life, the life lived heroically, imparts a tragic quality to Homer's poetry, for tragedy is "the representation of actions and life" which command deep interest and respect (σπουδαῖοι). Aristotle points out the most important differentia between Homer and Attic tragedy. The significance of these will become perhaps clearer if we first reduce the two poems, as far as is possible, to a tragic pattern.

"From Iliad and Odyssey can be made one tragedy, each, or not more than two." Bywater thinks the phrase, "not more than two" applies to the *Odyssey*, because it has a "double" plot. The language of Aristotle, however, hardly permits this limitation.[6] And of course Aristotle did not mean the material for more than two plays, but the plot or plots as developed in essential episodes.[7] We begin with a tragic pattern of the *Iliad*.

THE WRATH OF ACHILLES

DRAMATIS PERSONAE. Achilles, Patroclus, Herald of Agamemnon, Briseis (mute), Thetis, Phoenix, Odysseus, Ajax, Antilochus, Priam.

The scene is laid before the quarters of Achilles. The chorus consists of captive Trojan women, slaves of Myrmidon leaders (cf. IX, 664-668).

PROLOGOS. Achilles tells Patroclus of the quarrel and of Agamemnon's threat. A herald enters and leads away Briseis. Achilles prays to Thetis, who appears, forecasts the plan of Zeus as certain, and bids Achilles remain but take no part in the fighting. She leaves to go to Olympus.

PARODOS. The captives have heard that Achilles will return at once to Phthia; they enter to inquire if this is true. Theme: Dread of exile, with loss of all hope of ransom, added to their present wretched lot.

EPEISODION I. Phoenix in a Messenger's rhesis tells Achilles a few essential facts from Books II-V, and more particularly of the success of Hector (VIII). Exit. Enter Odysseus and Ajax as envoys of Agamemnon. Agon between Odysseus and Achilles (as in IX). Exit Odysseus to report at once to the council. Reënter Phoenix. The agon continues as in IX. Ajax leaves in sorrow. Phoenix goes within after telling Achilles about the wounded hero (Machaon), whom he had seen but did not recognize (XI, 597 f.). Achilles summons Patroclus from within, and sends him to Nestor's quarters (XI, 602-617).[8]

STASIMON I. Eris and the Litae (IV, 440-445; IX, 502-512); possibly the story of Meleager might be used (IX, 529-599).

EPEISODION II. Enter Patroclus weeping (XVI, 1 ff.). He tells of the success of Hector (XV). A brief agon follows. Enter Phoenix with the news that the ship of Protesilaus is burning (XVI, 112-124). Achilles consents to send Patroclus with the Myrmidons. His libation and prayer. He solemnly warns Patroclus not to pursue the Trojans to the city.

STASIMON II. Friendship's meaning and value, illustrated by several myths. A long ode is required by the action of XVI and XVII.

EPEISODION III. Antilochus enters and briefly describes the pertinent parts of the fighting of XVI-XVII. Exit to help in the defense of the body of Patroclus. Lyrics, Achilles and Cho. Thetis enters; the dialogue as in XVIII, 73-137. She instructs Achilles about the formal reconciliation with Agamemnon, and leaves for Olympus to obtain the new armor. Antilochus reënters, and persuades Achilles, though unarmed, to appear at the trench. Exeunt. A short chorikon or lyric dialogue. Reënter Achilles with the body of Patroclus. Brief kommos and dialogue, shortened by Achilles' eagerness for vengenace. The body is taken within, accompanied by Achilles.

STASIMON III. Honor, a noble aim in life, but human judgment is prone to error.

EPEISODION IV. Phoenix enters and tells Chorus of the reconciliation (XIX), the battle, and the death of Hector. Enter Achilles in his chariot dragging the body of Hector. Lyrics and dialogue, Achilles, Phoenix, and Chorus. Achilles describes the burial which he proposes for Patroclus, and promises to throw Hector to the dogs.

THE POET: REALIST AND IDEALIST 235

STASIMON IV. A short ode on the evil of overmuch vengeance.

EXODOS. Thetis enters: Zeus, angered by the persistent outraging of Hector's body, commands Achilles to give it back. Priam is already on the way. Mother and son converse together as if for the last time (cf. XXIV, 141 f.). Exit Thetis. Enter Priam. The dialogue is given, XXIV, 486-570. Exit Priam with the body. Enter Phoenix, to whom Achilles reviews the frustration of his life. The old man tries in vain to comfort him with the thought of fame.

EXODION, as in the *Antigone*.

A plot similarly outlined might in the hands of a skillful dramaturge become an Attic tragedy. The chorus must be Euripidean in the looseness of its connection with the action. Some of the parts assigned to Phoenix and Antilochus might be given to an unnamed Messenger. Otherwise the only essential departure from the *Iliad* is the use of Phoenix at the end in the rôle of Theseus in the *Oedipus at Colonus*. Homer leaves the tragic end of Achilles implicit, because the *Iliad* concludes with a different but equally complete tragedy, to which we turn:

HECTOR

DRAMATIS PERSONAE. Priam, Polites, Hector, Helen, Antenor, Hecuba, Andromache, Messenger A, Polydamas (or Messenger B), Idaeus.

The scene is before the palace of Priam. Sisters and sisters-in-law of Hector, and other Trojan ladies of rank, form the Chorus.

PROLOGOS. Enter Hector by parodos, to whom Priam from within. Hector urges an engagement: Priam opposes. Polites enters with tidings of the advance of the Greek army. Exeunt Hector and Polites to marshal the army; Priam remains.

PARODOS. The Chorus enters to ask Priam if the rumor is true that the enemy is approaching the city in force. Theme: War, the length and hardships of the present war, or the cause of it.

EPEISODION I. Helen enters on her way to the Tower. Her dialogue with Priam, as in III, 162-242. Exit Helen. Antenor enters. A brief agon: To give up Helen or to continue the war (using VII, 348-353, III, 202-224, XI, 125-142). Reënter Helen, accompanied by a strange attendant slave. She describes the meeting of the two armies, and the single combat between Paris and Menelaus; as the latter was on the point of victory a dust storm came on; when it passed, Paris had disappeared. Priam urges Helen to enter the palace and wait. She excuses herself, and with conflicting emotions, ill concealed, goes towards the palace of Paris. Priam goes into the palace.

STASIMON I. Theme suggested by the exit of Helen and by her previous words: Ἔρως.

EPEISODION II. Enter Hector from the field; Hecuba from within. Hector tells of the breaking of the truce and the success of Diomede (IV-V), and bids her offer sacrifice to Athena. She goes out. Enter from the Tower, Andromache, and Astyanax in the arms of an attendant. The dialogue as in VI, 407-493. Exeunt.

STASIMON II. A Euripidean ode on woman as the cause of war and the chief sufferer from it.

EPEISODION III. A Messenger enters from the battle. In his dialogue with Priam—or perhaps with Hecuba—he gives selected incidents from the fighting described in VIII-XV, ending with complete confidence in Hector's success.

STASIMON III. HYPORCHEME. The hope of victory after gloom and almost despair. The Chorus then divides into two groups, one hopeful, the other apprehensive. (A long choral passage is needed because of the amount of action which intervenes.)

EPEISODION IV. Polydamas enters breathless from the field. He tells the Chorus, and then Priam, such incidents of XVI-XXI as would most concern Hector, that is, the death of Cebriones; the death of Patroclus; the pride of Hector in wearing the arms of Achilles; Achilles at the Trench; his own warning to Hector (XVIII, 254-283. In the tragedy this warning must be to retreat at once, now that Achilles is ready to fight). Polydamas has caused the gates to be opened and already more than half the army has entered the city. But Hector is not among them. Exeunt Polydamas and Priam to the Tower.

STASIMON IV. Prayer to Apollo (perhaps referring to his part in the death of Patroclus) to keep Achilles back until Hector and the rest of the army are safe within the wall. The *Iliad* readily provides materials for the ode.

EPEISODION V. Idaeus enters from the Tower. He tells Hecuba of Priam's plea to Hector; of the pursuit, and the death of Hector, whose body Achilles is now dragging to the ships; of Priam's agony of grief and his struggles to free himself and go forth to the Greek camp to beg Achilles for the body. Hecuba is about to go to the Tower, when Priam enters struggling with attendants. Hecuba calms him. He goes within overwhelmed with grief. Enter Andromache. Kommatic passage, Andromache, Hecuba and Chorus (XXII, 430-515). Reënter Priam. He tells of the command of Iris, and, in spite of the doubts of Hecuba, goes out to take chariot for the Greek camp.

STASIMON V. Love of country; Hector the patriot, whose death has robbed the city of its only hope.

EXODOS. Enter Priam with the body on a bier. Lyric passage with Hecuba, and brief rhesis (Ω, 349-693). Hecuba and Priam go within to prepare for the funeral; the body remains. Enter Andromache, and then Helen. Kommos (Ω 725-745, 762-775). Exeunt into the palace with the body.

These two outlines, *tours de force* as they are, show clearly, I think, that Aristotle was aware that there are two complete tragedies in the plot of the *Iliad*. It is hard to see, however, how a second "tragedy" can be carved out of the *Odyssey*. The Return, because of the widely separated places at which much of the action takes place, and because so much of the rest of the action is narrated by a character, is not adapted to the Attic theater (except in an Aristophanic comedy—which the Odyssey is not). Nor is the succession of scenes sufficiently progressive in the tragic interest. After the arrival at Scheria, the adventures of Odysseus would be an anticlimax if the play should end with his arrival on the island of Ithaca. Even the Vengeance would offer insuperable difficulties, I think, to the Attic tragic poet. The journey of Telemachus—which is essential in Homer's account—would tax even an Aeschylus to conceal or to ignore convincingly the lapse of time which it demands. The chorus presents another difficulty. The Suitors —whom, except for the leaders, Hentze likens in function to a tragic chorus—are slain; women slaves did not, and could not, witness the slaughter, and male slaves must have taken sides in the struggle; and, since the outer gate was made fast, no neutral Ithacans could be present. Still further, Attic tragedy was reluctant to remove "the fourth wall," and (perhaps less so) to transfer to the court of a building what really occurred within. But most of the action of the Vengeance is carried on "within four walls." In view of these difficulties, prudence forbids a layman to sketch a pattern by which the undoubtedly dramatic material of the major plot of the *Odyssey* could have been acted in the Attic theater. For this reason we shall use only the two outlined tragedies of the *Iliad* in trying to see more clearly the difference between Homer and Attic tragedy.

We notice first the significance of the gods in the action which we have sketched. This was confined to Thetis, the plan of Zeus and his command to Achilles and to Priam, and Aphrodite in the form of the unknown slave of Helen (a mute, and unnecessary). All these could be eliminated if one might deviate from Homer's way of describing causality. Let Thetis be a mortal woman, highly revered, like some Diotima, for her unusual wisdom, and brought to Troy with Achilles because, for example, of a prophecy that Troy could not be taken without her presence. Then no plan of Zeus will be needed: Thetis, speaking with authority, will tell Achilles that without him the Greeks are no match for Hector. Thetis herself will induce her son to give back Hector's body. Priam, without a divine command, will carry out his first purpose—to go to Achilles, and Polyctor's son, the young Myrmidon whose form Hermes assumes (XXIV, 397), will have told Achilles or Thetis that Priam is on the way. The two tragedies will lose none of the tragic by this change. Homer's gods are due to the time spirit; human nature remains virtually the same whether the equation of human life be Man +gods +Fate $=x$, or heredity +environment +Chance $=x$. But Homer uses his gods in the *Iliad* for a second purpose, which violates one of the canons of Attic tragedy. Two tragic actions are sometimes blended into a single drama, as in the *Antigone*, but never into three. In the *Iliad* the gods enact a third tragedy, lacking only the tragic τέλος, as it must: there can be no completeness in the life of the ever-living.

A more far-reaching difference is the chorus. It is true that a poet might write all the lyric passages, using thoughts, images, and myths in Homer. Nor does Homer lack the chorus: the Muses, the dancers on the shield of Achilles and at the Phaeacian games, and mourners. But these are not constant attendants on the life which Homer pictures. Life is not all storm. The soul of man, like his physical heart, suffers systole and diastole, though not with the same regularity. This alternation Homer provides: the feast on Goat Island after the storm; the Phaeacian episode between the hardships of the Wanderings and the danger at home; the Tricking of Zeus and the scenes on the shield of Achilles, between stormy incidents. And most of the remaining action is not that which calls for lyric. Only a small portion of life demands expression in song and in rhythmized movement. The limitation to action and situation appropriate to the lyric intensity of emotion hemmed in Attic tragedy in many ways. From it, directly or indirectly, arose the conventions: of time and place, of the irremovable fourth wall; and of the disregard of off-scene action which does not immediately concern the characters themselves. Akin to convention was the limitation in the number of the human characters and the restriction of expressive physical action largely to the patterned movements of the chorus. Other tokens of our universal existence all but vanish in Attic tragedy. Most human beings spend at least one-third of their existence in eating and sleeping. This large part of life was ignored in the action which the spectators saw. So was nature, with rare exceptions, like the *Oedipus at Colonus*. Attic tragedy in its recognition of the external realities of life was far removed from Homer's realism. The distance between the two was as that which separates one of the pediments of Pheidias from some of the frescoes at Cnossus.

Life in the Age of Pericles had reached another peak, and with it, poetry. But tragedy, the full and final flowering of Greek poetry, because it lyricized—in the larger sense—the epic myths, concentrated and limited the heroic life to its most intense experiences. Its function was to "purge" the tragic emotions, and did not include also the participation in the full heroic life. So in its picture of life, tragedy revealed, as it were, the Many in the One (the tragic mask is evidence); Homer, the One in the Many. Tragedy was synthesis; Homer, analysis.

In the course of time the chorus vanished; the scene could be changed at will, and the action ceased to be timeless. The cast grew larger, and physical action was more freely presented. Several threads could be twisted into a single plot, and the grave and the gay were no longer incongruous, nor the common incidents of life meaningless. When this time had come, and with it, Shakespeare, another poet who could see and picture the largeness of human life, tragedy became almost Homeric.

The difference that remains is largely due to the "spectacle," which Aristotle did not regard as strictly belonging to the poet's art (*Poetics* 1450b 16, 1453b 3). If all the performances of *Hamlet* could have been recorded and could be reproduced on the screen, it would appear how little the visual representation of the characters and the action belongs to Shakespeare, and how much to the actors and the producer. And even the ὄψις for which Shakespeare wrote his plays presented life with a different kind of realism from that of Homer. ὀφθαλμοὶ τῶν ὤτων ἀκριβέστεροι μάρτυρες.[9] The eyes give a more exact picture of the external world than the ears. The opposite of ἀκριβῶς is τύπῳ.[10] The oral utterance generalizes; the spectacle must either particularize or remove itself from reality by the use of symbol. The particular confines the receptive imagination of the audience; the general permits the listener to picture the scene and the action in terms of his own experience transmuted into an image at the suggestion of the poet's words. For this reason the aesthetic pleasure derived from a Messenger's narrative in Euripides was undoubtedly greater than if the action had been presented on the scene. Furthermore, the generalizing power of the spoken word greatly extends the limits of the action which it can describe. Hence epic must always surpass tragedy in "breadth." In "breadth" lies its superior excellence. Tragedy has never written the heroic life with the largeness of Homer. It may plumb depths as great, but the wide expanse of living is beyond its sphere.

The contrast between Homer and tragedy in this respect, and at the same time the closeness with which Homer pictures life—which is what we mean by realism—may be illustrated by observing the great steps by which tragedy and the epic have reached their present state of development. At first, in Greece, both tried to picture heroic life as real, and both derived their medium of expression from the early tendency to burst forth into song at moments of great emotion caused by present experience or past memory. We may indicate the evolution of song along these two lines by a diagram (see next page).

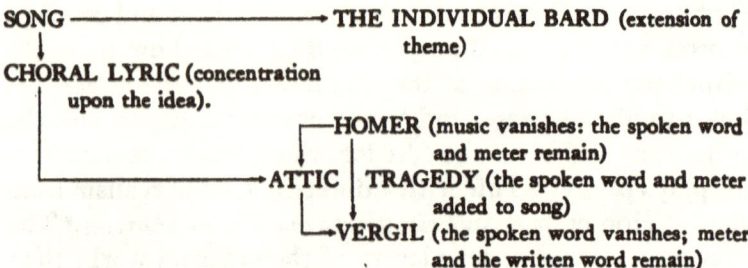

SHAKESPEARE (music vanishes; the spoken word and meter remain)
Mourning Becomes Electra (meter vanishes; the spoken word remains)
Les Misérables; *The Forsyte Saga* (meter vanishes; the printed word remains)

Both song and written prose are near and at the same time remote from normal utterance. Music and rhythm are farther removed than prose, but song, because it is oral, is nearer to life than prose reduced to visual symbols. The symbols give the reason time to act, to identify and combine particulars, and to place the whole more exactly in the experience. Hence, written prose is the medium of expression of a scientific "exactness" (ἀκρίβεια), as well as of rational generalization. Song, on the other hand, poetically idealizes the contents of emotional experience.

In the progress from the idealism of poetry to the realism of science, Attic tragedy is nearer its origin in keeping the music of song, and Homer is nearer in using oral utterance —which tends to generalize—where tragedy employs the particularizing "spectacle."

Attic tragedy is farther from reality also because it relies in large measure on convention to produce a unity in the combination of lyric, dramatic, and epic elements. Homer blends the three poetic manners: He speaks now in the third poetic "person," now in the second, and now in the first, and again, using all degrees of each manner in all sorts of combinations. In this he closely approaches modern scientific realism, which sees no compartments in the mind or its contents.

Attic tragedy presents a picture of life which is further abstracted from reality because it confines its attention closely to man, and neglects nature. Homer saw that nature is inseparable from human existence. His greater realism in this respect was due to his age.

Attic tragedy, if we regard Sophocles as its most typical representative, was produced, like the *Aeneid*, at one of the culminations of human culture. Homer, on the contrary, lived on a very low plane of culture, but between two mountain peaks, Minoan Cnossus and Periclean Athens. He was a Greek, and his theme and heroes were also Greek. But into the Greek tradition before him had passed something of Minoan culture. Today we can identify in Homer two Minoan characteristics: a poetic realism which pictured man in his natural surroundings, and nature herself; and an avoidance of "scientific" or "pessimistic" realism, in refusing to portray cruelty and obscenity—a refusal which Sir Arthur Evans regards as one of the evidences of high culture among the Minoans.

Homer is thus the mediator between two cultures. Tradition, carrying back in some way not yet explained, to the earlier peak of civilization, showed him the reality of life in its setting of nature, and the meaning of life in the daily round as well in its momentous crises. Tradition, too, because the poetic view of life was not yet clouded by the scientific, imparted to life the quality of sublimity. If we knew the Heroic Age of Greece only through fifth-century art and poetry, we should hardly think of it as the Golden Age. It was the poetry of Homer, far more than that of Hesiod, which lifted life into a realm of gold.

Since the time of Aristotle, perfection in a finite world has often been defined as the balance between two extremes. With Homer, poetry closely approached this balance in many ways. In his verse and his formulas, small and large, is rigid Law; in the wide variations in both, a close approach to Freedom within the law. In place, time, and characters Homer employs the Many; but so that the resulting picture of life is complete and One. The same is true of his themes and manner. Andrew Lang only voiced the opinion of the ancients when he said that Homer, in a sense, contained the whole of Greek literature. Plato recognized that the poet's manner was a mean between the dramatic and the narrative; this is still clearer today, when the difference between oral utterance and the written word is better understood. Homer is at once Humanist and Naturalist; both realist and idealist. To human beings life is still the ultimate reality, and the ultimate problem of realistic science. Realism in literature can go no farther than Homer did in imparting life to a picture of the past. But Homer was a poetic realist. He created a life that never was on land or sea. The men of his times did not care to know; they were content to enter into and make their own a mythos of life. Homer's mythos magnifies life by poetizing it. He is a realist in imparting life to his mythos, an idealist in painting that life large.

NOTES

Notes to Chapter I

[1] Eustathius, 745, 52, on I 189.

[2] Odysseus has used the word "comrades" throughout the Apologue, except once, ι 59, where the contrast with "Ciconians" justifies the use of "Achaeans."

[3] For other passages containing similar praise of the poems, see Finsler, *Homer*, I, 337 f.

[4] Paul Friedländer, "Lachende Götter," *Die Antike* X (1934), 219, is one of the first of modern scholars to deny this. He, however, assumes a *Vorlage* for Hera's oath (Ξ 271-280), p. 218.

[5] Phoenix has a reason for doing this when he is about to tell the tale of Meleager (I 524): he is no poet, and the tale is told for its moral.

[6] τά τε παλαιὰ καὶ τὰ καινά: the Chorus to Aeschylus and Euripides, Ar. *Frogs*, 1107.

[7] *H.S.C.P.* XLI (1930), 138.

[8] Parry changed to conviction what had been only a strong impression. Cf. S. E. Bassett, *T.A.P.A.* XLVIII (1917), 95.

[9] *T.A.P.A.* LXIV (1933), 181.

[10] *H.S.C.P.* XLI (1930), 146.

[11] *H.S.C.P.* XLIII (1932), 6.

[12] Pl. *Phaedrus*, 275 A, Jowett's translation (3d ed.).

[13] *What Plato Said*, 287.

[14] *H.S.C.P.* XLI (1930), 147, 146.

[15] η 177a (= ε 95), found by Ludwich in U¹, U⁵, seems to be necessary, although the vulgate lacks it. See Walter Arend, *Die typischen Scenen bei Homer* (Berlin, 1933), 70, Anm. 1. But see also Pierre Chantraine, "Remarques sur l'emploi des formules dans le premier chant de l'Iliade," *Rev. des Etudes Grecques* XLV (1932), 121-154.

[16] "Les doctrines de cette espèce ressemblent un peu aux cultures de bactérie, qui ne fleurissent pas dans le milieu de tous les jours, mais, placées dans le *medium optimum*, se maintiennent pendant un temps indéfini."—G. M. Calhoun, "Nausicaa et Aristarque," *Rev. des Etudes Homériques* IV (1934), 10.

[17] The lesser Ajax is hardly a major hero; the two Aiantes are given, together, the titular vocative. For the details, see Thilde Wendel, "Die Gesprächsanrede im griechischen Epos und Drama der Blütezeit," *Tübinger Beiträge* VI (1929), 49-50; for the omission of the vocative, S. E. Bassett, *A.J.P.* LV (1934), 140-152.

[18] L. A. Morrison, "A Day with the Golden Treasury," *Adelphi* (London), June, 1925.

[19] From an article by the author, "Scientist and Humanist in Homeric Criticism," *Class. Weekly* XX (1926), 39.

[20] Cf. Pl. *Resp.*, 607 B.

[21] *Republic* 399 A, Jowett's translation.

NOTES TO CHAPTER II

[1] E.g., *Isthmians* 2, 34; 8, 57; *Ol.* 10, 96.
[2] Cf. *Anthol. Pal.* 7, 42; Propertius, 3, 3, 1-6.
[3] *Posthomerica* 3. 594, 785.
[4] Käte Friedemann, "Die Rolle des Erzählers in der Epik," *Unters. zur neueren Sprach- u. Literaturgeschichte*, n. f. VII (1910), 33-54.
[5] Most of the Messenger's narratives in Attic tragedy, especially in Euripides, begin with ἐπεί, "When," and the place is immediately mentioned unless it is readily inferred.
[6] Hermann Fraenkel, "Die Zeitauffassung in der archaischen griechischen Literatur," *Beilageheft zur Zeitschr. f. Aesthetik u. allg. Kunstwissenschaft*, Bd. 25 (1931), 97-117. Homer never refers to Father Time, and χρόνος is never used in the nominative case in the Homeric poems.
[7] R. G. Kent, "The Time Element in the Greek Drama," *T.A.P.A.* XXXVII (1906), 39-52.
[8] "Die Behandlung gleichzeitiger Ereignisse im antiken Epos," *Philologus*, Supplementband VIII (1901), 418.
[9] "Epische Gesetze der Volksdichtung," *Zeitschr. f. deut. Altertum* LI (1909), 8.
[10] *Merrily We Roll Along.* See *The Literary Digest*, October 13, 1934.
[11] As Aristotle noticed (*Poetics* XXIV, 1459b 23).
[12] Hector, O 484, sees Teucer's bow broken. But Teucer has already gone to his quarters and now has his spear (vss. 478-483).
[13] Homer never mentions the death of a son or husband before the eyes of a mother or wife; not so Vergil and Quintus, nor Aeschylus nor Euripides. See S. E. Bassett, "The Pursuit of Hector," *T.A.P.A.* LXI (1930), 147-149.
[14] Franz Stürmer, in Drerup's *Homerische Poetik*, III (1921), 600-601, has collected a list of such "*Deckszene*" in the *Odyssey*.
[15] The plague rages nine days (A 53); Thetis must wait twelve days for the return of the Olympians (A 493). Achilles drags the body of Hector about the tomb of Patroclus for twelve days (Ω 31), and nine days are spent in providing wood for the pyre of Hector (Ω 784). The two days during which the dead are buried and the Greek wall is built are similar in description. In the *Odyssey*, the hero spends four days in building the raft, seventeen on his voyage toward Phaeacia, and two in the water after Poseidon has shattered the raft. In the narratives by the characters, intervals devoid of action are common.
[16] Stürmer, *op. cit.* 337 and Anm. 1.
[17] Claude Bragdon, *Scribner's Magazine* XCVI (1934), 42-43.
[18] Except in some parts of the Apologue; and never on shipboard.
[19] Most recently by Walter Arend, "Die typischen Scenen bei Homer," *Problemata*, Heft 7 (1933), 127: Homer dünkt die Welt so schön und feingeordnet auch in den einfachsten Vorgängen, dass er diese wieder und wieder erzählen konnte.
[20] The entrance and exit of a character, parallel scenes while the narrative passes over a bare stretch, like the sleeping of Odysseus in ζ and the second dinner of the Suitors (β, see above, p. 45), and brief summaries of minor action at Ithaca in β and δ, are not included.

[248]

Notes to Chapter III

¹ *The Intimate Notebooks of George Jean Nathan* (New York, 1932), p. 4.
² For the *Aeneid*, cf. S. E. Bassett, "The Inductions of the Iliad, the Odyssey, and the Aeneid," *Class.Weekly* XXVII (1934), 105-110, 113-118; for the *Nibelungenlied*, e.g., Friedemann, *op. cit.* 15, and particularly, as representing the general feeling of scholars, G. H. Needler, *The Nibelungenlied, Translated into English Rhymed Verse* (New York, 1904), p. xxviii, "The Iliad is essentially narrative and descriptive.... : the Nibelungenlied is essentially dramatic."
³ For the "dramatic" effect of the Homeric poems, see below, Chap. VIII.
⁴ For the dramatic recitation of Homer, cf. Felix Bölte, "Rhapsodische Vortragskunst," *Neue Jahrb.* XIX (1907), 571-578; Victor Bérard, *Introd. à l'Odyssée*, I (1924), 75-165; idem, *La Résurrection d'Homère: Le Drame Epique* (1930), 1-100.
⁵ G. R. Throop, "Epic and Dramatic [I, II]," *Washington University Studies*, V, Humanistic Series (1917), 1-32; XII, Humanistic Series (1924), 67-104.
⁶ Only 45 per cent of its verses are direct speech; the number of speeches per dialogue never exceeds seven (Homer has twenty-four dialogues of eight or more speeches each), and only once do as many as three speakers participate.
⁷ Richard Heinze, *Virgils epische Technik* (3d ed., 1928; Leipzig), 404 ff.
⁸ Axel Olrik, "Epische Gesetze der Volksdichtung," *Zeitschr. f. deut. Altertum* LI (1909).
⁹ Dialogues with three speakers, 31; with four, 18; with five, 5; with six, 2; with seven, 1; and with eight, 1.
¹⁰ *Der Dialog*, I (1895), 14 f.
¹¹ The exact figures are of little value. It is not always clear where a dialogue begins and ends. The continuity of the narrative prevents any hard-and-fast analysis into "scenes."
¹² Exceptions are found at o 194-201—a single speech, however—and rarely in the Apologue.
¹³ Actually, 482:477 verses, omitting the Boar Hunt as ἔξω τοῦ μυθεύματος.
¹⁴ To this should be added four tales not told in a dialogue: the song of Demodocus about Ares and Aphrodite; the story of the daughters of Pandareus, told by Penelope in her prayer (υ 66 ff.), and the Boar Hunt and the ancestry of Theoclymenus, told by the poet in digressions.
¹⁵ The "bungling" of Agamemnon seems to be further hinted at by the word πυκινήν which the poet applies to his scheme for testing the spirit of his army (B 55). Mülder ingeniously rationalizes this scheme, explaining Agamemnon's motive as due to his recognition that his treatment of Achilles had made him unpopular. Homer, however, says not a word of this, either in the account of the quarrel or in describing the thoughts of Agamemnon. Besides, his only other use of πυκινήν βουλήν is to characterize the offer made by Hector of the horses of Achilles to any Trojan who would bring him news of the actions at the Greek camp (K 302).

Notes to Chapter IV

[1] In the present century there have been growing protests; Drerup, *Homerische Poetik*, I, 444-466.
[2] Käte Friedemann, "Die Rolle des Erzählers in der Epik," 1-32.
[3] *Ueb. naive u. sentimentalische Dichtung* (Säkul. Ausg.) XII, 183. Friedemann, op. cit., 3.
[4] Charles Sears Baldwin, *Ancient Rhetoric and Poetic* (New York, 1924), 196.
[5] *Littell's Living Age*, April 1, 1930, 157 f.
[6] X 202 f., χ 12-14. The similar question of Menelaus in the tale of Proteus (δ 443) cannot entirely ignore Telemachus, to whom the tale is told; nor can that of Odysseus (κ 573 f.) ignore his Phaeacian audience.
[7] The only exception seems to be Circe's account of dangers that lie before Odysseus (μ 39-110). This, however, is instructions, not a narrative.
[8] Thersites (B 221), Scamandrius (E 53), Dolon (K 318), Antiphus (Δ 107), Harpalion and the sons of Hippotion (N 646, 794), Euphorbus (Π 810), Polydorus (T 411), Ctesippus (υ 291), Leiodes (φ 148).
[9] The cap of Meriones worn by Odysseus, which has become famous for its archaeological interest (K 271), the breastplate of Dolops (O 534), the cup of Achilles (Π 228), the bar of Achilles' gate (Ω 457), the wine cellar and granary of Odysseus, with its stewardess (β 348), the white stones where Neleus used to sit (γ 411), the shield of Laertes (χ 186); also the dog Argus, ρ 296.
[10] O 274, Φ 495, are not exceptions. Apollonius and Quintus follow Homer in this respect. Nonnus seems to have been the first in Greek epic to use the imperfect and pluperfect in similes.
[11] *Die Odyssee* (Munich, 1924), 17.
[12] Cf. Carl Rothe, *Die Odyssee als Dichtung* (Paderborn, 1914), 59.
[13] Also B 783; in speeches, T 96, 416, Ω 615.
[14] In the account of Hera's toilet (Ξ 170-186) imperfects take the place of present tenses. This is exceptional.
[15] Finsler, *Homer* (2d ed., 1918), II, pp. xvii and 194 f., mentions many attempts, beginning with that of Jean Boivin, 1715; to which should be added Leaf, *The Iliad* (2d ed., 1902), Appendix I, and J. L. Myres, *Who Were The Greeks?* (1930), 517-525, who discusses the Geometric symmetry of the scenes.
[16] Λ 24-28, 33-40, 632-635, λ 609-614, τ 228-231.
[17] That κυανέην (vs. 564) denotes material rather than color (as the ancient commentators understood it) is possible. If so, it is the only unmistakable technical detail in the whole description.
[18] Eust. 1162, 44; E. M. 189, 12.
[19] Δ 223 f., ἔνθ' οὐκ ἂν βρίζοντα ἴδοις Ἀγαμέμνονα δῖον, οὐδὲ καταπτώσσοντ', οὐδ' οὐκ ἐθέλοντα μάχεσθαι.
[20] Eust. 465, 31, on the passage.
[21] *Menex.* 239 D, 240 D, δεῖ δὴ αὐτήν (sc. τὴν ἀρετήν) ἰδεῖν . . . , ἐν ἐκείνῳ τῷ χρόνῳ γενόμενον λόγῳ . . . ἐν τούτῳ δὴ ἄν τις γενόμενος γνοίη, οἷοι ἄρα ἐτύγχανον ὄντες τὴν ἀρετὴν οἱ Μαραθῶνι δεξάμενοι τὴν τῶν βαρβάρων δύναμιν.
[22] Cf. Gildersleeve and Miller, *Syntax of Classical Greek*, I, 172, n. 3.
[23] In speeches, in the *Iliad*, 1:20 vss.; in the *Odyssey* (without the Apologue), 1:21 vss.; in the narrative, *Iliad*, 1:41 vss.; *Odyssey* (without the Apologue), 1:58 vss.
[24] *Grundfragen der Homerkritik* (3d ed., 1923), 430.
[25] Arend, op. cit. 106-115.
[26] Karl Hentze, "Die Monologe in den homerischen Epen," *Philologus*, n.f. XVII (1904), 12-30; Friedrich Leo, "Der Monolog im Drama," *Abhandl. d. königl. Gesell. d. Wiss. zu Göttingen, philol.-hist. Kl.*, n.f. X (1908), 1-6.
[27] This has been discussed by the writer in *T.A.P.A.* LXI (1930), 130-149.

Notes to Chapter V

[1] *Times and Tendencies* (Boston, 1931), 92-112.
[2] XIX, 340, αἱ μὲν τοίνυν ἄλλαι δυνάμεις ἐπιεικῶς εἰσιν αὐτάρκεις, ἡ δὲ τοῦ λέγειν, ἂν τὰ παρ' ὑμῶν τῶν ἀκουόντων ἀντιστῇ, διακόπτεται.
[3] Giuseppe Fraccaroli, *L'Irrazionale nella letteratura* (Turin, 1903), 397.
[4] G. M. Calhoun, "Homeric Repetitions," *Univ. Calif. Publ. Class. Philol.* XII, 1-25; *idem.*, "The Art of Formula in Homer—ἔπεα πτερόεντα," *Class. Philol.* XXX (1935), 215-227.
[5] G. E. Duckworth, *Foreshadowing and Suspense in the Epics of Homer, Apollonius, and Vergil* (Princeton Univ. Press, 1933).
[6] E.g., Charon, Canto III; Francesca and Paolo, Canto V. This is realism of a different kind: Dante cannot know the name when first he sees them.
[7] Theoclymenus enters, ο 223; his name is given at verse 256. But no character in the poem knows or uses the name.
[8] *Etude sur l'Iliade d'Homère* (1888), 493 ff., 536 ff.
[9] "Dismissing the Assembly in Homer," *Class. Jour.* XXVI (1931), 458-460.
[10] *Pap. Oxyr.* 1086, on B 763, σημειοῦται δὲ ὅτι διὰ παντὸς ὁ ποιητὴς οὕτως εἰς τὰ ὕστερα πρότερος ἀπαντᾷ κατὰ ἰδίαν συνήθειαν. The papyrus is dated about the middle of the first century B.C.
[11] *Ad Att.* I, 16, 1. Pliny (*Ep.* 3, 9, 28), when about to answer a question which he had passed over, says, "Hoc facit Homerus."
[12] E.g., from the *Odyssey* alone, η 238 ff., λ 160 ff., 170 ff., 210 ff., 492 ff., ξ 115 ff., ο 347 ff., 509 ff., ω 106 ff., 288 ff.
[13] E.g., ζ 209 ff., η 163 ff., θ 389 ff., ν 404-ξ 1, ο 75 ff.
[14] νῦν δέ. Commentators miss the point; it is not temporal, but denotes disappointed expectation. "We came to win honor for you (expecting honor from you), but I am to receive only insult. *Such being the case*, I will return home."
[15] E.g., *Medea* 475 ff., 526 ff., Soph. *Electra*, 526, 558. Cf. also J. T. Lees, "Δικανικὸς Λόγος in Euripides," *Univ. of Nebraska Studies* (1892), 380, 385, 396, 399.
[16] G. W. Elderkin, *Aspects of the Speech in the Later Greek Epic* (Baltimore, 1906), 45 ff.
[17] *Harvard Studies in Classical Philology* XXXI (1920), 56, for evidence that Crates identified the deuteron proteron of Aristarchus with chiasmus.
[18] Georg Lehnert, *De scholiis ad Homerum rhetoricis* (Leipzig, 1896), 1 ff.
[19] 390, 2, and 496, 14.
[20] Possibly Aristotle inverts as much as Plato; see below, n. 27.
[21] *Lysis* 203 A; cf. *Prot.* 309 B, *Phaedrus* 227 A.
[22] I find not a single inversion, but at 233 A there are six consecutive antitheses.
[23] S. E. Bassett on Aristotle *Poetics*, 1459b 15, in *Classical Studies Presented to Edward Capps* (Princeton, 1936), 9 ff.
[24] English translators of Greek authors often substitute the antithetic order for a Greek inversion. Rawlinson, Hdt. III, 99; Rogers, Ar. *Frogs*, 3, 5 = 20, 30; Jowett and Shorey not infrequently.
[25] *Sacred Literature* (London, 1820).
[26] Thomas Boys, *A Key to the Book of Psalms* (London, 1825), 29, 35, 39.
[27] The fondness for inversion in the Hebrew poets, and in Plato and Aristotle, may be partly due to another reason. Naegelsbach finds in antithesis and chiasmus the two basic principles of word order in literary Latin prose, ab ab, or ab ba. These principles must obviously govern the arrangement of words wherever there is a strong tendency towards pairing, as in the *sermo quadrata*. Here the perpetual use of antithesis would be unendurably monotonous, and chiasmus is frequently desirable. It follows that wherever the thought deals with pairs of ideas, the inverted order is likely to be used, unless, as in Attic oratory, the antithesis is consciously preferred. In Hebrew poetry the antithesis is very common; the chiastic

[251]

order may therefore be due partly to the desire to avoid monotony. So in Plato and Aristotle frequent occasions for discussing the differentia of opposites, or of contrasted things and ideas, increase the opportunities for the inverted order. Yet, both in Plato and in Aristotle—and much more in Homer—the avoidance of monotony fails to explain a large proportion of the inversions.

I am indebted to my student and friend, Miss Helen F. Bellows, for directing my attention to the work of Professor Lund: (1) "The Presence of Chiasmus in the Old Testament," *Am. Jour. Sem. Lang. and Lit.* XLVI (1930), 104-126; (2) "The Presence of Chiasmus in the New Testament," *Jour. of Relig.* X (1930), 74-93; (3) "The Influence of Chiasmus on the Structure of the Gospels," *Anglican Theol. Rev.* XIII (1931), 27-48; (4) "The Literary Structure of Paul's Hymn to Love," *Jour. of Bib. Lit.* L (1931), 266-276; (5) "Chiasmus in the Psalms," *Am. Jour. Sem. Lang. and Lit.* XLIX (1933), 281-312; (6) *Outline Studies in the Book of Revelation* (Chicago, 1935).

[28] G. Fraccaroli, *L'Irrazionale nella letteratura*, 401 ff.; Rothe, *Die Ilias als Dichtung*, 209, Anm. 2; S. E. Bassett, "Sir Arthur Conan Doyle and Homer," *Class. Weekly* XXIV (1930), 42.

[29] Adolph Roemer, "Aristarchea," in E. Belzner, *Homerische Probleme*, I (1911), 179.

[30] BT on Π 844, ὃ δὲ ᾔδει ὁ ποιητής, τοῦτο τῷ ἡρωικῷ προσώπῳ περιέθηκεν. This is also the explanation of Roemer, "Die Homerexegese Aristarchs in ihren Grundzügen," *Studien zur Geschichte und Kultur des Altertums*, XIII (1924), 234 f. He assigns it to Aristarchus, but, apparently overlooking this scholium, says he cannot find in our sources any formulation of the principle.

[31] *Die Bedeutung der Widersprüche für die homerische Frage* (Berlin, 1894), 6-10.

[32] Since Fraccaroli, it has been generally recognized that the poet may keep matters secret from the characters, but never from the audience.

[33] I 701-703. Hence Düntzer rejected these verses.

[34] P 186; Π 279 does not explain his knowledge. There the poet refers also to the armor of Automedon. It was not the armor, but the Myrmidons, that made the Trojans think Achilles was fighting.

[35] Zeus and Poseidon must at times see in order to know (Θ 397, Ο 6; ε 283). Ares and the Sun God must be told (N 521 f., Ο 110 ff.; μ 374 f.)

[36] Ο 90 f., ἀτυζομένη δὲ ἔοικας·/ἢ μάλα δή σ' ἐφόβησε Κρόνου πάϊς.

[37] *Odyssee* (2d ed.) 584, 518.

[38] χ 140. The hearer learned at τ 1-33. As for Odysseus' knowledge (σ 281-283), the poet has told us (vss. 158-161) that Athena had put it into the heart of the Queen to appear before the Suitors, "that she might be honored more than before by her husband and son."

[39] *Hom. Unters.* 105, Anm. 15.

[40] Schol. BT on Z 326 explains the resentment of Paris as we have done, but fails to suggest how Paris could have known of the hatred of the Trojans.

[41] Ε 349, ἦ οὐχ ἅλις ὅττι γυναῖκας ἀνάλκιδας ἠπεροπεύεις; Γ 399, δαιμονίη, τί με ταῦτα λιλαίεαι ἠπεροπεύειν;

[42] I 392 (Achilles loquitur), καὶ ὃς βασιλεύτερός ἐστιν. I, 160 (Agamemnon loquitur), ὅσσον βασιλεύτερός εἰμι.

[43] Cf. the repeated words of Achilles, ὅ τ' ἄριστον Ἀχαιῶν οὐδὲν ἔτεισας (ἔτεισεν), A 244, 412.

[44] *Geschichte der griechischen Literatur*, I, 1 (1929), 124 and Anm. 2.

[45] Note on ε 79. Cf. *Commentationes Homericae* (Leyden, 1911), 31 ff.

[46] Note on κ 277 (Odysseus does not explain how he knew it was Hermes who met him), sed talia reticere poeta Odyssea non fuit solitus.

[47] ν 363, π 161, 208-212, ρ 10, τ 27, 287, 360, χ 491.

Notes to Chapter VI

[1] πρὸς μὲν γὰρ ἓν ἅπαντα συντέτακται, *Metaph.* 1075a 18.

[2] Cf. Rhys Carpenter, *The Esthetic Basis of Greek Art* (New York, 1921), 133-152.

[3] A 214, ὕβριος/εἵνεκα/τῆσδε· σὺ δ'/ἴσχεο,/πείθεο δ'/ἡμῖν. This verse the ancient grammarians regarded as bad because the feet and the words so nearly coincide. Cf. Eust. 740, 5.

[4] C. M. Lewis, *The Principles of English Verse* (Oxford Univ. Press, 1929).

[5] S. E. Bassett,"Versus Tetracolos," *Class. Philol.* XIV (1919), 216-233.

[6] S. E. Bassett,"'Ολιγομερία and Πολυμερία," *Class. Philol.* XII (1917), 97-101. I owe Mr. Alexander Shewan also a dikolos, εἵλετο δ'ἔγχος/ αὐτοκασίγνητος δυωκαιεικοσίμετρον.

[7] ἀεὶ καινόν.

[8] For a fuller discussion, see the writer's article,"The Theory of the Homeric Caesura According to the Extant Remains of the Ancient Doctrine," *A.J.P.* XL (1919), 343-372; cf."The Caesura—A Modern Chimaera," *Class. Weekly* XVIII (1925), 76-79.
Since the publication of these articles, some progress has been made towards recognizing the poet's freedom within the law. Hermann Fraenkel, "Der kallimachische und der homerische Hexameter," *Nachr. d. Gesellsch. d. Wiss. zu Göttingen* (1926, philol.-hist. Kl.), 197-229, says (228): "Die Sinnesstruktur des Hexameters war fest durch ihre Gründung auf die Harmonie und die absolute Schönheit; und sie war schmiegsam durch ihre Freiheit." A. W. de Groot, *Mnemosyne*, ser. 3, II (1935), "Wesen und Gesetze der Caesur," 81-154, remarks (105) that Goodell and Wilamowitz forgot that there are no metrical laws, but only metrical tendencies.

[9] Westphal, Usener, and Chaignet cite Aristotle, *Metaph.*, 1093a 30, as evidence to the contrary.They are wrong, as the writer has shown, "'Right' and 'Left' in the Homeric Hexameter," *Class. Philol.* XI (1916), 458-460.

[10] The Great Anonymous, W. Studemund, *Anecd. Var.* (Berlin, 1886), I, 215, 25.

[11] Cf. the well-known verse in Hector's reply to Ajax, H 238,

οἶδ' ἐπὶ δεξιά, οἶδ' ἐπ' ἀριστερὰ νωμῆσαι βῶν/ἀζαλέην.

[12] We need to know, for example, (1) what proportion of Homer's verses contain a single unit of thought, and how many two or three; (2) the form which this thought takes, whether it is verbal (i.e., a sentence), or nominal, or adjectival, or adverbial; (3) the use of this thought-unit verse, in simple narrative, the speeches, and exposition; and (4) the context: how often this kind of verse occurs at the beginning or end of a speech or paragraph, and to what moods they are suited and to what unsuited.

[13] *T.A.P.A.* LX (1929), 215.

[14] *H.S.C.P.* III (1892), 91-129; cf. *Introduction to the Language and Verse of Homer* (Boston, 1885), 83 f.

[15] S. E. Bassett, "Notes on the Bucolic Diaeresis," *T.A.P.A.* XXXVI (1905), 111-124; idem,"The Hephthemimeral Caesura in Greek Hexameter Poetry," *ibid.* XLVIII (1917), 85-110. The pauses within the first dipody have not yet been studied sufficiently.

[16] So of Tlepolemus (E 632), when otherwise it would not be clear whether he or Sarpedon spoke; of the new speakers, Antinous, Eurymachus, and Leocritus (α 383, 399, β 242).

[17] Seymour discovered this principle, citing α 11-16. But cf. α 97-101, A 11-15, 17-21; 44-50, X 440-448, *et passim*.

[18] "The man who has been properly trained in Latin and Greek has little need for italics."—Presidential Address before the Classical Association, 1926.

[253]

[19] S. E. Bassett,"The So-called Emphatic Position of the Runover Word in the Homeric Hexameter," *T.A.P.A.* LVII (1926), 116-148.

[20] Ferdinand Brunetière, "Le caractère essentiel de la littérature française," *Etudes Critiques* V (Paris, 1903), 259.

[21] The Catalogues provide the best examples, about thirty pairs of this kind, as against only four or five with both nouns qualified; and at least a dozen trios of names, the last only being qualified, whereas there is only a single instance in which the first of the three alone has an epithet (520).

Two nouns, the second being qualified by an adjective, B 496, 501, 503, 519, 559, 571, 573, 575, 583, 584, 591, 603, 605, 607, 615, 632, 633, 646, 683, 695, 717, 729, 749, 757, 830, 842, 858, 876; both nouns qualified, 508, 570, 640, 696; three nouns, the last only being qualified, B 497, 498, 502, 532, 537, 561, 592, 606, 712, 739, 836, 855; the first alone qualified, B 520.

[22] Franz Dornseiff, *Pindars Stil* (Berlin, 1921), 33.

[23] Not all are of different metrical value, as Parry's law of economy in the traditional formula demands. The following are interchangeable: μώνυχες and δίζυγες, καλλίτριχες and χρυσάμπυκες, κεντρηνεχέες and Πυλοιγενέες. The longer adjectives are extremely easy to form. Any poet trained to improvise would have no difficulty in producing them.

[24] Dornseiff, *op. cit.* 36.

[25] If we use the v. l. ὑψαύχενες, E 772.

[26] Cf. Paul Cauer, *Das Altertum im Leben der Gegenwart* (2d ed., 1915), 47; Dornseiff, *op. cit.* 35.

[27] Dornseiff, *op. cit.* 40 f.

[28] E.g., Aesch. *Pers.*, 424; Soph. *Antig.*, 424; Eurip. *Bacchae*, 1056, 1066, 1090.

[29] Schol. T on M 41.

[30] Georg Finsler, *Homer in der Neuzeit* (Leipzig, 1912), 249.

[31] Arthur Platt, *Jour. Philol.* XXIV (1896), 28 ff., was the first to make this clear. He thereby removed the so-called anachronisms from Homer.

[32] My authority for this interpretation of δαίμων—which is never thus used in the narrative—is Professor Campbell Bonner.

[33] Essay on *Paradise Lost*, Arber's Reprints, p. 57.

[34] It rains, and the wind blows, on the first night of Odysseus' stay with the Swineherd (ξ 457 f.).

[35] J. C. Shairp, *Studies in Poetry and Philosophy* (Edinburgh, 1868), 53 ff. The shepherd in the similes has been mentioned; for the vagrant, cf. Γ 33, E 597, Π 263.

[36] C. T. Winchester, *Some Principles of Literary Criticism* (1899), 275.

[37] *Op. cit.* 275.

[38] By Professor J. W. Mackail, *Lectures on Greek Poetry* (London, 1910), 97.

Notes to Chapter VII

[1] Judging by the *Eumenides*, Prometheus must have consented to make peace with Zeus in exchange for honor as Fire God at Athens.

[2] ἐξ ἁλός, λ 134, ψ 281, "away from," is exactly paralleled by ἐκ πατρίδος, o 272, both phrases being used with the copula.

[3] Aristotle, *Rhetoric*, III, 14, 6.

[4] That is, if the ancient interpretation of α 19 is to be followed. See *A.J.P.* XLIV (1923), 343, and *Class. Weekly* XXVII (1934), 107.

[5] Cf. the unreadiness of Zeus to bring about the fated return of Odysseus, α 17, 32, 65, or to send Hermes to Ogygia at once; cf. α 84 f. with ε 23, 29. The first speech of Zeus, α 32-43, betrays a character disinclined to action.

[6] The only βουλὴ Διός in the *Iliad* is the avenging of Achilles' slighted honor. Apollo caused the quarrel, and the poet nowhere says that Zeus was the cause of the war. Hence the motif of the *Cypria* cannot be transferred to the *Iliad*.

[7] So the absence from home of Helen (Ω 765) and of Odysseus (β 175) has lasted twenty years—a very long time: the number is "round" rather than historical. Cf. below, n. 50.

[8] A 545-550.

[9] Friedländer, "Lachende Götter," *Die Antike* X (1934), 214 f.

[10] Scott, *The Unity of Homer*, 226.

[11] By Sarpedon (E 485), by Helenus (Z 73-76, 80-82), by Cebriones (Λ 523-530), by Polydamas (M 61-79, N 735-744), and by Glaucus (Π 538-547, P 142-168). The Asius episode (M 108-172), to which critics used to object, shows clearly what might have happened to Hector but for the advice of Polydamas.

[12] Cf. Θ 497-541 with 470-472, M 231-236 with Λ 192-194.

[13] Scott, *Unity*, 233 ff.; idem, *A.J.P.* XXXV, 309 ff.

[14] S. E. Bassett, "That Young Prig, Telemachus," *Sewanee Rev.* XXVIII, 160-171.

[15] Compare Θ 541 with O 719, A 410-412 with Π 17 f.

[16] Eustathius, 1103, 52, observes that Hector shows the same ungenerous depreciation of the services of the Lycians (P 220-226)—the "Myrmidons" of the Trojan army—that Agamemnon shows for what Achilles has done for him and Menelaus in the previous fighting. Hector "bullies" Paris (N 769-773) and Melanippus (O 552), his cousin and a distinguished warrior.

[17] S. E. Bassett, "Hector's Fault in Honor," *T.A.P.A.* LIV (1923), 117-127.

[18] But cf. Aristotle, *Eth. N.*, 1123b, 35: τῆς ἀρετῆς γὰρ ἆθλον ἡ τιμή.

[19] "Ector pitous of nature."—Chaucer, *Troilus and Criseyde*, I, 113.

[20] E. g., O 496-499, P 223 f.

[21] He tactfully uses the plural (I 112), but the reference is to Agamemnon; cf. vs. 97, ἐν σοὶ μὲν λήξω.

[22] ἀντί νυ πολλῶν λαῶν ἐστιν ἀνήρ, I 116 f.

[23] Δ 360-363; Z 521-529; θ 406-409.

[24] S. E. Bassett, "The Ἁμαρτία of Achilles," *T.A.P.A.* LXV (1934), 51.

[25] Ibid. 54-58.

[26] C. M. Bowra, *Tradition and Design in the Iliad* (Oxford, 1930), 19, regards them as "sacred suppliants." But they neither bring the tokens nor assume the posture of "suppliants," nor do they appeal in the name of the god of the suppliant.

[27] August Nauck, *Tragicorum graecorum fragmenta* (Leipzig, 1889; reprinted 1926), p. 861:

οὐκ ἦν ἄρ' οὐδὲν πῆμ' ἐλευθέραν δάκνον
ψυχὴν ὁμοίως ἀνδρὸς ὡς ἀτιμία.

(J. T. Allen, *Univ. Calif. Publ. Class. Philol.* XII [1936], 29 f.).

[28] Eust. 1087, 25.

[29] S. E. Bassett, *T.A.P.A.* LXI (1930), 141-145.

[30] The sources of the scholiasts, with a single exception, incline to the latter in-

terpretation, ABT on X 395; Schol. B prefers the former, but admits the possibility of the other. Eustathius (1276, 1), always ready to point the moral, insists that Homer disapproves of the actions.

³¹ S. E. Bassett, *T.A.P.A.* LXIV (1933), 44 f.
³² E. Buchholz, *Homerischen Realien*, II, 1 (Leipzig, 1881), 326 f.
³³ See *T.A.P.A.* LXIV (1933), 47-50, for a score of instances.
³⁴ τῷ καὶ ἀτασθαλίῃσιν ἀεικέα πότμον ἐπέσπον.
³⁵ The five Trojan contingents in the attack on the wall (M 88-102) were *ad hoc*, cf. vss. 87, 88, as were the leaders of each contingent. The language used in the other three Catalogues shows clearly that the poet is describing an earlier organization: for the Trojan Catalogue, cf. B 805, οἷσί περ ἄρχει; for the Myrmidons, cf. Π 168-172; for the Achaeans, see below.
³⁶ There are only three unnamed minor heroes in the *Iliad*, M 92, N 211, 394.
³⁷ There are mentioned by name 243 of the 318 heroes definitely mentioned as slain in the fighting. See Seymour, *Life in the Homeric Age*, 617, who cites von Hahn; cf. Karl Frey, *Hektor* (Bern, 1895), 1 f.
³⁸ By Odysseus, seven Lycians (E 678 f.); by Hector and Ares, six Greeks (E 705-707); by Teucer, eight (Θ 274-276); by Hector, nine (Λ 301-303); by various Greek leaders, eight (Ξ 511-516); by various Trojans, eight (O 329-342); by Patroclus, nine (Π 694-696); by Achilles, seven (Φ 209 f.).
³⁹ In the following groups one or more named heroes do not appear again: Γ 146-148, Ucalegon; N 790-792, Orthraeus, Polyphetes, Palmys, and Ascanius (only elsewhere in the Catalogue, vs. 862); P 216-218, Deisenor, Mesthles, and Ennomus (the last two only elsewhere in the Catalogue, vss. 864, 858); Π 173, 186, 193, Menesthius, Eudorus, Pisander, leaders of Myrmidon contingents.
⁴⁰ BT on N 643 mentions ten names applied to two or more characters. I have noted twice as many more: Agelaus, Alastor, Areilycus, Areithous, Antiphus, Anchises, Apisaon, Bias, Borus, Chromius, Dolops, Epistrophus, Helenus, Hippodameia, Iphitus, Laodice, Oenomaus, Oileus, Opheltius, Orestes, Ormenus, Orsilochus, Pelagon, Periphas, Tlepolemus.
⁴¹ See above, Chap. I, pp. 14 ff.
⁴² Cf. Wilhelm Schmid, *Philologus* LXXX (1924), 67 ff.
⁴³ The rendezvous at Aulis, mentioned by Odysseus (B 303), may have suggested this beginning. The anachronism in placing the Boeotians in Boeotia nearly a century too early exists only under the assumption that Homer possessed the viewpoint of the historian and that he had some of the latter's apparatus. In the time of Homer the Boeotians had lived for centuries where he places them.
⁴⁴ See p. 255, n. 7.
⁴⁵ T. W. Allen, *The Homeric Catalogue of Ships* (Oxford, 1921), 156-159.
⁴⁶ Except for the Catalogue, Diomede is mentioned only once in Α-Γ, and then only as the son of Tydeus (B 406). We may compare the introduction of Patroclus as the son of Menoetius (A 307).
⁴⁷ In 40 of the 48 books of the two poems, all except H, Θ, N, T, X, ν, τ, ψ, an interesting new character, not a mute, enters the action for the first time.
⁴⁸ M. P. Nilsson, "Götter und Psychologie bei Homer," *Archiv f. Religionswissenschaft* XXII (1923-24), 373 f.
⁴⁹ Wilhelm Nestle, "Anfänge einer Götterburleske bei Homer," *Neue Jahrb.* XV (1905), 161-182; Engelbert Drerup, *Das fünfte Buch der Ilias* (Paderborn, 1913), 394-420; cf. Drerup, *Homerische Poetik*, I (1921), 226-231, 414-422.
⁵⁰ Cf. P. Waltz, "L'exagération numerique dans l'Iliade et dans l'Odyssée," *Revue des études homériques* III (1933), 9.
⁵¹ "Lachende Götter," *Die Antike* X (1934), 209-226.
⁵² M. P. Nilsson, *A History of Greek Religion* (Oxford, 1925), 171.
⁵³ M. P. Nilsson, *The Mycenean Origin of Greek Mythology* (1932), 244. Friedländer, however, denies this, *op. cit.*, 219.

Notes to Chapter VIII

[1] ν 125-187; cf. *Class. Philol.* XXVIII (1933), 305-307.
[2] *L'Evolution des genres.*
[3] William Morris,"The Haystack in the Floods."
[4] P. J. Macdonell,"The Tactics of Odysseus," *Greece and Rome* V (1936), 115.
[5] The length is merely "heroic," as is that of the 22-cubit pike of Ajax; yet most commentators interpret both measures as historical.
[6] ἐκ μὲν 'Ιλιάδος καὶ 'Οδυσσείας μία τραγῳδία ποιεῖται ἑκατέρας ἢ δύο μόναι. Gudeman notes that ἑκατέρας must be taken with the following phrase; otherwise the reference of the latter to one or the other of the poems would be made clear.
[7] Gudeman on Ar. *Poetics*, 1459b 2, 1462b 3.
[8] Achilles should leave in anger, and after a difference with Ajax. The regular limitation to three actors of importance makes the exit of Odysseus necessary. The exit of Phoenix is then needed only that he may see Machaon.
[9] Heraclitus, Frg. 101a, Diels (2d edition).
[10] John Burnet, *The Ethics of Aristotle* (1900), XLIV, n. 1.

INDEX

INDEX

Achaeans, 30, 32, 36, 77, 101, 109, 121, 122, 181, 193, 198; noblest of the, 137, 195
Achilles, 10, 29, 36, 43-44, 47, 50, 66-67, 69-70, 72, 77, 78, 87, 91-92, 99, 101, 102, 103, 119, 123-124, 132, 137, 175, 176-177, 181, 182, 185, 186, 187, 193, 216-217, 220, 229, 231, 238; shield of, 31, 94-99, 123, 156, 166, 239; treatment of Hector's body by, 36, 43, 193, 194, 202, 203, 204, 205, 206, 207, 230; rage of, 43, 207; funeral of, 43; exults over Hector, 75; pursuit of Hector by, 108-109, 206; wrath of, 136, 196, 207; death of, 176, 193; ruling passion of, 183; preëminent in manly qualities, 187; tragedy of wrath of, 187; and Hector contrasted, 188 ff.; love of, for Patroclus, 191, 206; tragedy of, 192-193; ideals of honor of, 195-196, 197, 199, 200, 201, 207; desertion of, by friends, 198; will face Hector, 201, 202; bemoans own shortcomings, 201-202, 207; slaughter of Trojan youths by, 202, 203, 205, 206; return of spear to, 203; followed code of Heroic warfare, 203-207 *passim;* condemned, 204; anguish of, 206; return of, to battle, 215; Ajax called "second to," 216; attitude of Diomede toward, 216-217; wins glory by death, 223
Aeneas, 73, 87, 92, 100, 112, 136, 138, 185, 217, 218
Aeneid, 24, 59, 82, 117, 142, 146, 193
Aeolus, 151 *passim*
Aeschylus, 7, 51, 60, 61, 128, 163, 165, 175, 176, 202, 238
Agamemnon, 43, 49, 71, 77, 94, 99, 100, 102, 103, 121, 123, 134, 136, 137, 175-176, 178, 180, 181, 185, 188, 191, 194, 195, 198-199, 204, 207, 209, 216, 220; shade of, 10, 176, 178; insult by, 181, 195, 202, 217; no apology offered by, 195-196, 198; penitence of, 196; has but one good quality, 196-197; standards of, contrasted with those of Achilles, 198 ff.
Ajax, 58, 62
Ajax, 66, 91, 101, 124, 132, 136, 139, 186, 190, 197, 198, 207, 213, 216; plea of, to Achilles, 200-201; the lesser, 213
Ajaxes, two, 112
Alcestis, 58, 65
Alcibiades, 5, 27
Alcinous, 10, 30, 73, 231; palace of, 50, 89; Garden of, 88
Alexandrian: criticism, 115; critics, 130, 145, 165, 227
Amphimachus, 91, 214
Andromache, 35, 36, 63, 70, 78, 98, 129, 142, 148, 177, 190, 191, 206, 230
Antenor, 118, 119, 139, 152; proposal of, 134-135; debt to, 197
Anticleia, 121, 134
Antigone, 156, 192, 204, 239
Antilochus, 99, 101, 136, 188, 190, 212, 216
Antimachus, 118, 119, 204
Antinous, 101, 107, 130, 139
Aphrodite, 101, 129, 133, 136, 238; cestus of, 91, 224; Loves of Ares and, 31, 222
Apollo, 30, 40, 65, 85, 120, 122, 130, 132, 136, 181, 185, 196; slaying of Achilles by, and Paris, 193; part of, in death of Patroclus, 202

INDEX

Apologue: in Homer, 10, 57, 62, 63, 73, 78, 137; in Vergil, 73
Archelochus, 132, 139
Arend, 46
Ares, 65, 110, 111, 133, 139, 185, 225; Loves of, and Aphrodite, 31, 222
Arete, 121-122
Argives, 10, 49, 100, 185
Argonautica, 54, 61
Aristarchus, 20, 105, 120, 121, 124, 125, 127, 130
Aristophanes, 12, 48, 116, 146
Aristotle, 6, 33, 44, 54, 61, 78, 82, 115, 141, 145, 176, 182, 201, 207, 219, 229, 233, 240, 243; on Homer's dramatic manner, 59; inverted order used by, 126; comparison made by, 173-174
Arnold, Matthew, 47
Artemis, 117, 121, 138, 225
Asius, 75, 101, 106, 210
Astyanax, 206, 232
Athena, 38, 40, 41, 45, 49, 52, 69, 90, 92, 103, 104, 110, 120, 122, 133, 135, 136, 138-139, 140, 176, 184, 185, 194, 195; spear of, 31, 91; interference by, in plans of Ares, 65; speeches of, in *Odyssey*, 76; sacrifice to, 76; appearance of, to Achilles, 102; plan of, 186; trickery of, 202-203
Attic tragedy, 14, 33, 44, 48, 49, 50, 61, 62, 65, 78, 144, 165, 174-175, 178, 233, 238, 239, 240, 242, 243
Audience: Homer's, 10, 27, 82, 115, 116, 177, 215; silent partner in the drama, 114, 131; coöperation of, 128-129, 135; motivation supplied by, 130 ff.; Greek, 185, 197, 215

Baldwin, the Hon. Stanley, 154
Baldwin, C. S., 84
Beauty: of nature, 141; varied rhythmic, 148; imparted by Homer, 158
Beggar, 11, 45, 54, 67, 68, 71, 101, 105, 135, 139, 177, 178
Beowulf, 179
Berenson, Bernard, 155
Bergk, 89
Boar Hunt, 69, 208
Bossuet, 155
Bougot, 37, 94 f., 119
Bowra, 193, 204
Briseis, 91, 103, 123, 136, 191, 195
Bucolic diaeresis, 153

Caesura, the, 145-149 *passim*
Calchas, 194, 219
Calhoun, 115
Calypso, 40, 120, 133, 137, 138, 139, 221; isle of, 41, 42, 52, 53; cave of, 88
Cap of Hades, 104, 133, 139

Cassandra, 75, 93, 175
Catalogues, 19, 29, 30, 120, 184, 208, 209, 211, 212; geographical completeness the aim of, 212, 228; source of, 212
Cauer, 105
Cebriones, 75, 205, 216
Cesarotti, 95
Charis, 215, 219
Chryseis, 194
Chryses, 132, 181, 198
Cicero, 6, 120, 126
Circe, 11, 120, 139
Clytemnestra, 196-197
Code of Heroic warfare, 203, 204, 207
Continuity: of life, 42; of time, 44, 119; of place, 48, 52, 119; of narrative, 49; of ideas, 119
Creon, 156, 192, 204
Cronus, 107, 133
Curse of the Atridae, 175
Cyclops, 58; episode, 91, 220; isle of, 117. *See also* Polyphemus

Dactylic: hexameter, 141, 142; rhythm, 143, 144. *See also* Hexameter; Rhythm
Dante, 24, 117, 182
Deiphobus, 211, 216
Demodocus, 31, 32, 73, 105, 118, 222
Demosthenes, 114, 115, 165
Derivationist school of metricians, 146
Diapeira, 74
Dido, 73, 117, 118
Diomede, 40, 72, 73, 86, 87, 92, 103, 106, 107, 110, 130, 131, 133, 136, 184-185, 188, 202, 216-218
Diomedeia, 208; is "episodic," 215; typifies course of the Trojan War, 219
Dionysius of Halicarnassus, 146, 214
Dionysiaca, 61
Dionysus, 48, 111; cult of, 29
Dissectors, 20, 115
Divine Comedy, 24, 182
Divine: guidance, 181; interference, 65, 101, 133, 194, 203, 220, 221; intervention, 103, 136, 138, 168, 182, 220; purpose, 103
Divinity in Homer, 220
Dolon, 101, 130, 131, 188, 219
Doloneia, 19, 130
Dörpfeld, 42
Drama, 26-27 *passim*; difference between epic and, 48; Attic, 58; characteristic feature of, 60; of Thespis, 60; Homer's approach to, 65; presentation of, 82; contribution of silent partner to, 114; epic, 208, 215, 220

Dramatic: Homer's, epic, 85; illusion, 59; manner, 62, 82; motivation, 137; poet, 27; technique of, epic, 64
Drerup, 3, 95, 116

Einstein, 33
Embassy, 91; speeches of, 124; Achilles' reply in, 136, 197; failure of, 195; Achilles' ideal of honor revealed in, 197; episode, 220
Enjambement, 154 f.
Epic: purpose of, 9; narrative, 36-37, 51; unity of time, 42-44; difference between, and drama, 48; drama, 48, 208, 215; Homer supreme among, poets, 59; description of, 82; oral, poet, 83, 114; Homer's dramatic, 85; *hyporcheme*, 98-99; written, 114; irony, 135-136; Homer true to his conception of, 178; theme, 179 ff.; early, 227
Epic illusion: in Homer, 27-28 *passim*, 41, 87; creation of, 56; break in, 87, 129, 137; continued, 88. *See also* Chap. IV
Epipolesis, 110, 215, 217
Episode: first Olympian, 77; interpositions at end of, 106; contrary implications of, 207-219 *passim*; function of, in epic drama, 220; Phaeacian, 239
Epithet. *See* Homeric epithets
Eumaeus, 39, 54, 72, 85, 103, 135, 139, 177, 228, 232
Eumenides, 175
Euphorbus, 91, 100, 132, 219
Euripides, 51, 58, 62, 70, 75, 124, 128, 163, 220, 241
Eurycleia, 67, 68, 69, 106, 135, 138, 160, 177
Eurymachus, 107, 229
Eustathius, 96, 121, 125, 126, 130

Finsler, 95, 119
Formulaic: language, 44-45; verses, 151, 152
Fraccaroli, 131 *passim*
Fraenkel, Hermann, 33
Friedländer, Paul, 222
Frogs, 48, 111, 128

Gilgamesh epic, 128
Gin, Pierre, 166
Glaucus, 40, 86, 93, 106, 107, 132, 136, 191, 214, 216, 217, 222; challenges Diomede, 218; speech of, 219
Greece: culture of, 5; Heroic Age of, 173, 243; and standards of, 193, 194, 207; Heroic leaders of, 186
Greek: army, 112, 201, 212, 213; audience, 185, 197, 215; Catalogue, 120-121, 209, 211, 212, 213, 215; criticism, 146; epic, 12, 61; fleet, 213; leaders, 210, 212, 215; literature, 6, 77, 84, 127 f., 244; memory in historical times, 16; myths and legends, 12, 14; names, 146; scholars, 3, 20; scholarship, 2; tradition, 5, 13, 243; wall, 100, 106, 132, 185, 186, 208

Greeks, 77, 111, 112, 135, 136, 140, 184, 198, 201, 214, 215, 216, 218, 224, 238; success of, in first battle, 184; repute of Hector among, 186

Grimm, H. F., 95

Hebrew: account of Creation, 8-9; Psalmist, 174

Hebrew literature: parallelism of thought in poetry of, 126-127; inverted order in, 127 *passim*; inclination in earliest, 127 f.; "introverted parallelism" in, 127, 128

Hector, 35-36, 40, 43, 44, 50, 54, 63, 65, 70, 75, 78, 80, 91, 92, 100, 101, 112, 122, 129, 132, 133, 134, 135, 175, 182, 184-185, 186, 195, 199, 203, 204, 210, 211, 215-218 *passim*, 220, 226, 230; death of, 35, 39, 51, 98, 99, 148, 193, 203; laments for, 35, 175; dragged by Achilles, 36, 43, 129, 193, 203, 205, 206, 207, 230; funeral of, 43; a living individual, 79; body of Patroclus dragged by, 104, 205; pursuit of, by Achilles, 108-109, 206; helmet of, 136, 232; wrath against, 176, 179; burial of, 177, 188; devotion of, to country and family, 183, 187; term and limit of Trojan success revealed to, 184; transfer of the Wrath to, 185; the instrument of Zeus, 186; genius of Homer in presenting, 187 ff.; Achilles and, contrasted, 188 ff.; prayer of, 191; treatment of body of, by Achilles, 194, 202, 203, 204, 206; Achilles will face, 201, 202; compassion for, 202; Athena's deception of, 202, 203; pity for, 203, 206; Zeus gives glory to, 215; Ajax fears, 216; human weaknesses of, 218; shield of, 232; tragedy of, 235 ff.

Hecuba, 35, 36, 148, 186, 190, 230

Helen, 39, 72, 106-107, 134, 135, 136, 162, 175, 177, 186, 190, 193, 197, 217, 238

Helenus, 76, 211, 216

Hephaestus, 71, 89, 92, 95, 225

Hera, 65, 77, 90, 101, 102, 122, 129, 132, 133, 152, 183-184, 185, 186; battle between Zeus and, 185; Homer's portrait of, 223-226

Heracles, 48, 54, 71, 93; Choice of, 189; life on Olympus when, lived, 223

Heraclitus, 232

Herder, 18

Hermes, 40, 41, 42, 52, 64, 80, 88, 91, 122, 133, 137, 139, 215, 219, 221, 239

Hermogenes, 144, 146

Herodotus, 12, 31, 82, 126

Heroes, Age of, 175. *See also* Greece

Hesiod, 29, 160, 243

Hexameter, 15, 17, 142; dactylic, 141, 142; Homer's, 145, 146; long, 159

Higher: Criticism, 1, 2, 3, 4, 121; Critics, 7, 122, 133

Hirzel, 62-63

Homer, 1-12 *passim*; audience of, 10, 82, 114-119 *passim*, 129, 131, 135, 137; came at peak of Greek epic, 12; invention of, 13, 14, 56, 211; supremacy of, 14, 18, 59; language of, 14, 143; formulas of, 14, 45, 115, 116, 150; style of, 15, 47; poetry in time of, 15-16; originality in, 16, 18; poetry of, 17, 20, 243; not a single poetic mood, 19; rejection of verses of, 20 ff.; position of, between two cultures, 24, 243; meaning of past to, 24-25; is unique, 27; epic illusion in, 27-28, 86; Muses and the Muse of, 28-31 *passim*; devices used by, 32; narrative of, 32, 42; time relative in, 33, 38; the primitive in, 34, 40, 45, 46, 115, 116, 231;

method and genius of, estimated, 36 f.; realism in, 37, 50, 117, 140, Chap. VIII; avoidance of "flat stretch" by, 40-41, 45; use of modern method by, 41; flat spaces in, 42, 43, 47, 107, 108; approach of, to epic unity of time, 42; repetition in, 45, 75, 86-87, 115, 116, 137; prevents monotony, 45; function of meals in tales of, 47; action in poems of, 47, 53 f.; movements characteristic of, 47-48, 64; unity of place in, 48, 49, 51, 52, 55; multiplicity of, 48; freed from artificial laws of unity, 48-49, 243-244; similes in, 48, 75, 87, 88, 94, 109-112 *passim*, 118, 164-172 *passim*; journeys in, 53 ff.; showed tragedy the way, 58; debt to, 59, 60; charm of, 59, 150, 163; illusion of personality in, 59; poetic manners in, 59 ff.; use of direct speech by, 60; dramatic character of, 60, 62; epic of, identified with tragedy, 61; dialogues of, 60, 61, 62, 64, 65, 70, 71, 72, 74, 75, 86, 102, 104, 106, 130, 207; speeches in, 62, 75, 76, 77-78, 87, 102, 103, 109, 112, 123, 124; single speeches in, 64, 74, 75-76, 106, and categories of, 76; attention of, to rest, 64; approach of, to drama, 65; used tale within tale, 71; power of, to impart reality of life, 72, 227; distinctive characteristic of, 81; art of, 81, 112, 197-198; oral medium used by, 82; dramatic epic of, 85; effect of tale of, on listeners, 85, 115; manner of, 86, 115, 131; description of places by, 88; interruption of narrative by, 91; description of major hero by, 92; miniature portraits by, 93-94; shield of Achilles described by, 94-99, 123; introduction of extraneous matter by, 99; interpositions of, 99, 113, 131; concentrates emotional tension, 101; is purely subjective, 102, 103, 112; use of objective method by, 103; refuses to dramatize undramatic material, 106; epithets of, 116, 158-164 *passim*; contrasted with Vergil, 117, 118; continuity of ideas in, 119, 123, 124; hysteron proteron of, 120, 122-126 *passim*; inversion of order by, 122 ff.,' 126; "threaded speech" of, 124; gift of narrative of, 129-130, 137; technique of motivation of, 130 ff., 134 ff.; mastery of plot and detail the same in both poems of, 140; verse of, closely follows nature, 141; measure of, remains dactylic, 142, 143-144; change of rhythm in, 143, 144; verses of, shackled with the caesura, 145 ff.; matchless rhythm of, 147; arrangement of thoughts of, 150 ff., 154 ff., 157; begins with the new, 151; fondness of, for bucolic diaeresis, 153; enjambement in, 154; tonal quality of verses of, 156 f.; saw life exalted, 158; gift of, to poetry, 164; epic of, differs from Milton's, 167; compared with Wordsworth, 168-169, 172; attitude of, toward nature, 168, 243; compared with Sappho and Alcman, 171; Aristotle's comparison of poems of, 173; method of composition of, 174; literary unity of poems of, 174, and completeness in, 174, 176; the "father" of tragedy, 175; true to his conception of epic, 178; new literary invention used by, 182; genius of, in presenting Hector, 187 ff.; Achilles and Hector contrasted by, 188 ff.; reveals the soul of his characters, 191; was *philachilleus*, 192, 203; the first and one of the greatest tragic poets, 207; use of the "episodic" by, 207-208, 219; Diomede one of the greatest creations of, 217; divine interference natural in, 220-221 *passim*; devout religious attitude revealed by, 221; gods of, 222, 239; ethical philosophy of, 223; the first great humanist, 223, 244; approach of, to the particular, 231; tragic quality in poetry of, 233 ff.; alternation provided by, 239; contrast between, and tragedy, 241; blends three poetic manners, 242; was a poetic realist, 241

Homeric: courtesy, 224; criticism, 208; dialect, 156; enjambement, 154 ff.; hysteron proteron, 120, 122-126; manner, 90, 115; narrative, 34, 47, 50, 102, 120, 220; new, Problem, 1; principle of divine interference, 181-182; Question, 1, 2, 5, 7; repetition, 115, 116; scholars, 1, 2, 3, 40, 94, 120, 154, 224; scholarship, 14, 22; theory of, style, 115; triad, 116
Homeric epic, 26-27, 155; completeness of, 207, 208
Homeric epithets, 116, 158-163; of the horse, 161, 162; of the ship, 162; need new examination, 163-164
Homeric poems, 3, 7, 9, 12, 19, 94, 114, 129, 173, 203; one great maker of, 7; Muses and Muse of Homer revealed by, 29-30; time element in, 33 f.; the primitive in, 34, 40, 45, 46, 115; recitation of, 60; aim of, 84; appeal of, 115; most unique feature of, 164; "idyls" contained in, 165; literary unity of, 174; completeness in, 174; action in, 174, 230; endings of, 178; no prolonged torture in, 230; reduced to a tragic pattern, 233 ff.
Homeric poetry: antecedents of, 3; study of, 4, 20; minor problems of, 149; three qualities of, 173; at its best, 214; tragic quality in, 233
Homeric similes, 48, 75, 87, 93, 94, 109-111, 112, 118, 164, 168, 169; function of, 165-167 *passim;* detachment of, 166
Human Life Writ Large, 24-25, 56, 114, 174, 182, 221, 230

Idaeus, 64, 79, 80
Ideas, continuity of, 119, 123, 124
Idomeneus, 75, 92, 132, 191
Iliad, 1, 4, 5, 7, 10, 17, 19, 21, 22, 24, 31, 33, 34, 35, 39, 43, 49, 50, 52, 55, 63, 78, 112, 118, 121, 137, 175, 182, 196, 212, 217; Tricking of Zeus, 12, 53, 129, 133, 224, 239; brief compass of action of, 42; the plague in, 43, 181, 220, 221, 230; use of crowds in, 51; full of action and conflict, 62, 65; speeches in, 63; dialogues in, 63, 65; theme of, 63, 70, 181, 227; single speeches of, 63, 75-76; a tale of war, 69; tale within the tale of, 71-72; characters addressed in, 85; tragedy of, 92, 187, 193; similes in, 93, 166, 168; pattern of, 119; personal combats in, 131; dramatic irony in, 135; gods as *dramatis personae*, 138-140, 177, 183, 221-225; looks forward, 176; aim of narrative speeches in, 178; induction of, 179; two prayers in, 191; *immitis Achilles*, 193, 202; episodes in, 208, 216, 219, 220; proper names in, 211; realism and idealism in, 227 f.; tragic pattern of, 233 ff.; two outstanding tragedies of, 238; a third tragedy in, 239. *See also Odyssey*
Illusion of: continuous time, 44; historicity, 28 ff.; personality, 56, 57, 58, 59; real life, 42, 47; reality, 36, 48, 57, 74; vitality, 32, 47 f.
Iphigenia in Tauris, 70
Iphition, 75, 132
Iris, 40, 65, 77, 122, 132, 139, 214, 220
Ithaca, 39, 40, 50, 52, 64, 88, 103, 108, 140, 179, 228; palace at, 49
Ithacan assembly, 37, 51

Jebb, John, Bishop of Limerick, 127 *passim*
Jowett 13

Kalevala, 160, 179
Kipling, 165, 223
Kirchhoff, 121, 133-134

Laertes, 38, 39, 56, 70, 103, 121, 133, 177, 229
Lang, Andrew, 84, 193, 244
Latin grammarians, 146
Leacock, Stephen, 143, 156
Lehrs, 89
Lessing 3. 45
Literary: foundation of, edifice, 1-2; greatest single, fact, 2
Literature: creative, 2; Greek, 6, 77, 84, 127 f., 244; epic poetry was, itself, 8, 36; great creators of, 18-19; transmission of, 20; Homer's exalted place in, 28, 84; biology of, 57; comparative, 126; early Hebrew, 126 f.; the metaphor in, 165; comparison in, 165; Hera the first scold in, 224; realism in, 227, 244
Lowell, 50, 140
Lowes, 12
Lowth, Bishop Robert, 126
Lucian, 6, 33, 44
Lund, Nils W., 127
Lycaon, 101, 132, 202, 203, 204
Lyrical Ballads, 167
Lyric poetry, 26-27
Lysias, 5, 126

Mackail, 171
Melanthius, 39, 107, 133, 229, 230
Melantho, 67, 107
Meleager, 71, 86, 103, 199
Menelaus, 39, 50, 79, 85, 86, 100, 101, 103, 106, 111, 125, 132, 135, 156, 184, 190, 191, 196, 197, 204
Menestheus, 213
Menesthius, 93, 211
Menexenus, 126
Menoetius, 91, 202
Mentes, 103, 140
Meriones, 112, 191, 197
Milton, 9, 24, 31, 149, 167, 178; epic of, differs from Homer's, 167
Motivation-by-the-audience, 133
Muse: of Epic Poetry, 23; contribution of, in Homer, 28, 30, 31, 85; of Homer, 28-29, 31, 178; of the Old Comedy, 48
Muses: of Helicon, 29; of Hesiod, 29; of Homer, 29-30; influence of, 29; of Olympus, 29; revealed by Homeric poems, 29-30; traditional, of Poetry, 29; gift of, 30
Myres, 96

INDEX

Myrmidon: Catalogue, 208, 213; contingents, 209, 211
Mythos, 22, 57, 182, 208, 244

Narration: basic principles of, 28; development of primitive, 115
Narrative: Homer's impersonal, 28; Homeric, 34, 37, 47, 50, 102, 120, 220; technique of Homer, 35, 130; mastery of art of, 55; difference between oral and written, 73; oral, 74, 80, 86, 102, 105, 109, 112, 118, 137, 220; written, 74; interruptions of, 91; oral epic, 94; places where, alone will not suffice, 107; success of a, 129; technique, 130-131; principle, 131; contrast between simile and, 167, 169; two reasons for a, 178
Nausicaa, 90, 103, 117, 163, 222
Necyia, 6, 55, 175; Second, 176, 178
Nestor, 9, 64, 76, 79, 80, 86, 92, 104, 119, 136, 139, 162, 178, 185, 188, 196, 204, 209, 216, 231
Nibelungenlied, 59, 179, 210, 229
Niceratus, boast of, 17
Nilsson, 220
Niptra, 67-70, *passim*
Nireus, 58, 213, 214

Objectivity: Homer's, 81; two meanings of, 81
Oceanus, 103, 133, 166
Odysseus, 30, 32, 38, 44, 46, 49, 50, 52, 53, 54, 57-58, 73-74, 75, 101, 103, 105, 106, 108, 117, 121, 122, 124, 131-139 *passim*, 151, 153, 163, 177, 188, 196, 201, 204, 216-217, 220, 221, 229, 231, 237; wanderings of, 13, 32, 54-55, 105, 120; dramatic entrance of, into home, 39, 48; vengeance of, 51; as envoy to Achilles, 66 ff.; raft of, 91, 133, 161, 162; insults endured by, 107; slaughter of Suitors by, 135, 205, 231, 238; prayer of, 152; return of, 169, 177; reward of, 177; friend of Achilles, 190, 197, 198; dismissed by Achilles, 200; greatness achieved by, 202
Odyssey, 1, 4, 5, 7, 17, 18, 19, 31, 33, 45, 107, 179, 196, 223; parallelism of action in, 35, 40; description of future action in, 41; brief compass of action of, 42; climax of, 48; compared with the *Iliad*, 49 ff., 63, 69 ff., 75-76, 138 ff., 182 f., 212; charm of, 52; art of narrative in, 55; makes greater use of dialogues, 62, 64; advance in technique of, 64; theme of, 64, 70, 181, 187; a tale of domestic intrigue, 69; tales in, 72; characters addressed in the *Iliad* and, 85; inversion of order of events in, 120 ff.; argument for different authorship of, 137; complements the *Iliad*, 175; last verse of, denotes finality, 176; interest in narratives of, 178; architectural principle of, 186 f.; plan of, revealed in the first scene, 187; episodes in, 208; realism in, 227, 228
Oedipus at Colonus, 176
Oedipus Rex, 58, 70, 182, 192
Ogygia, 41, 44, 56, 64, 106, 139
Old Testament, 59, 127, 160, 179, 220
Olrik, Axel, 34

270 INDEX

Olympian: Muses, 29; family, 65, 223, 225; first, episode, 77; intervention, 220
Olympians, 65, 182, 219, 221, 225, 228; Hera prevailed over the, 77; are not spirit but power, 223
Olympus, 13, 30, 49, 52, 53, 71, 90, 133, 167, 177, 183, 220, 223, 224, 226, 228
Orthryoneus, 75, 93, 132

Pandarus, 99, 104, 131, 136, 184, 219
Paradise Lost, 24, 174
Parallelism: of thought in Hebrew literature, 126 f.; "introverted," 127, 128
Paris, 64, 78, 79, 101, 133, 134, 135, 184, 185, 211
Parry, Milman, 14, 15-18 *passim*, 19, 20, 115, 116, 150, 155
Patrocleia, 92
Patroclus, 66, 67, 85, 91, 92, 101, 105, 130, 132, 176, 185, 188, 190, 192, 212, 216, 217, 232; shade of, 43, 140; burial of, 43; Cebriones slain by, 75, 205; Sarpedon slain by, 75, 136; death of, 99, 201, 202, 203, 207; body of, dragged by Hector, 104, 205; retreat with body of, 111-112; laments for, 175; funeral of, 176; victorious, 186; armor of, 189, 211; Achilles prays for, 191; Achilles' statement to, 200; pyre of, 202, 205; Achilles' duty to, 204
Penelope, 67-70 *passim*, 105, 106, 107, 121, 130, 133, 134, 135, 138, 160, 163, 196, 220, 230; fame of, 10; Dream of, 140; part of, in poem, 177
Pentecontaetia, 102
Pericles, 17; Age of, 240; *Funeral Oration* of, 102
Perrault, 165
Personality: center of, 58; intangible, 57; elements of, 57; illusion of, 57, 58
Phaeacia, 53, 55, 65
Phaedrus, 16, 126
Philoctetes, 210, 212, 213, 230
Phoenix, 58, 66, 69, 71, 124, 178, 190, 191, 192, 197, 199, 200, 201, 219, 229
Phorcys, harbor of, 88, 108, 139. Phorcys Harbor, on page 88, is a misprint.
Pindar, 14, 29, 30, 71, 162, 163, 165, 214
Pisistratus, 50, 158, 176
Place, continuum of time and, 119. *See also* Continuity
Plato, 5, 6, 13, 17, 27, 29, 34, 60, 62, 100, 125; dialogues of, 7, 102; souls of, 23; "harmonies" of, 24; identified Homer with drama, 59; Homer's rival in Greek literature, 77; inverted order used by, 125-126
Platonic: Question, 5; Socrates, 77; style of, dialogue, 7
Plutarch, 145
Poet: meaning of, 8; dramatic, 27; epic narrative practiced by, 36-37; art of, 240
Poetic: devices, 52; manners in Homer, 59; Muse of all, tradition, 29; spell of, illusion, 26; unique form of, expression, 165
Poetry: in Homer's day, 7-8; aim of, 8; of Homer, 15, 243; war between, and science, 23-24; Muse of Epic, 23; spell of, 26; lyric, 26, 27, 157, 169; traditional Muses of, 29; made distinct from prose, 141; minor problems of Homer's, 149; knowledge of essence of, 163; Homer's gift to, 164; similes as pure lyric, 169-170; essence of all our greatest, 221; after Homer, 229; Greek, 240

Poiesis, 8, 141, 227
Polites, 104, 211, 220
Polydorus, 132, 205
Polyphemus, 57, 58, 153. *See also* Cyclops
Poseidon, 9, 31, 91, 181, 185, 210, 215, 224
Praxiphanes, 120
Presbeia, the, 66-67, 69-70
Priam, 35, 36, 47, 50, 64, 79-80, 98, 118, 175, 178, 188, 197, 211, 214, 217, 224, 229, 231, 238, 239; dialogue between, and Achilles, 63, 65, 70; sons of, slain by Achilles, 132; grief of, for Hector, 190
Proems, 9, 31, 32, 151, 180, 183
Prometheus Bound, 62, 183
Protagoras, 126
Proteus, 78, 156
Pursuit of Hector, 108-109, 206
Pylus, 38, 51, 54, 56, 64, 103, 135, 158, 177
Pythagoras, 5

Quarrel, the, 91, 123, 176, 185, 194, 198, 201, 217; cause of, 180-181
Querelle, 164, 166
Quintus Smyrnaeus, 29, 124

Rahmenerzählung, 72, 74
Realism: in Homer, 37, 50, 117, 140, 227, 229, 231, 232, 240, 241; scientific, 230, 242; in literature, 244
Republic, 5, 6, 7, 19, 126, 174, 229
Rhythm, 141, 142; anapaestic, 144; dactylic, 143, 144; trochaic, 143, 144; change in, 143, 144; variety of, in Homer, 146, 154; matchless, of Homer, 147
Rothe, Carl, 3, 20, 95, 130, 131, 134
Ruth, 83, 84, 86; Book of, 59, 83-84, 103

Saint-Évremond, 166
Sainte-Beuve, 9
Sappho, Homer compared with, 171
Sarpedon, 75, 101, 132, 136, 139, 185, 186, 191, 217-218, 222, 223
Schiller, 81-82
Schmid, Wilhelm, 137-138
Scholia, 120, 121
Scholiast, 13, 120, 130
Schwartz, Eduard, 90
Science: search for knowledge of, 2; method of, 3, 4; war between, and poetry, 23-24
Scott, John A., 1, 3, 5
"Scourge of Homer," 156
Separatist hypothesis, 5

Separatists, 20, 52
Seymour, Thomas Day, 150
Shairp, Principal, 168-169 *passim*
Shakespeare, 78, 80, 81, 82, 147, 197, 221, 241
Shield of Achilles, 31, 94-99, 123, 156, 166, 239
Shorey, 13, 16
Similes. *See* Homeric similes
Slaughter, the, 39, 51, 106, 135, 152, 231; of Trojan youths, 202, 203, 205, 206
Sleep God, 53, 219, 224
Socrates, 5, 7, 17, 27, 28, 60, 89, 100, 126, 129, 164; Platonic, 77
Sophocles, 50, 58, 62, 67, 79, 176, 182, 197, 204, 230
Sparta, 41, 52, 56, 64, 104, 135
Sun God, 137
Suppliants, 60
Swineherd, 39, 53, 56, 71, 135, 188, 231
Symposium, 89

Telemachus, 14, 31, 37, 38, 40, 41, 45, 50, 51, 52, 103, 121, 134, 140, 160, 176, 177, 204; journey of, 45, 53, 54, 76, 104, 135; instrument of Athena's plan, 186
Telemachy, 175
Tennyson, 142, 159, 165
Teucer, 212, 216
Themis, 133, 215, 219, 225
Themistocles, 17
Theoclymenus, 87
Theogony, proem of, 29
Theomachy, 210, 225
Thersites, 49, 58, 91, 92, 162, 219, 225, 229, 231
Thespis, 12; drama of, 60
Thetis, 47, 99, 103, 176, 183, 184, 193, 224, 238, 239
Throop, Chancellor, 61
Thucydides, 12, 126, 230
Time: arrangement of, intervals, 43; continuous, 44, 48, 119; in Homeric poems, 33-34; unity of, 42, 44, 55
Tragedy: epic of Homer identified with, 61; with a happy ending, 70; *hyporcheme* of, 99; "father" of, 175; contrast between Homer and, 241
Trojan: allies, 209; Catalogue, 209, 214; elders, 210; families, 118-119; heroes, 176; plain, 91, 167, 222, 228; slaying of, youths, 202, 203, 205, 206; success, 184; women, 36, 54, 105, 190, 202
Trojan War, 24, 31, 74, 80, 87, 94, 105, 151, 166, 181, 205, 219, 223, 228
Trojans, 101, 109, 111, 112, 119, 120, 135, 181, 186, 192, 193, 198, 202, 210, 218, 224; victorious, 215, 216, 217; Hera's hatred against, 224
Troy, 43, 65, 80, 219, 228, 238; doom of, 77, 184; Elders of, 118; fall of, 176, 224; Hector's visit to, 215; story of, complete, 175; walls of, 108, 109; women of, 163, 190

INDEX 273

Truce, 79, 125, 176; breaking of, 175, 184, 215; broken by Zeus, 136; terms of the, 77

Ucalegon, 118, 211
Unification of places, 52
Unity of Homer, The, 1
Unity: of place, 48, 49, 51, 52, 55; of time, 42, 44, 55

Van Leeuwen, 100, 118, 131, 137-140 *passim*
Varius, 82
Varro, 145, 146
Vengeance, 37, 202, 204, 206, 207
Vengeance, the, 107, 186, 238
Vergil, 9, 24, 31, 61, 73, 82, 88, 117, 118, 142, 143, 162, 178
Verszwang, 152, 160
Voice of the Past, 31, 56, 114

Wanderings of Odysseus, 13, 32, 54-55, 74, 105, 120, 239; dramatic climax, of, 137
Wilamowitz, 20, 134, 193, 217
Wild-Goat Island, 122-123, 239
Wooden Horse, 73, 118
Wordsworth, 167, 168; lyrics of, compared with Homer's similes, 168-169, 172
Wrath: cause of, 136; against Hector, 176, 179; ruinous, 180, 187; tragedy of, of Achilles, 187 ff., 233 ff.; of Agamemnon, 194 f.; first outburst of, of Achilles, 196
Wrath, the, 151, 169, 177, 216, 221; cause of, 175; deadliness of, 176; last event in tale of, 177; beginning of tragedy of, 180; persons effecting the outcome of, 182; end of, 184; transfer of, to Hector, 185; concluding scenes of, 206; incidents which occurred before, 213

Zephyrus, 139, 151
Zeus, 32, 37, 38, 47, 49, 101, 122, 137, 178, 189, 193, 197, 205, 217, 222, 223, 224-226 *passim;* Tricking of, 12, 53, 129, 133, 224, 239; crossing the purpose of, 71; speeches of, 76; command of, 77, 122; truce broken by, 136; Odysseus prays for sign from, 152; caused wrath to be ruinous, 180; plan of, 180, 181, 183-187 *passim*, 216, 219, 238; Hector the instrument of, 186, 187; gives glory to Hector, 215
Zielinski, 34, 35

www.ingramcontent.com/pod-product-compliance
Lightning Source LLC
Chambersburg PA
CBHW021657230426
43668CB00008B/655